What People Are Saying About

*"Trusting a recipe often comes down to trusting the source.
The sources for the recipes are impeccable;
in fact, they're some of the best chefs in the nation."*
BON APPETIT MAGAZINE

"Should be in the library—and kitchen—of every serious cook."
JIM WOOD—Food & Wine Editor—San Francisco Examiner

*"A well-organized and user-friendly tribute to many of the state's
finest restaurant chefs."*
SAN FRANCISCO CHRONICLE

*"An attractive guide to the best restaurants and inns,
offering recipes from their delectable repertoire of menus."*
GAIL RUDDER KENT—Country Inns Magazine

"Outstanding cookbook"
HERITAGE NEWSPAPERS

*"I couldn't decide whether to reach for my telephone and make reservations
or reach for my apron and start cooking."*
JAMES MCNAIR—Best-selling cookbook author

"It's an answer to what to eat, where to eat—and how to do it yourself."
THE MONTEREY HERALD

*"I dare you to browse through these recipes
without being tempted to rush to the kitchen."*
PAT GRIFFITH—Chief, Washington Bureau, Blade Communications, Inc.

Books of the "Secrets" Series

COOKING SECRETS
from around the
WORLD

PAMELA A. MCKINSTRY

BON
VIVANT

Library of Congress Cataloging-in-Publication Data

Cooking Secrets From Around The World

Copyright ©1997
Millennium Publishing Group
97-071562
ISBN 1-883214-15-7
$15.95 softcover
Includes indexes
Autobiography page

Cover photograph by Robert N. Fish
Cover design by Morris Design
Food styling by Susan Devaty
Editorial direction by Judie Marks
Illustrations on pages 6-7 by Robin Brickman
All other illustrations by Krishna Gopa
Type by Cimarron Design

Published by Bon Vivant Press
a division of The Millennium Publishing Group
PO Box 1994
Monterey, CA 93942

Printed in the United States of America

Contents

My Bon Vivant Lifestyle

Food and travel are the two driving passions in my life and I've managed to create a lifestyle and a career around them. Through a combination of persistence, luck and hard work, I succeeded in the restaurant business, creating and operating three restaurants over a 16-year period.

A wonderful bonus of my seasonal summer restaurants was that I had seven months a year at leisure. With the advent of autumn and cold weather, Nantucket empties and I was free to travel.

For six years my focus was on Europe and Asia, where my love of food and professional interest in cooking played a key role in my travels. In 1986, my husband Mark and I went to Africa, a trip that indelibly changed my life. After a few years of working my way down the continent, I realized that my interest in the bush, instead of waning over time, was becoming an obsession. I now live and work in Zambia, where I help manage the Chinzombo Safari Lodge.

None of my restaurants ever fit into a neat category like French or Vegetarian or Californian. I liked the freedom of an eclectic approach and so my menus defied a single descriptive label. My recipes are associated with all types of cuisine, borrowing ideas and ingredients and techniques to create an inventive, varied menu distinguished by my own sense of style and flair. I chose the "homemade" approach to restaurant cooking, both because I love the actual act of cooking and because the results are so tasty.

The criterion by which I judge a dish is first and foremost its flavor. Too often, recipes fail to impress or rise above mediocrity, not because of poor ingredients or faulty technique, but because they lack a flavor focus or what I call pizzazz. Complexity of taste is vital, whether it be a simple lemon mousse bursting with tart piquancy or an Indian curry redolent with twelve spices, each complementing and building upon the others to create a subtle yet unforgettable marriage of flavors.

My recipes depend upon one or two ingredients to create this intensity of flavor. For a sauce, it is usually homemade stock or fresh herbs. It might be a period of marination or something as simple as cooking with a real vanilla bean. Whatever it is, there needs to be some element of the dish that will give it distinction and impact.

The recipes in this cookbook run the gamut from simple to complex, ordinary to extraordinary; from everyday, old-fashioned classics to grandiose finales. The collection is eclectic and encompasses a potpourri of cuisine, from around the world to the original in your kitchen. It's my hope that once you try some of these "foreign" dishes, they'll become a favorite part of your repertoire.

Here's to good food from around the world!

– Pam McKinstry

Favorite Recipes

§

Breakfast and Brunch

AMERICAN
Blueberry Muffins, 19
Bookstore Pâté, 20
Brunch Casserole, 21
Chicken Hash, 22
Chicken Sausage Patties, 23
Cranberry-Orange
   Muffins, 24
French Scrambled Eggs, 26
Island Berry Pancakes, 29
Maple French Toast, 31

Morning Glory Muffins, 33
Orange Oat Waffles, 34
Scrambled Egg Surprise, 36
Tomato and Pesto
   Quiche, 38
Upside-down French
   Toast, 39

AFRICAN
Avocado Bread, 18
Ham and Pasta Frittata, 28
Lemon-Banana Juice, 30

EUROPEAN
Eggplant Gratin, 25
Pain Perdu, 35
Melanzane Sandwich, 32
Spinach Cheese Puffs, 37

FAR EAST
Fruit Salad with Fragrant
   Syrup, 27

§

Appetizers

AMERICAN
Artichokes Vinaigrette, 41
Butternut Ravioli with
   Sage Cream, 64
Crab Cakes with
   Rémoulade Sauce, 45
Lobster Mousse, 49
Oysters in Champagne
   Sauce, 52
Oysters Rockefeller, 53
Pesto and Prosciutto
   Palmiers, 54

AFRICAN
Ethiopian Chicken Legs, 47
Samoosas, 58

EUROPEAN
Asparagus Riso, 41
Country Pâté, 44
Grilled Mozzarella, 48
Mussels Provençal, 51
Polenta Pizzas, 55
Rotolo di Prosciutto and
   Formaggi, 57

Spinach and Herb
   Gnocchi, 62
Spinach Ravioli and
   Gorgonzola Sauce, 64

FAR EAST
Pot Stickers, 56
Satay Sticks, 60
Spicy Orange Shrimp, 61

❧
Soups and Salads

❧
Fish and Seafood

§ Meat

§ Poultry

❦
Pasta

❦
Vegetables and Accompaniments

Desserts

❦
Pantry

Menu Planning

Page numbers are given for the recipes in this book

SUNDAY BREAKFAST
Mimosas
French Scrambled Eggs, 26
Chicken Sausage Patties, 23
Maple French Toast, 31
Fruit Salad with Fragrant Syrup, 27

A MEXICAN FIESTA
Strawberry Margaritas
Guacamole and Tortilla Chips, 222
Chilled Cantaloupe Soup, 71
Chiles Rellenos, 108
Black Bean and Corn Salad, 67
Mango Shortcake, 190

BRUNCH FOR A CROWD
Lemon-Banana Juice, 30
Morning Glory Muffins, 33
Brunch Casserole, 21
Spinach Cheese Puffs, 37
Smoked Turkey Salad à la Waldorf, 83
*Roasted Pepper and Bean Salad
Amandine, 81*
Fruit Salad with Fragrant Syrup, 27
Brioche Bread Pudding, 166

A MOVABLE FEAST
Country Pâté, 44
Ethiopian Chicken Legs, 47
Tomato Pesto Quiche, 38
New Potato Salad, 78
Black Bean and Corn Salad, 67
Ginger Crinkle Cookies, 183
Pumpkin-Date Tea Bread, 193

INTERNATIONAL HORS D'OEUVRES PARTY
Cheese Tray
Spicy Orange Shrimp, 61
Samoosas, 58
Chicken Satay Sticks, 60
Oysters Rockefeller, 53
Pesto and Prosciutto Palmiers, 51

SUMMER LUNCHEON
Pimm's Cup
Red and Yellow Gazpacho, 80
Confit of Duck Salad, 72
Avocado Bread, 18
*Luscious Lemon Mousse with
Raspberry Sauce, 188*

A MEDITERRANEAN CELEBRATION

Arugula Ravioli with Salsa Fresca, 231

Lamb Provençal, 114

Creamy Polenta, 149

Eggplant Gratin, 25

Braised Fennel, 145

Tiramisù, 199

MANZE CAMP BUSH DINNER

Gin & Tonics

Zanzibar Chicken Soup, 87

Beef Curry, 111

Rice

Poppadoms

Condiments

Bananas à la Foster, 164

AN AUGUST BARBECUE

Sangria

Spicy Orange Shrimp, 61

Grilled Chicken Prego, 128

Basmati Pilaf, 143

Grilled Zucchini with Basil Butter, 153

Sliced Farm Tomatoes with Crumbled
Feta and Balsamic Vinaigrette

Sun-dried Cherry and Peach
Crumble, 198,
with Ginger Ice Cream, 184

DINNER IN CAPETOWN

Oysters on the Half Shell

Bobotie, 106

Yellow Rice

Malay Sweet Potatoes, 154

Sautéed Spinach

Cape Brandy Pudding, 167

SPECIAL OCCASION

Champagne

Délices de Nantucket, 90

Veal Chops with Tarragon Glaze, 119

Mascarpone Mashed Potatoes, 155

Fresh Asparagus

Sautéed Wild Mushrooms

Decadent Truffle Cake, 175

CHRISTMAS DINNER

Eggnog

Lobster Mousse, 49

Tenderloin of Beef with Shiitake Cognac
Sauce, 118

Garlic Potato Gratin, 152

Creamy Swiss Chard, 150

Buttered Carrots

Fruit Cake, 182

MY FAVORITE DINNER
Oysters in Champagne Sauce, 52

Green Salad with Pears,
Stilton & Walnuts

Confit of Duck with
Lemon-Caramel Sauce, 125

Haricots Verts

Nectarine Chutney, 226

Spicy Roasted New Potatoes, 160

Volcano Cake, 205

APRÈS SKI PARTY
Hot Mulled Wine

Vegetable Crudités

Grilled Vegetable Lasagna, 134

Chili for a Crowd, 107

Rice

Garlic Bread

Green Salad

Caesar Salad, 68

Caramel Fudge Brownies, 168

A YANKEE DINNER
Lobster and Corn Chowder, 77

Cured Pork Chops with
Maple Glaze, 110

Buttermilk Mashed Potatoes, 146

Oven Roasted Vegetables, 157

Gingerbread, 185

A SIMPLE AUTUMN LUNCH
Hot Cider

Harvest Bisque, 76

Pork and Cranberry Sandwich, 116

German Potato Salad, 74

Persimmon Pudding Cake, 192

AN INDIAN OCEAN REPAST
Samoosas, 58

Chicken Madagascar, 124

Basmati Pilaf, 143

Snow Peas with Sesame

Frozen Passion Fruit Pie, 181

EAST MEETS WEST
Pot Stickers, 56

Tuna with Fennel-Pepper Crust and
Ginger Beurre Blanc Sauce, 103

Creamy Polenta, 149

Oven Roasted Vegetables, 157

Tropical Trifle, 203

A TASTE OF ITALY
Cinzano

Spinach and Herb Gnocchi, 62

Crusty Bread

Shrimp Scampi, 98

Asparagus Riso, 42

Broccoli with Olive Oil & Garlic

Italian Chocolate Torte, 187

Breakfast & Brunch

Avocado Bread

Blueberry Muffins

Bookstore Pâté

Brunch Casserole

Chicken Hash

Chicken Sausage Patties

Cranberry-Orange
   Muffins

Eggplant Gratin

French Scrambled Eggs

Fruit Salad with
   Fragrant Syrup

Ham and Pasta Frittata

Island Berry Pancakes

Lemon-Banana Juice

Maple French Toast

Melanzane Sandwich

Morning Glory Muffins

Orange Oat Waffles

Pain Perdu

Scrambled Egg Surprise

Spinach Cheese Puffs

Tomato and Pesto Quiche

Upside-down French
   Toast

Avocado Bread

Yield: 1 loaf
Preparation Time:
  20 Minutes
Baking Time:
  One Hour
Preheat oven to 350°

  ½ cup butter, softened
  1 cup sugar
  2 avocados, mashed
  2 tsps. fresh lemon juice
  ½ cup buttermilk
  2 eggs
  2 cups flour
  ½ tsp. salt
  ½ tsp. baking soda
1½ tsps. baking powder
  ¼ tsp. cinnamon
  ¼ tsp. ground cloves
  1 cup chopped walnuts

In my experience, when you need an avocado it is either hard as a baseball or you have an overabundance of ripe specimens. On those latter occasions, turn your bounty into avocado bread. These luscious fruits, masquerading as vegetables, are not just for salads and sandwich spreads. Much like carrots and zucchini, avocados make a moist and delicious tea bread that only improves with age.

Butter a 9 × 5-inch loaf pan. Cream the butter and sugar in a large bowl; mash the avocados with the lemon juice and add to the creamed butter and sugar mixture.

In a separate bowl, beat the eggs with the buttermilk until blended and add to the avocado. Then sift together the flour, salt, baking soda, baking powder and spices; add the dry ingredients to the batter, stirring to thoroughly combine. Finally add the nuts and turn the batter into the prepared loaf pan.

Bake in the middle of a hot oven for 55 to 65 minutes or until a skewer inserted into the center of the bread comes out clean. Cool on a rack and then turn out.

☆

Blueberry Muffins

Tender, light muffins that never fail to elicit praise! The secret is the buttermilk. If you handle the batter properly, it creates a tender and moist product. It took me three months to develop and perfect this recipe but I've never encountered a better muffin. By the way, fresh cultivated blueberries do not work well in this recipe as they are too dry. The batter is basic for any muffin—add other spices and fruits to create your own variations.

Sift the flour, sugar, salt, baking powder, baking soda and lemon rind into a large bowl. Set aside.

In a separate bowl whisk the eggs, buttermilk and oil until combined. Add this mixture to the dry ingredients and stir until the batter is just mixed. Gently fold in the blueberries and distribute evenly. It is essential that you do not stir the batter too much or the muffins will not be tender.

Line a muffin tin with paper liners or grease the muffin pan. Spoon the batter into the prepared pan, filling each cup to the brim. Sprinkle each muffin with ½ tsp. granulated sugar, if desired.

Bake for 20 minutes, then remove the muffins from the pan and finish cooling on a cake rack.

Yield: 14 to 16 Muffins
Preparation Time:
   15 Minutes
Baking Time:
   20 Minutes
Preheat oven to 375°

   3¼ cups flour
1½ cups granulated sugar
   1 tsp. salt
   4 tsps. baking powder
   1 tsp. baking soda
   1 Tbsp. grated lemon
      rind
   2 eggs
   2 cups buttermilk
½ cup vegetable oil
   1 cup frozen blueberries

Bookstore Pâté

Serves 6
Preparation Time:
  15 Minutes
Baking Time:
  40 Minutes
Preheat oven to 350°

  2 lbs. ground ham
  2 lbs. ground pork
  2 eggs, beaten
  ¾ cup catsup
  ¼ cup Dijon mustard
  1 large yellow onion,
     minced
  1 cup bread crumbs,
     homemade
  ½ cup milk
  1 tsp. white pepper

Bookstore Pâté is really meatloaf. In my restaurant we had difficulty persuading customers to try anything as ho-hum as meatloaf, so we changed the name and voilà—it became a best seller. I use it mainly for sandwiches, served in warm slices on pumpernickel bread with Dijon mustard, tomatoes and lettuce. You can also form the mixture into cocktail meatballs. Bake them in the oven and serve with a sweet-hot mustard sauce. Ask your butcher to grind the ham and pork for you. Be careful to choose a ham that is not too salty.

In a large bowl combine the meats, eggs, catsup and mustard and mix well. You may find that using your hands is the easiest method to achieve this.

Add the remaining ingredients and mix thoroughly.

Transfer the pâté to an ungreased loaf pan and bake for 40 minutes. Pour off and discard any juices that accumulate in the pan.

Serve hot or allow the pâté to cool and then unmold it and wrap it tightly in plastic. Refrigerate or freeze.

Brunch Casserole

A do-ahead breakfast or brunch dish that is great for a large gathering. Dozens of variations are possible on this theme: substitute cubes of ham for the sausage, add a layer of sautéed peppers, onions and asparagus, or make a vegetarian version without any meat.

utter a 9 × 13-inch baking pan or a 2 qt. ovenproof casserole dish. Arrange the bread cubes on the bottom of the pan.

Mix 1 cup of cheese with the mustard, paprika and sour cream. Add the sausage meat, making sure that it's been well drained or your casserole will be greasy. Spread this mixture on top of the bread cubes.

Whisk the eggs with the milk; season with salt and pepper. Pour the custard into the pan and sprinkle with the remaining one cup of cheese. Cover with plastic wrap and refrigerate overnight.

The next morning preheat your oven to 350°. Bake in the middle of the oven for 45 to 50 minutes or until set, puffed and golden. Cool 15 minutes before cutting.

Serves 8
Preparation Time:
  30 Minutes
(note refrigeration time)
Baking Time:
  45 Minutes
Preheat oven to 350°

 1 **loaf French bread, cubed (about 6 cups)**
 2 **cups sharp cheddar cheese**
 ½ **tsp. dry mustard**
 ½ **tsp. hot paprika**
 ½ **cup sour cream**
 ½ **lb. sausage, cooked, crumbled and drained**
 8 **eggs**
 ½ **cup milk**
 ½ **tsp. salt**
 ½ **tsp. pepper**

Chicken Hash

Serves 8
Preparation Time:
  15 Minutes
Cooking Time:
  20 Minutes

- ½ cup oil or butter
- 1 large yellow onion, finely minced
- 2 cups cubed raw potatoes (or cooked)
- 2 cups diced cooked chicken
- 2 cups stuffing, cubed or crumbled
- ¼ cup minced fresh parsley
  Salt and cayenne pepper to taste

Leftovers were the catalyst for this recipe. Now I find that I always cook more chicken and stuffing than I need, just so there will be plenty on hand for hash the next morning. The proportions aren't critical, so if you have less stuffing or more potatoes than suggested here, don't worry, just make the hash with what you have. Needless to say, turkey works equally well.

D ivide the oil between 2 heavy skillets and heat. Cook the potatoes, if raw, in one pan and the onions in the other until both are tender and golden. You may need to add more oil for the potatoes. If they are already cooked, however, just sauté them until they are hot and crispy.

Combine the onions and potatoes in your largest skillet and add the chicken and stuffing, cooking over medium high heat until the mixture is hot. Season with the parsley and spices. Serve hot.

Chicken Sausage Patties

In these days of low-fat, low-cholesterol dining, bacon and sausages have all but disappeared from breakfast plates. This recipe is ideal for those who love sausage but loath the high fat content of commercial brands.

Cut the pork into 1-inch cubes and arrange in a single layer on a tray or plate. Freeze the meat until it is firm on the outside, but not frozen through. Repeat this procedure with the chicken (on a separate plate).

In a food processor, grind the partially frozen pork until it is coarsely chopped. Add the chicken and the remaining ingredients and process for 15 seconds to mix. Unless you have a large-capacity food processor, this will necessitate two batches.

Lightly flour your hands and form the mixture into eight, ½-inch-thick patties. The sausage may be frozen at this point; defrost completely before cooking.

To serve, heat a large skillet, preferably non-stick, until it is hot. Add the patties but do not crowd the pan. Cook over medium heat for four minutes and then carefully flip and cook another three or four minutes. Serve immediately.

Serves 8
Preparation Time:
  20 Minutes
Cooking Time:
  20 Minutes

12 oz. raw pork
    tenderloin
 1 lb. raw, boneless and
    skinless chicken
 1 Tbsp. brown sugar
1½ tsps. salt
 ¾ tsp. white pepper
 ¼ tsp. cayenne pepper
 ½ tsp. sage
 ¼ tsp. allspice

★

Cranberry-Orange Muffins

Yield: 16 Muffins
Preparation Time:
  20 Minutes
Baking Time:
  30 Minutes
Preheat oven to 375°

  ¾ cup butter, softened
  1 cup sugar
  2 eggs
1¼ cups chopped
    cranberries, fresh or
    frozen
    Grated rind of 1 orange
  3 cups flour
  ½ tsp. baking soda
  1 Tbsp. baking powder
  ½ tsp. salt
  1 tsp. nutmeg
1½ cups plain non-fat
    yogurt

This is a departure from my normal muffin recipe, which relies on buttermilk as a tenderizing agent. I was trying to create a low-fat muffin for a change, and so experimented with yogurt in its place. This doesn't qualify as a low-fat treat, I'm afraid, because of the butter, but it is less sweet than most muffins.

In a large bowl cream the butter and sugar until smooth and fluffy. Add the eggs, one at a time, beating well after each addition. Stir in the cranberries and orange zest.

Sift the dry ingredients and add to the bowl in three additions, alternating with the yogurt. Do not overmix or the muffins will be tough.

Line a muffin tin with papers or butter the cups. Fill each cup to the top and sprinkle each muffin with a teaspoon of sugar, if desired.

Bake in the middle of oven for 30 minutes or until the muffins are set and golden.

Eggplant Gratin

I cater for so many vegetarians on safari that I'm always on the lookout for interesting meatless dishes. This casserole is one of my most popular brunch or lunch items. Grilling the eggplant saves calories and fat grams, and I particularly like the smoky flavor it imparts. If you're in a hurry or ripe tomatoes are out of season, skip the homemade sauce and use a purchased "gourmet" substitute. I haven't specified any one type of cheese—a combination of several, like Parmesan, fontina and mozzarella, works well. The gratin keeps in the refrigerator for several days before or after baking; it also freezes well.

Cut the eggplant into ⅓-inch slices. Sprinkle lightly with salt on both sides and arrange the slices on a rack that has been set into a baking tray. Allow the eggplant to sit at room temperature for 30 minutes to extract excess moisture.

Meanwhile, make a tomato sauce by heating about 2 Tbsps. of oil in a saucepan and sautéing the onion until it is soft and translucent. Add the garlic and tomatoes and cook for 5 minutes over high heat, stirring frequently. Then, add the wine, thyme, oregano and salt. Cover the pan and lower the heat so that the sauce maintains a gentle simmer. Cook for 45 minutes to 1 hour or until the tomatoes have softened and the sauce has concentrated in flavor. Add the parsley and basil and remove from the heat.

Pat eggplant dry, brush with oil and grill, bake or fry.

Spread a layer of tomato sauce on the bottom of a 9 × 9 inch baking dish. Cover with a layer of eggplant and top with some of the cheese. Continue layering your ingredients in this manner, finishing with a top layer of cheese.

Bake for 30 minutes or until the gratin is bubbling hot. Remove from the oven and let sit for 10 minutes before serving.

Serves 4
Preparation Time: Sauce:
20 Minutes
Cooking Time:
1½ Hours
Preheat oven to 350°

- 1 **eggplant**
  Salt
- ½ **cup olive oil**
- ¾ **cup finely diced yellow onion**
- 3 **cloves garlic, minced**
- 10 **ripe Roma tomatoes, diced (about 5 cups)**
- ½ **cup red wine**
- 1 **tsp. dried thyme**
- 1 **tsp. dried oregano**
- 1½ **tsps. salt**
- 1 **Tbsp. minced fresh parsley**
- 1 **Tbsp. minced fresh basil**
- 3 **cups shredded cheese**

★

French Scrambled Eggs

Serves 6
Preparation Time:
  5 Minutes
Cooking Time:
  5 Minutes

  1 dozen eggs
  ¼ cup milk
  1 tsp. salt
  ½ tsp. white pepper
  ⅓ cup cream cheese,
    softened
  1½ Tbsps. fresh parsley,
    minced
  1½ Tbsps. fresh dill,
    chopped
  2 Tbsps. butter

Although I don't eat eggs and never have, I do enjoy cooking them. For years my customers just raved about this creation and everyone wanted to know the "secret." There is really nothing to it—the cream cheese makes the eggs creamy and the fresh herbs add flavor. Improvise with what you may have on hand.

I n a large deep bowl, lightly whisk the eggs, milk, salt and pepper. In another bowl, mash the cream cheese with the parsley and dill until well-blended.

In a large skillet, preferably non-stick, heat the butter until it is sizzling, but not brown. Pour in the egg mixture and, over low to medium heat, gently stir the eggs until they just begin to thicken. Immediately add the herbed cream cheese in several chunks and stir constantly until the eggs are set and creamy.

Fruit Salad With Fragrant Syrup

Jazz up fruit with an exotic syrup redolent of the Orient. Homemade fruit salad is worth the effort and always makes a beautiful addition to a special breakfast or brunch. The fruits listed here are just suggestions: use whatever you like that's in season. The Fragrant Syrup recipe makes about one cup. The amount you add to the salad is a matter of personal preference. I usually double the recipe and keep a jar on hand in my refrigerator.

Heat the water and sugar in a small pan and stir to dissolve. Add the remaining syrup ingredients and simmer over low heat for 15 minutes. Turn off the burner, cover the pan and let the syrup cool to room temperature. When cool, strain into a clean bowl. Remove the vanilla bean and, using a small knife, scrape the seeds into the syrup.

Make the fruit salad by cutting the pineapple, melons, mango and peaches into bite-sized, uniform pieces. Add the grapes, blueberries, orange juice and Fragrant Syrup to taste. At this stage you may refrigerate the salad for several hours if desired. Just before serving add the banana and kiwi fruit.

Serves 10
Preparation Time:
  45 Minutes
Cooking Time:
  15 Minutes

Fragrant Syrup:
1 1/3 **cups water**
  1 **cup sugar**
    Grated rind of 1 lime
    Juice of 2 limes
  1 **cinnamon stick, broken**
  2 **star anise**
  8 **cardamom pods, crushed**
  1 **vanilla bean, split**

Fruit Salad:
  1/2 **fresh pineapple**
  1/2 **cantaloupe**
  1/2 **honeydew melon**
  1 **mango**
  2 **peaches or nectarines**
  1 **cup seedless grapes**
  1 **cup blueberries**
  1 **cup fresh squeezed orange juice**
  1 **banana**
  2 **kiwi fruit**

Ham and Pasta Frittata

Serves 6
Preparation Time:
   10 Minutes
Cooking Time:
   30 Minutes
Preheat oven to 350 °

   2 **Tbsps. butter**
   ½ **cup minced scallions**
      or leeks
   1 **cup diced ham**
   ¾ **cup cooked spaghetti**
      or other pasta, cut into
      one-inch lengths
   10 **eggs**
   ½ **cup milk**
   1 **tsp. salt**
   ½ **tsp. white pepper**
   ½ **cup grated Parmesan**
      cheese

If you aren't familiar with frittatas, it's time you experimented with this versatile egg dish. Basically, a frittata is an open-faced omelet begun on the stove top and finished in the oven. If you are pressed for time, you can skip the stove-top step and just cook the frittata from start to finish in the oven. The variety of ingredients is limitless. Frittatas are a great way to use up leftovers, which is how this version came about!

Melt the butter in a 12-inch non-stick skillet. Sauté the scallions or leeks until soft, then add the ham and the chopped pasta and continue cooking until just heated through.

Meanwhile, in a bowl whisk the eggs with the milk, salt and pepper. Pour the custard over the ingredients in the skillet and cook the frittata over medium heat until the bottom sets. Do not stir and do not rush the process.

Sprinkle the top of the frittata with the Parmesan cheese and place the skillet in the center of your preheated oven. Please note that if your skillet has a plastic handle, you must wrap this in several layers of aluminum foil to prevent a melt down. Bake the frittata for 15 to 25 minutes, or until set, puffed and golden.

Carefully slide the frittata onto a serving platter, cut into wedges and serve hot or at room temperature.

Island Berry Pancakes

These pancakes are a world removed from those thick, doughy disks that seem to be ubiquitous these days. In this recipe, the cornmeal and beaten egg whites rescue the pancakes from that fate. Orange juice and zest lend a lively flavor to the batter and the combination of berries is superb. Be sure to cook these pancakes very slowly and to handle them gently, as they are extremely light and delicate.

Sift the cornmeal, flour, baking soda and powder, salt and sugar together in a large bowl. Stir in the grated orange rind and the nutmeg.

In a smaller bowl, whisk the buttermilk, orange juice, egg yolks and oil until combined.

Meanwhile, beat the egg whites in a clean, dry bowl until they form soft peaks.

Add the liquid ingredients to the dry mixture and stir to just combine. Fold in the egg whites.

Heat an electric griddle or set a large skillet on your stove over low heat.

Lightly oil the pan and when hot, spoon about 2 Tbsps. of batter onto the griddle. Spread the batter slightly and then sprinkle a few blueberries and cranberries on top. Repeat with the remaining batter and berries.

Cook very slowly for about 4 minutes, or until you see tiny bubbles forming on the surface of the pancakes. Flip carefully and cook another minute or two. Serve with hot maple syrup and whipped butter.

Yield: 12 Pancakes
Preparation Time:
   15 Minutes
Cooking Time:
   5 Minutes
Preheat griddle to 350°

   ½ **cup yellow cornmeal**
   ½ **cup flour**
   ½ **tsp. baking soda**
   ½ **tsp. baking powder**
   ⅛ **tsp. salt**
   5 **Tbsps. sugar**
      Grated rind of 1 orange
   ¼ **tsp. nutmeg**
   ¾ **cup buttermilk**
   ¼ **cup orange juice**
   2 **eggs, separated**
   5 **Tbsps. vegetable oil**
   ½ **cup frozen blueberries**
   ½ **cup frozen cranberries,**
      sliced
      Hot maple syrup,
      optional
      Whipped butter,
      optional

Lemon-Banana Juice

Serves 4
Preparation Time:
  5 Minutes

  6 ripe bananas
  ½ cup sugar
  1 cup fresh lemon juice,
    chilled
  1½ cups ice cold water

Break away from orange juice and try this healthy, refreshing and unusual breakfast drink. The recipe comes from Chinzombo Safari Lodge in Zambia.

Cut the bananas into small chunks and purée in a blender or food processor until smooth.
  Add the remaining ingredients and blend completely. Taste and adjust for sweetness and consistency as desired.

Maple French Toast

Here's an easy dish for a special breakfast or brunch, one which I never serve without requests for the recipe! All the work is done the day before—in the morning you simply bake the concoction. The fruit may be varied to suit your taste and the season. Bananas work well, especially in combination with berries.

Grease a 9 × 13-inch ovenproof baking pan.
Trim the crust from the French bread and cut the loaf into ½-inch cubes. Place half of the bread into the prepared pan. Scatter the cream cheese cubes atop the bread, cover with the fruit, and then top with the remaining bread.

In a bowl whisk together the eggs, milk, maple syrup and sugar. Pour this mixture over the contents of the pan, cover with plastic wrap and refrigerate overnight.

Discard the plastic wrap and cover the pan with a piece of aluminum foil. Bake in the middle of a 350° oven for 30 minutes, then remove the foil and continue baking for an additional 30 minutes or until the French toast is golden and puffed.

Serve immediately with hot maple syrup.

Serves 10
Preparation Time:
  20 Minutes, plus
  overnight refrigeration
Baking Time:
  One Hour
Preheat oven to 350°

  1 **loaf French bread**
 16 **oz. cream cheese,**
    cubed
  1 **cup fresh blueberries**
  1 **cup fresh strawberries,**
    sliced
 12 **eggs**
  2 **cups milk**
 ½ **cup real maple syrup**
  2 **Tbsps. sugar**

Melanzane Sandwich

Serves 4
Preparation Time:
  20 Minutes
Cooking Time:
  10 Minutes

  1 **large eggplant**
  ¼ **cup olive oil**
     Salt and pepper to
     taste
  4 **sandwich baguettes or**
     bulky rolls
  ¼ **cup pesto (see recipe**
     page 230)
  1 **ripe tomato, sliced**
  1 **ball fresh milk**
     mozzarella, sliced

Melanzane *is Italian for eggplant, which is combined to delicious effect in this sandwich with mozzarella cheese, pesto and tomato. The eggplant can be grilled a day or two in advance, refrigerated and returned to room temperature before assembling. If you can find* mozzarella di bufola, *this is the ultimate cheese to use, although fresh milk domestic mozzarella will be fine.*

Slice the eggplant lengthwise into ¼-inch thick slices. Peeling is not necessary unless you so desire.

Brush both sides of the eggplant slices with olive oil and season lightly with salt and pepper.

Grill over a hot flame until tender but not mushy, about 6 minutes.

Slice the sandwich rolls in half. Spread the cut surfaces with pesto; you won't need much, as it is very powerful.

Plan on 2 pieces of eggplant for each sandwich. Arrange on the bread, top with slices of tomato and cheese and cover with the remaining half roll.

★

Morning Glory Muffins

You might say that I made my reputation on these muffins. I developed this recipe in 1978 for my first restaurant, the Morning Glory Café. The muffins were an instant success and the recipe has been reprinted countless times in magazines, cookbooks and newspapers. In 1991 it was chosen as one of Gourmet's 25 favorite recipes from the past 50 years. Morning Glory Muffins are now sold all across the United States in doughnut shops and trendy coffee houses. I even make them on safari in Africa, although we call them something else because morning glory has a naughty connotation in the British empire.

The combination of fruits and carrots keep the muffins moist. They really do taste better one or two days after baking, mellowing like a fruit cake. I especially like them with cream cheese and honey, although purists would disagree.

Sift together the sugar, flour, cinnamon, baking soda and salt into a large bowl. Add the coconut, fruit, carrots and nuts and stir to combine.

In a separate bowl whisk the eggs with the oil and vanilla. Pour this mixture into the bowl with the dry ingredients and fruit and blend well.

Spoon the batter into cupcake tins lined with muffin papers. Fill each cup to the brim. Bake for 35 minutes at 350°, or until a toothpick inserted into the center of a muffin is withdrawn clean.

Cool the muffins in the pan for 10 minutes, then turn out and finish cooling on a rack. These muffins need 24 hours for ripening to develop their full flavor. They also freeze extremely well.

Yield: 16 Muffins
Preparation Time:
   30 Minutes
Baking Time:
   35 Minutes
Preheat oven to 350°

1¼ cups sugar
2¼ cups flour
1 Tbsp. cinnamon
2 tsp. baking soda
½ tsp. salt
½ cup shredded coconut
½ cup raisins
1 apple, shredded
8 oz. crushed pineapple, drained
2 cups grated carrots (4 large)
½ cup pecans or walnuts
3 eggs
1 cup vegetable oil
1 tsp. vanilla

Orange Oat Waffles

Serves 6
Preparation Time:
  15 Minutes
Cooking Time:
  5 Minutes

  8 Tbsps. butter, melted
  4 egg yolks
1½ cups buttermilk
  ½ cup oatmeal
1½ cups flour
  1 tsp. baking soda
  2 tsp. baking powder
  1 tsp. salt
  ¼ tsp. nutmeg
    Grated rind of
    3 oranges
  4 egg whites
  ⅓ cup sugar

Orange juice and oatmeal add an unusual twist to an old breakfast favorite. These waffles are light and tender due to the addition of beaten egg whites and buttermilk. The batter does not hold well because the egg whites lose their volume over time, but it can be refrigerated and used the following day with no loss in taste. Serve with hot maple syrup and whipped butter.

Combine the melted butter, egg yolks and buttermilk in a small bowl. Grind the oatmeal to a fine powder in a food processor or blender. Mix the oat flour, flour, baking soda and powder, salt and nutmeg in a large bowl. Add the orange rind.

Pour the liquid ingredients into the dry and stir just to combine. Do not overbeat.

Beat the egg whites until foamy and then add the sugar gradually, beating until stiff. Lighten the batter with about 1/3 of the egg whites and then carefully fold in the remainder.

Preheat your waffle iron and follow the manufacturer's directions for cooking.

Pain Perdu

Pain Perdu is French for lost bread and refers to a practice of "reviving" stale bread by soaking it in an egg batter and then sautéing it for French toast. Any firm bread works well, such as French or Italian; brioche and challah are ideal. Serve with hot maple syrup and whipped butter.

Serves 6
Preparation Time:
  10 Minutes
Cooking Time:
  10 Minutes

- 1 **cup heavy cream**
- ½ **cup half and half**
- 2 **eggs**
- ½ **cup orange juice**
- 2 **Tbsps. honey**
- 2 **Tbsps. Grand Marnier**
  or orange liqueur
- 1 **tsp. cinnamon**
- ½ **tsp. nutmeg**
- ½ **tsp. grated orange rind**
- 12 **pieces firm bread**
  (Portuguese, French,
  brioche, etc.) cut at
  least ½-inch thick
- ¼ **cup clarified butter**

I n a large bowl, whisk the cream and half and half with the eggs until combined. Add the orange juice, honey, Grand Marnier, spices and orange rind and whisk thoroughly. Add the bread slices to the bowl and let them soak for several minutes on each side. You don't want the bread to be dry inside, but if you leave it in the batter too long, it will fall apart.

Liberally brush a griddle or large skillet with clarified butter and heat until hot. Over a low to medium heat cook the bread until golden brown, then flip and finish cooking on the other side. Add more butter as necessary. Do not crowd the pan; cook in batches if necessary. The pain perdu may be held in warm oven for 15 minutes before serving.

Scrambled Egg Surprise

Serves 2
Preparation Time:
  10 Minutes
Cooking Time:
  5 Minutes

  2 **cups fresh spinach**
    leaves, firmly packed
  6 **eggs**
  ¼ **cup milk or half and**
    half
  ⅛ **tsp. salt**
  2 **pinches white pepper**
  1 **Tbsp. butter**
  ½ **cup grated Swiss**
    cheese

Plain scrambled eggs are so boring! The very blandness of eggs makes them a perfect foil for almost any ingredient. Stir constantly while the eggs are setting up so that they remain loose and creamy. Other combinations in lieu of the spinach and Swiss cheese suggested here include smoked salmon, dill and crème fraîche; tomato, bacon and cheddar; or Parmesan, parma ham and sautéed mushrooms. Raid your refrigerator and use up odds 'n ends!

P lace the spinach in a large skillet with 1 tablespoon of water. Cook over moderate heat until the spinach is wilted. Turn out onto a chopping board and roughly mince the spinach into bite-sized pieces. Set aside.

Vigorously whisk the eggs with the milk and salt and pepper in a medium-sized bowl.

Melt the butter in a non-stick skillet and when the butter is hot and bubbling, add the egg mixture. Cook very slowly over low heat, stirring constantly. When the eggs are halfway set up, add the cheese and continue stirring until totally cooked.

Mix the spinach into the scrambled eggs and serve immediately.

Spinach Cheese Puffs

I've been making these spinach cheese puffs for years in my restaurants and they are as popular today as they were a decade ago. They make a delicious luncheon entrée and of course can be made bite-sized for party hors d'oeuvres. I have not had much success with storing uncooked puffs. They get very soggy and the filo dough is so delicate that it just flakes apart. If you are making bite-sized puffs, you will have better luck freezing them, but I recommend serving the entrée-sized spinach cheese puffs the day you make them. They are very time-consuming but are worth the effort.

Drain the thawed spinach thoroughly and then squeeze out all the excess moisture with your hands.

In a large bowl, mix the spinach with the cheeses, eggs, herbs, bread crumbs, scallions, lemon juice and spices.

Remove the filo dough from its wrapper and unroll onto a damp towel. Cut the filo dough in half widthwise and refrigerate or freeze half the dough for another occasion.

Each spinach cheese puff will require 4 sheets of dough. Place 1 sheet of filo on a flat surface, brush it with some of the melted butter, then cover it with another sheet of dough. Brush this piece of filo with butter, cover with another sheet of dough, then butter this and top with the fourth sheet of filo. Do not butter the top layer.

Spread about ½ cup of the spinach filling along the bottom edge of the filo stack, stopping short of the side edges. Loosely roll up the dough to form the puff. Repeat with the remaining filling and filo dough.

To cook, place the puffs on a lightly greased baking sheet and brush the tops with melted butter. Bake at 350° for 20 minutes or until the puffs are golden. Serve with a garnish of sour cream and lemon wedges.

Yield: 12 Puffs
Preparation Time:
  1½ Hours
Baking Time:
  20 Minutes
Preheat oven to 350°

- 2 10-oz. packages frozen chopped spinach, thawed
- 1 lb. ricotta cheese
- 8 oz. feta cheese, crumbled
- ¾ cup Parmesan cheese, finely grated
- 6 eggs, beaten
- ½ cup fresh minced parsley
- ⅓ cup fresh minced dill
- ¾ cup fine bread crumbs
- 1 bunch scallions, minced
  Juice of 1 lemon
- 1 tsp. salt
- ½ tsp. fresh ground pepper
- ¼ tsp. nutmeg
- 1 pkg. Filo or phyllo dough
- 1 cup unsalted butter, melted

Tomato and Pesto Quiche

Serves 6
Preparation Time:
   15 Minutes
Baking Time:
   45 Minutes
Preheat oven to 325°

  15 **cherry tomatoes**
1½ **cups ricotta cheese**
 ⅓ **cup crème fraîche or
     sour cream**
 ⅓ **cup cream cheese,
     softened**
 ½ **cup finely grated
     Parmesan cheese**
 ⅓ **cup fresh minced basil**
  1 **egg**
  2 **egg yolks**
 ½ **tsp. salt**
 ¼ **tsp. white pepper
     9-inch pastry shell,
     prebaked**
 ⅓ **cup Pesto (see recipe
     page 230)**

Although quiche no longer enjoys the popularity of its heyday in the '70s, it is still awfully darn good. Maybe real men don't eat it, as the amusing book by that title would have us believe, but there are many who still think it's a terrific choice for lunch or a light supper. Make it in individual tart pans and call it a flan and you have a lovely appetizer course.

Cut each tomato in half horizontally and gently squeeze out the juice and seeds. Place the tomatoes on a rack, cut side down, and let them drain until you are ready to assemble the quiche.

Mix the ricotta, crème fraîche, cream cheese and Parmesan in a medium-sized bowl until smooth. Beat in the basil, the egg and yolks, and the salt and pepper.

Transfer the cheese-custard mixture to the prebaked pastry shell.

Arrange the cherry tomatoes, cut side up, on top of the filling, lightly pressing on the tomatoes to set them in place.

Bake the quiche in a 325° oven for 45 minutes or until the custard has set. Remove the quiche and cool on a rack for 30 minutes.

Fill the center of each tomato shell with pesto. Serve at room temperature.

Upside-down French Toast

I generally make French toast when I have company. It's always a big hit, perhaps because few people have the time or inclination to make it at home these days. This recipe is terribly simple. It is baked rather than fried, eliminating the need to stand over a stove while your guests are seated at the table. Please note that this French toast does need to be assembled the day before serving.

Combine the butter, brown sugar and corn syrup in a pan. Stir over medium heat until the butter melts and the sugar dissolves. Let the sauce boil for 2 minutes without stirring.

Pour the sauce into a 9 × 13 × 2-inch glass baking dish, tilting to coat the bottom surface. Set aside to cool.

Trim the crusts off the bread and discard. Arrange the slices in two layers in the baking dish, cutting the bread to fit as necessary.

Place the half and half, eggs and vanilla in a bowl and whisk to combine; pour this custard over the bread. Cover the dish with plastic wrap and refrigerate overnight.

Bake the French toast at 350° for 30 to 40 minutes, or until it is golden brown and puffed.

Remove from the oven and let cool for 10 minutes before serving. To serve, cut into 6 portions, removing each with a spatula. Invert the pieces so that the sugar topping faces up. Serve with warm maple or fruit syrup.

Serves 6
Preparation Time:
  20 Minutes
(note refrigeration time)
Baking Time:
  35 Minutes
Preheat oven to 350°

  ½ **cup butter**
  1 **cup dark brown sugar, firmly packed**
  2 **Tbsps. light corn syrup**
 12 **slices firm white bread (like Pepperidge Farm toasting white)**
1½ **cups half and half**
  6 **eggs**
  1 **tsp. pure vanilla extract**

★

Appetizers & First Courses

Artichokes Vinaigrette

Asparagus Riso

Butternut Ravioli with
Sage Cream

Country Pâté

Crab Cakes with
Rémoulade Sauce

Ethiopian Chicken Legs

Grilled Mozzarella

Lobster Mousse

Mussels Provençal

Oysters in Champagne
Sauce

Oysters Rockefeller

Pesto and Prosciutto
Palmiers

Polenta Pizzas

Pot Stickers

Rotolo di Prosciutto and
Formaggi

Samoosas

Satay Sticks

Spicy Orange Shrimp

Spinach and Herb
Gnocchi

Spinach Ravioli with
Gorgonzola Sauce

Artichokes Vinaigrette

In the winter I live in the heart of artichoke country where dense fields of silvery-green, knee-high bushes march along the roadsides for miles. Artichokes twice the size of softballs sell for a dollar apiece at local farm stands. Blessed with this bounty, hardly a day goes by that I don't eat one of these low-calorie, vitamin-packed vegetables. Although the idea of cooking a fresh artichoke seems daunting to some people, in truth, there is nothing more basic.

Serves 4
Preparation Time:
  15 Minutes
Cooking Time:
  30 Minutes

  4 **large artichokes**
  1 **lemon, juiced**
  1 **tsp. salt**
  1 **cup French Poodle**
     Vinaigrette (see recipe
     page 221)

Wash the artichokes and cut off the stems. Rub the leaves and the base with the lemon juice. In a large pan add 1 inch of water, the salt and any residual lemon juice. Arrange the artichokes, stem side down. Cover the pan and steam over medium-high heat for approximately 25 minutes. The cooking time will vary depending on the size of your artichokes. When cooked, a knife will easily pierce the bottom and the leaves will pull off without a struggle. Avoid over-cooking the artichokes.

Transfer the artichokes to a platter and let stand upside down until cool.

When cool enough to handle, remove all of the leaves from the artichokes. Select approximately twenty of the best leaves from each artichoke and set these aside.

Use a small spoon to scrape the inedible hairy chokes from the artichoke bottoms.

Place each bottom in the center of an 8-inch plate. Arrange a ring of the reserved leaves around the bottoms, creating 2 or 3 layers.

When ready to serve, fill the bottoms with vinaigrette and drizzle a small additional amount along the base of the leaves.

Asparagus Riso

Serves 6
Preparation Time:
  20 Minutes
Cooking Time:
  40 Minutes

¾ lb. fresh asparagus
1 cup water or broth
½ cup butter
1¼ cups finely minced
   yellow onion
4 cloves garlic, minced
3 cups riso pasta (prefer
   De Cecco 74)
5 to 6 cups strong
   chicken stock (recipe,
   page 70)
1 cup white wine
2 cups freshly grated
   Parmesan cheese
   Salt and pepper to
   taste

Riso is a rice-shaped pasta that I sometimes use in place of Arborio rice for a risotto-style dish. The cooking technique is identical to making risotto but the end result is much lighter. It makes a nice first course, or served in more generous portions, a satisfying, single-dish supper. Often I make this version with the addition of fresh crab meat and cream. As with risotto, anything goes!

Peel the asparagus and reserve peelings and stalk ends. Cook asparagus until just tender; do not overcook. Remove the spears from the pan and set aside. Add the peelings and stalk ends to the cooking water or liquid and reduce to ½ cup. Strain and reserve.

Heat butter in a large skillet and when hot, add the onion. Sauté for about 8 minutes or until the onion is tender and translucent.

Add the garlic and the pasta and stir for 2 minutes.

Add 1 cup of hot chicken stock to the skillet and cook slowly over low heat until the liquid is absorbed. Next add the cup of wine and cook until it evaporates. In the same manner, add the reserved asparagus liquid, then continue adding the stock in half-cup increments, cooking until absorbed before adding the next installment. Stir frequently.

When the riso is tender, stir in 1½ cups of the Parmesan and heat through. Cut the asparagus spears on the diagonal into 1-inch pieces and gently mix into the pasta.

Season to taste with salt and pepper and serve immediately. Garnish with the remaining Parmesan cheese.

Butternut Ravioli with Sage Cream

Silky, slightly sweet squash purée is an unusual but delicious filling for pasta. This dish is not for dieters, the sauce being the ultimate in richness, but it does make a sensational first course for a special occasion meal.

Cut the squash in half. Scoop out the seeds and discard. Place on a baking sheet, cover with foil and roast for 75 to 90 minutes, or until very soft.

When the squash has cooled enough to handle, scrape the flesh into a strainer set over a bowl. Let the squash drain for at least four hours, preferably overnight. Reserve whatever juices exude.

Measure out 2 cups of squash and place in a food processor. Purée.

Reduce the rendered juice over high heat to 1 Tbsp. Add juice to the squash, along with the remaining ingredients, pulsing to blend. Refrigerate the mixture for at least 4 hours before using.

Form the raviolis as described on page 231.

The Sauce:
In a small skillet brown the butter with the sage until it is nutty.

Transfer to a large skillet and add the cream. Cook over medium heat for 20 minutes or until the cream has reduced and thickened slightly.

Add the cheese and stir to melt. Season to taste with salt and pepper.

To Serve:
Bring a large pot of lightly salted water to a boil. Add the raviolis and poach for 3 minutes if fresh, 6 minutes if frozen.

Sauté the walnut pieces with the butter until warmed through. Salt lightly.

Place a small pool of sauce on each serving plate. Arrange 6 raviolis on top and drizzle with a little more sauce.

Garnish with the walnuts and fresh sage leaves.

Serves 8; approximately 50 raviolis
Preparation Time: 20 Minutes
(note refrigeration time)
Cooking Time: 1½ Hours, total
Preheat oven to 375°

- 2 cups roasted butternut squash (about 1½ lbs.)
- 1 egg
- ¼ tsp. white pepper
- 1 tsp. salt
- ¼ tsp. nutmeg
- 2 Tbsps. brown sugar
- 1 recipe Ravioli Dough (see recipe page 231)

The Sauce:
- 2 Tbsps. butter
- 1 tsp. fresh sage, minced
- 3 cups heavy cream
- ½ cup fresh grated Parmesan
  Salt and fresh ground pepper

The Garnish:
- ½ cup walnut pieces
- 1 Tbsp. butter
  Fresh sage leaves

★

Country Pâté

Yield: 1 Loaf
Preparation Time:
  30 Minutes
(note refrigeration time)
Cooking Time:
  1¾ Hours
Preheat oven to 325°

  1 lb. bacon, sliced
  4 bay leaves
  4 slices white bread,
    crustless
  ½ cup heavy cream
  ½ cup Port or Cognac
  1 lb. chicken livers,
    drained
1½ lb. pork sausage
  1 tsp. thyme
  ¼ tsp. allspice
  ¼ tsp. white pepper
  ¼ tsp. nutmeg
  1 clove garlic, minced

Everyone likes this pâté because it doesn't have too strong a liver flavor. Double the recipe and freeze one loaf, as it's just as easy to make two loaves as one.

Separate the bacon slices and blanch them in boiling water for 1 minute to remove excess salt. Rinse in warm water and drain. Line the bottom and sides of a loaf pan with the bacon slices, letting the bacon hang over the edges of the pan. Place 2 bay leaves on top of the bacon. Set aside.

Tear the bread in pieces and place in a small bowl. Add the cream and port to the bread and let soak until the bread has absorbed the liquids. Next, coarsely grind the raw chicken livers and then mix the liver with the pork sausage in a large bowl. Add the saturated bread, the herbs, spices and garlic and blend until combined. Sauté 2 Tbsps. of the pâté mixture in a skillet and taste; adjust seasonings.

Spoon the pâté into the prepared loaf pan and place the remaining 2 bay leaves on top of the mixture. Fold the overhanging bacon strips onto the top of the pâté and cover with any remaining bacon slices.

Cover the pâté with a piece of aluminum foil and place in a bain-marie. To fabricate a bain-marie, simply fill a pan larger in all dimensions than the loaf pan with boiling water to halfway up the sides of the pâté. Place the loaf pan in the center of the water bath and bake for 1¾ hours or until the internal temperature reaches 160°.

Remove the pâté from the oven and let it cool for 15 minutes on a wire rack. Compress the pâté by weighting it with a brick or cans for at least one hour. When cool, unmold the pâté and wrap tightly in aluminum foil. Refrigerate 2 days before serving to allow flavors to develop or freeze for up to 3 months.

To serve, discard the bay leaves and any excess bacon. Slice the pâté with a serrated knife and serve with any of the following condiments such as Dijon mustard, sliced Bermuda onion, cornichons (French sour pickles), capers or sliced tomatoes. Serve it on pumpernickel bread, crackers or wafers.

Crab Cakes with Rémoulade Sauce

If you try only one recipe from this cookbook, it should be this one. It is my most frequently requested recipe and these crab cakes always rate rave reviews. They are tender and juicy and they'll melt in your mouth. Instead of conventional bread crumbs for a binder, I use a shrimp mousse, which gives them an ethereal lightness and fresh taste.

Purée the raw shrimp to a paste in a food processor. Add the egg white and heavy cream and pulse to blend.

Transfer the shrimp mousse to a bowl and add the crab, squeezed dry of all juice, the seasonings, mayonnaise and lemon juice.

Heat the olive oil in a small skillet and sauté the shallots, scallions and peppers for 3 minutes or until soft but not mushy. Add the contents of the skillet to the mixture in the bowl and refrigerate, covered, for at least 2 hours or overnight.

Place the bread crumbs on a plate. Form the cold crab mixture into small cakes and press into the crumbs to form a thin coating.

Heat the clarified butter in a non-stick skillet and when it is hot, add the crab cakes and sauté over medium heat for 4 minutes. Carefully flip the crab cakes and continue cooking for another 2 to 3 minutes.

Serve the crab cakes with a dollop of Rémoulade Sauce (recipe follows on next page) and garnish with a lemon wedge.

**Serves 4 as an entree;
6 as an appetizer
Preparation Time:
30 Minutes
(note refrigeration time)
Cooking Time:
10 Minutes**

6 oz. raw shrimp, peeled and deveined
1 egg white
¾ cup heavy cream
1 lb. crab meat, well drained
2 tsps. Worcestershire sauce
¼ tsp. salt
½ cup finely chopped parsley
½ tsp. Tabasco
¼ tsp. cayenne pepper
¼ cup mayonnaise
1 Tbsp. lemon juice
2 Tbsps. olive oil
2 shallots, finely minced
1 bunch scallions, finely minced
⅓ cup each finely minced yellow, red and orange pepper
2 cups fine bread crumbs
¼ cup clarified butter

Rémoulade Sauce
Yield: 2 Cups
Preparation Time:
  15 Minutes

  2 egg yolks
  1 Tbsp. Dijon mustard
  1 Tbsp. tarragon vinegar
  ¼ tsp. salt
  ⋅ Fresh ground pepper
  ½ cup olive oil
  1 cup vegetable oil
  ½ tsp. Tabasco
  ¼ tsp. cayenne pepper
  1 Tbsp. tomato paste
  1 tsp. lemon juice
  3 drops Angostura
    bitters
  ⅛ cup capers, chopped
  1 Tbsp. caper juice
  4 cornichons, finely
    minced
  2 Tbsps. heavy cream
  1 Tbsp. minced parsley

Rémoulade Sauce
In a clean bowl whisk together the yolks, mustard, vinegar, salt and pepper.

Add the oils very slowly, drop by drop at first, whisking constantly. You may add the oils a bit faster after the first ½-cup has been incorporated.

To this mayonnaise base add the remaining ingredients, blending well.

Refrigerate à maximum of 4 days.

☆

Ethiopian Chicken Legs

A staple of Ethiopian cooking is berbere, *a fiery spice paste, which lends this dish its uniqueness. Although chicken legs are specified here, thighs or wings or breasts also could be used successfully. The dish can be served hot or cold. As a matter of fact, you can cook the chicken a day ahead, refrigerate, and then reheat in a hot oven or under the broiler before serving.*

To prepare the *berbere* place all of the dried spices in a small skillet and cook over low heat, stirring constantly, for 4 to 5 minutes. The spices should become fragrant and hot to the touch. Add the red wine and stir to make a paste. Remove the skillet from the stove and add the orange juice and oil.

Dry the chicken legs with paper towels and then liberally coat the meat with the spice paste. Place the chicken in a plastic bag or in a baking pan, covered with plastic wrap, and chill for at least 24 hours.

When you are ready to cook the chicken, preheat your oven to 375°. Arrange the drumsticks on a baking tray so that the pieces do not touch or crowd one another.

Bake for 30 to 40 minutes or until cooked through, turning the chicken once during the cooking process. The cooking time will vary depending on the size of your drumsticks.

Serves 12
Preparation Time:
   30 Minutes
(note refrigeration time)
Cooking Time:
   45 Minutes
Preheat oven to 375°

   ½ tsp. ground ginger
   ½ tsp. ground cardamom
   1 tsp. ground coriander
   ½ Tbsp. ground turmeric
   ½ Tbsp. dry mustard
       powder
   ½ tsp. ground nutmeg
   ½ tsp. ground allspice
   ½ tsp. ground cinnamon
   ¼ cup Hungarian hot
       paprika
   1 Tbsp. cayenne pepper
1½ tsps. salt
   ⅓ cup red wine
   2 Tbsps. orange juice
   2 Tbsps. peanut oil
  24 small chicken legs

Grilled Mozzarella

Serves 6
Preparation Time:
  20 Minutes
Cooking Time:
  3 Minutes

12 **Swiss chard leaves**
12 **nuggets fresh milk**
    mozzarella at room
    temperature
12 **slices prosciutto ham,**
    paper thin
24 **leaves fresh basil**
    Extra virgin olive oil
    Fresh ground pepper

Simple but satisfying, this unusual preparation makes a terrific appetizer that is not too rich or filling. Blanched romaine leaves could be substituted for the Swiss chard if it's not available.

Cut off the thick white stems of the chard and discard. Blanch the Swiss chard in boiling water for 45 seconds and immediately refresh the leaves with ice cold water. Dry the leaves with paper towels. If the chard leaves are very large, cut them in half to create an approximate 4-inch square.

Place a leaf on a flat surface and top with a piece of prosciutto. The prosciutto must be trimmed so that it does not extend beyond the edges of the Swiss chard square.

Cover the prosciutto with 2 basil leaves and then place a nugget of mozzarella in the center of the packet. The cheese nuggets should be roughly 1½-inch square in size, or at any rate not so large that they can't be totally enclosed by the Swiss chard.

Drizzle a bit of olive oil over the mozzarella and then grind fresh pepper on top.

Wrap the cheese in the blanched leaf by pulling the sides in to the center and then folding the top and bottom of the leaf over the mozzarella. The cheese should not be visible. Repeat with the remaining Swiss chard leaves.

Heat the barbecue grill to its highest intensity. Brush the mozzarella bundles with olive oil before grilling. Grill 1½ minutes on each side and serve immediately.

Lobster Mousse

You will surely be greeted with rave reviews when you serve this splendid first course. It is a beautiful pink color and the mousse is so light and delicate that it just melts in your mouth. The recipe might look complicated, but it isn't, and the dish can be prepared in stages.

The mousse can be held in the refrigerator, uncooked, for 8 hours. The sauce is very delicate and will break if it gets too hot. If you make it in advance, place it in a warm thermos until you are ready to serve the mousse.

Place 2 inches of water in a large pot and bring to a boil. Put the lobster in the pan and cover lightly. Steam for 2 minutes only and then remove the lobster and plunge it into cold water to stop the cooking process.

When cool enough to handle, remove the meat from the lobster and cut it into one-inch pieces. Refrigerate, covered, until very cold.

Sauté the minced shallot in the butter until it is soft. Let cool.

Place the cold lobster meat and the minced shallot into the bowl of a food processor. Process until the mixture is totally smooth. Force the purée through a sieve to ensure a perfect texture and then return the lobster to the food processor bowl.

Add the egg white, salt and nutmeg and purée again.

Put the entire food processor bowl, including the steel blade in the refrigerator and chill for 30 minutes.

Return the bowl to its base and, with the machine running, pour in the heavy cream in a steady stream.

At this point, check the consistency of the mousse with a spoon. The mixture should be absolutely smooth and should fall from the spoon with a soft plop. Add more cream if needed to achieve the correct texture.

Spoon the mousse into 4 buttered 6 oz. ramekins or glass cups. Poach in a water bath in a 325° oven for 25 minutes or until puffed and set.

Beurre Blanc:
Combine the shallots, wine and vinegar in a saucepan and cook over medium heat until the liquid is reduced to 2 Tbsps.

Serves 4
Preparation Time:
  45 Minutes
(note refrigeration time)
Cooking Time:
  25 Minutes

1¼ lbs. live Maine Lobster
1 shallot, minced
1 Tbsp. unsalted butter
1 egg white
¼ tsp. salt
⅛ tsp. freshly ground nutmeg
1 cup heavy cream
Beurre blanc sauce, recipe follows
1 Tbsp. fresh minced parsley

Beurre Blanc:
2 Tbsps. minced shallot
½ cup dry white wine
⅓ cup white wine vinegar
2 Tbsps. heavy cream
½ lb. unsalted butter, cut into 16 pieces

Add the heavy cream and reduce by half.

Over very low heat whisk in one piece of butter at a time, waiting for each piece to melt before adding the next. Do not allow the sauce to become too hot or the emulsification will break.

To Serve:
Invert the ramekins onto warm plates and blot up any water that collects on the plates with a towel.

Spoon the Beurre Blanc Sauce over the mousse, garnish with parsley and serve immediately.

☆

Mussels Provençal

With the advent of aquaculture farms, mussels are now available year-round, and even better, they are raised to be beardless and sand-free. This recipe's success lies in a tasty broth, the secret of which is lots of butter and Pernod, a licorice-flavored liqueur. Unfortunately, Pernod is expensive, seems to come only in giant bottles, and has few other uses in cooking. Obviously, the mussels will still taste good even if you eliminate this ingredient, but if you plan on making this dish fairly often, I recommend adding Pernod to your liquor cabinet.

Scrub the mussels in cold water, using a small paring knife to scrape off any pieces of hairy beard that may be present.

Combine the wine, garlic and leeks in a skillet or pan large enough to accommodate the mussels. Bring to a boil, then add the mussels. Cover tightly and steam 3 to 5 minutes over high heat. Discard any mussels that have not opened after 5 minutes.

Add the tomatoes, Pernod, butter and parsley to the pan and cook, uncovered, over high heat for a few minutes to reduce the broth and concentrate the flavors.

Season as required and serve immediately, dividing the mussels and broth between the bowls.

Serves 4
Preparation Time:
  20 Minutes
Cooking Time:
  10 Minutes

1½ lbs. raw mussels
  2 cups dry white wine
  3 cloves garlic, minced
  ⅓ cup leek, thinly sliced
  2 ripe tomatoes, diced
  2 Tbsps. Pernod
  4 Tbsps. butter
  3 Tbsps. fresh minced
    parsley
    Salt and pepper to
    taste

Oysters in Champagne Sauce

Serves 4
Preparation Time:
 30 Minutes
Cooking Time:
 15 Minutes

 12 **fresh oysters in the shell**
 ⅓ **cup oyster liquor or fish stock**
 ¼ **cup champagne**
 1 **tsp. shallot, minced**
 ¼ **cup heavy cream**
 2 **egg yolks**
 2 **tsps. lemon juice**
 ¼ **tsp. salt**
 ¼ **tsp. white pepper**
 ½ **cup unsalted butter**
 3 **cups rock salt**
 ¼ **cup Parmesan cheese, freshly grated**

Open the oysters over a bowl in order to save the liquor contained within the shells. Discard the top or flat half of the shell. Strain the accumulated oyster liquor through wet cheesecloth or a paper coffee filter to remove dirt or shell particles that may be present. Place the liquor, champagne and shallots in a non-aluminum saucepan and cook until the liquid is reduced to ¼ cup. Add the heavy cream and reduce again until only ¼ cup of liquid remains.

Cook the oysters in a 350° oven on a sheet pan for 2 minutes or until the edges of the oysters just begin to curl. Do not overcook! Pour off any liquid that collects in the oyster shells and reserve.

In the bowl of a food processor or blender place the egg yolks, lemon juice, salt and pepper. Melt the butter in a small pan until it is sizzling hot, and with the machine running, pour in the butter in a slow, steady stream. Then slowly add the champagne reduction and any reserved oyster liquor you may have.

Place the oysters on a layer of rock salt on a sheet pan and cover each mollusk with some of the champagne sauce. The rock salt is used to form a bed for the oysters. If you have no rock salt, you might improvise with balls of aluminum foil to keep the oysters from tipping over.

Sprinkle with the Parmesan cheese, then broil until the sauce is bubbly and browned. Serve 3 oysters per person.

Oysters Rockefeller

Here is my version of a classic oyster dish that never fails to elicit praise from my guests. I used to serve Oysters Rockefeller as a luncheon entrée at one of my Nantucket restaurants. They were so popular that I had to take them off the menu because the kitchen staff revolted at having to open so many oysters. That is the most tedious step of this recipe, but the end result is worth the effort!

Squeeze the excess moisture from the thawed spinach and place the spinach in the bowl of a food processor. Add the parsley, scallions and anchovies to the spinach and process to roughly purée the greens.

Add the melted butter to the bowl of the food processor and purée until the mixture is smooth.

Transfer to a clean bowl, add the bread crumbs, Worcestershire and Pernod and stir to blend.

Place a layer of rock salt on a baking tray to form a bed for the oysters. If you have no rock salt you might improvise with balls of aluminum foil to keep the oysters from tipping over.

Open the oysters and discard the flat shell. Add any oyster liquor that collects to the spinach purée.

Arrange the oysters on the rock salt and broil for about 3 minutes or until the edges of the oysters just begin to curl.

Remove the tray from the oven and spoon a generous dollop of the spinach purée onto each oyster. Sprinkle with grated Parmesan, then run the oysters under the broiler for several minutes until the spinach is hot and the cheese browns. Serve immediately.

Serves 6
Preparation Time:
  One Hour
Cooking Time:
  5 Minutes

- 10 oz. frozen spinach, thawed
- 1 bunch parsley
- 1 bunch scallions
- 4 anchovies, mashed
- 1 cup unsalted butter, melted
- 2/3 cup bread crumbs
- 2 tsps. Worcestershire sauce
- 1 Tbsp. Pernod
- 24 oysters in the shell
  Rock salt
- 3/4 cup Parmesan cheese, grated

Pesto and Prosciutto Palmiers

Yield: 24
Preparation Time:
  15 Minutes
(note refrigeration time)
Baking Time:
  15 Minutes
Preheat oven to 425°

  1 **box Pepperidge Farm**
    frozen puff pastry
  ¼ **lb. thinly sliced**
    prosciutto
  ⅔ **cup pesto (see recipe**
    page 230)
  ¼ **cup freshly grated**
    Parmesan cheese

Here's a simple but elegant hors d'oeuvre idea that goes together in a snap. The technique translates to any number of filling permutations: wild mushroom duxelles or olive tapenade work particularly well.

Defrost the puff pastry sheets per package directions. Lightly flour a clean work surface and roll the pastry to make the sheets slightly thinner. Arrange a single layer of prosciutto on each of the sheets, leaving a ¾-inch border of pastry. Divide the pesto and spread atop the ham. Sprinkle with the Parmesan cheese.

Arrange the puff pastry so that the short edges are at the top and bottom. Fold the short sides in to the middle so that the edges meet in the center of the pastry. Fold each of these halves again so that the rolled edges meet in the middle. Now, fold these two sides together so that you have one long strip, six layers thick. Trim the ends off the pastry and then cut into ½-inch slices. Place on a buttered or parchment-lined baking sheet, spacing the slices at least 2 inches apart so they have room to spread. Cover the tray with plastic wrap and chill the palmiers for 30 minutes.

Bake in the middle of the oven for 12 to 15 minutes or until the palmiers are puffed, golden and crisp. Cool for a few minutes, then transfer to a wire rack. Serve hot or cold.

Polenta Pizzas

I'm always on the lookout for new hors d'oeuvres or appetizers because I find I get in a rut, serving the same old favorites at every party. This simple, do-ahead recipe has become a staple of my repertoire and it always garners acclaim. Cut the polenta into squares or diamonds of appropriate sizes depending on whether they are meant to accompany cocktails or serve as a starter or luncheon course.

Oil or butter a 9 × 13-inch baking pan and set aside. Bring the stock and water to a boil in a large, heavy-bottomed saucepan with the salt. Add the cornmeal in a slow, steady stream, stirring constantly to avoid lumps. Reduce heat and cook, stirring continually, for 15 minutes.

When the polenta is the consistency of thick porridge and pulls away from the sides of the pan when stirred, remove from the heat and add the butter and Parmesan cheese.

Pour the polenta into the prepared pan, carefully smoothing the top with a spatula or knife. Chill until firm, then cover with plastic wrap and allow the mixture to rest in the refrigerator overnight.

Cut the polenta into squares or diamonds or whatever shape you like. Place on a baking tray and broil one side of the polenta until hot, about 4 minutes. Watch carefully that it does not burn.

Remove the tray from the oven and top the unheated side of the polenta with a slice or two of prosciutto, cut or folded to shape. Spread a dollop of pesto onto the ham and then top with a combination of the two cheeses.

Return the pan to the oven and broil until the cheese melts. Serve immediately.

Serves 6 as first course;
  10 as an hors d'oeuvre
Preparation Time:
  15 Minutes
(note chilling time)
Cooking Time:
  20 Minutes

  2 cups chicken stock
  2 cups water
  1 tsp. salt
  1 cup coarsely ground
    cornmeal (polenta)
  2 Tbsps. butter
  1/3 cup grated Parmesan
    cheese
  1/2 lb. thinly sliced
    prosciutto ham
  1/2 cup pesto (see recipe
    page 230)
  1 cup grated mozzarella
    cheese
  1 cup grated fontina
    cheese

★

Pot Stickers

Yield: 70 Pot Stickers
Preparation Time:
One Hour
Cooking Time:
5 Minutes per batch
Special Equipment:
Pot sticker or
Chinese dumpling tool

1 lb. ground pork
10 scallions, finely
   minced
½ cup grated fresh ginger
   root
8 cloves garlic, minced
2 tsps. salt
¼ tsp. cayenne pepper
1 pkg. wonton wrappers,
   preferably round
2 Tbsps. vegetable or
   sesame oil
3 Tbsps. chicken stock

If you aren't spending your entire day at it, making pot stickers isn't too terribly tedious. The filling is versatile and I occasionally substitute chicken, duck or shrimp for the pork. They are a snap to cook and so flavorful that a fussy sauce is not really necessary. I like Ginger Beurre Blanc sauce (see recipe page 103), but if time is short, use soy or plum sauce instead.

Combine the pork, scallions, ginger root, garlic, salt and cayenne and mix thoroughly. Test the filling for flavor by sautéing a tsp. of the meat in a tiny bit of oil. Add more garlic, ginger, salt or pepper according to your taste.

If you don't have round wonton skins, cut them into circles. Drape one wrapper over your pot sticker gadget; lightly brush the edges with water.

Place a small dollop of the pork mixture in the center of the wrapper. Fold the tool in half to crimp the edges.

Transfer the pot stickers to a tray lined with wax paper. Do not stack or allow the pieces to touch one another. The pot stickers may be frozen at this point. Once they are rock hard, they can be transferred to plastic bags or containers for ease of storage.

Heat the oil in a large, non-stick skillet. When it is sizzling, add as many pot stickers will fit comfortably without undue crowding. Cook over medium-high heat for two minutes, or until the bottoms are crispy and browned.

Add the chicken stock to the pan and cover immediately. This will allow the pot stickers to steam through and finish cooking, about two more minutes.

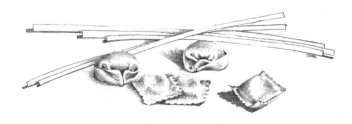

Rotolo di Prosciutto and Formaggi

Rotolo di Prosciutto and Formaggi is a fancy Italian name for an intriguing cheese "log." This is a visually stunning presentation that is really quite simple to assemble. It's essential that the prosciutto and zucchini are sliced paper-thin for ease in serving and eating. The flavors of this dish are most intense when served at room temperature, so be sure to remove the Rotolo from the refrigerator well in advance of serving. The Rotolo will keep for up to a week if wrapped tightly in plastic.

Place a double thickness of damp cheesecloth or a linen towel on a clean counter surface. Arrange the mozzarella slices on the cloth, overlapping the edges slightly to form a solid rectangle approximately 7 inches wide by 27 inches long.

Slice the fontina cheese and place it on an ovenproof plate. Melt the cheese in a microwave or conventional oven until it is soft and creamy.

Working quickly, spread the melted fontina over the mozzarella layer, taking care to cover the overlapping edges of the cheese slices. Generously grind fresh pepper over the entire surface.

Next, arrange half of the prosciutto ham in a single layer over the cheese.

Using a vegetable peeler, slice the zucchini lengthwise into very thin strips. Cover the ham with the zucchini, then top with a layer of basil leaves.

Cover the surface with the remaining prosciutto and then roll up the entire ensemble as tightly as possible, starting at the narrow, short end.

Wrap the Rotolo in the cheesecloth or towel and refrigerate overnight. Slice with a serrated knife and serve at room temperature on a pool of Tomato-Basil Vinaigrette. (See recipe page 234.)

Serves 8
Preparation Time:
  One Hour
(note refrigeration time)

1¼ lb. mozzarella cheese, sliced
¾ lb. fontina cheese
  Freshly ground black pepper
⅓ lb. prosciutto ham, sliced paper-thin
3 small zucchini
1 bunch fresh basil
  Tomato-Basil Vinaigrette
  (see recipe page 234)

Samoosas

Yield: 3 to 4 dozen
Preparation Time:
  1½ Hours
(note refrigeration time)
Cooking Time:
  filling: 15 Minutes

Filling:
  1 Tbsp. vegetable oil
  1 cup finely minced
    onion
  2 Tbsps. grated fresh
    ginger root
  3 cloves garlic, minced
  1 lb. ground beef
  ½ tsp. cayenne pepper
  ½ tsp. ground cardamom
  ¼ tsp. cinnamon
  2 tsps. curry powder, or
    more to taste
  1 tsp. salt
  ¼ tsp. ground cloves
  ½ tsp. ground cumin
  ½ tsp. ground coriander
    Juice of half a lemon
  1 Tbsp. finely diced
    dried apricot
  2 Tbsps. golden raisins

Pastry:
  4 cups flour
  1½ tsps. salt
  1⅓ cups solid shortening
  ⅔ cup ice water

  4 cups vegetable oil for
    frying

Similar to empanadas, *these spicy meat pastries of Indian origin are a ubiquitous cocktail staple in many parts of Africa. The filling lends itself to experimentation and versatility, so feel free to substitute pork, chicken, lamb, shrimp or vegetables (or any combination of these items) for the beef suggested here. Traditionally, the pastry for samoosas is similar to pie dough. Because they are deep fried, this results in a delicious but rather heavy, high-fat morsel. If you are concerned about calories and fat, substitute egg roll wrappers for the pastry; these are available in most supermarkets or from Oriental markets.*

eat the oil in a large skillet and sauté the onion, ginger root and garlic over moderate heat for 4 or 5 minutes.

Add the remaining filling ingredients and cook for 10 minutes or so, or until the beef is cooked. Drain off any excess fat and set the mixture aside to cool. Taste and adjust seasonings if desired.

To make the pastry, place the flour and salt in the bowl of a food processor and pulse to blend. Add the shortening and mix thoroughly. With the machine running, add about ½ cup of ice water and pulse to incorporate. Check the consistency of the dough and add more water by the teaspoon until the pastry just holds together when you pinch a bit between your fingers. Transfer the dough to a floured surface and divide it into four pieces, flattening each one into a patty. Cover with plastic wrap and refrigerate 1 hour. If you do not have a food processor, make the pastry in a bowl, following the same basic procedure; use two knives or a pastry blender to cut the shortening into the flour mixture.

To form the samoosas, roll one of the pastry disks into a thin sheet. Use a 4-inch circular ring to cut out as many rounds as possible from the dough.

Place a dollop of meat filling on one half of each circle, brush the edge of the pastry with water and then fold in half to make a crescent shape. Do not overfill the samoosas or they will split apart during the frying stage. Crimp together the edges of the dough with a fork. Repeat with all of the remaining pastry dough and filling. Please note: if you are using egg roll wrappers instead of the traditional pastry, cut the sheets in half and make triangular-shaped samoosas. Use water to seal the edges; crimping is not necessary.

At this stage the samoosas can be frozen for several months if desired. Arrange them on sheet trays so they do not touch and freeze until solid. Then, bag or store them in an air-tight container. Do not defrost before cooking.

To cook, heat enough oil in a skillet or saucepan to deep fry the samoosas. You will need oil to a depth of at least 1 inch. Bring the temperature of the oil to 375°, then fry the samoosas in small batches until golden brown. Drain on paper towels and serve hot or at room temperature. I like to accompany them with mango chutney.

★

Satay Sticks

Yield: 12 to 16 skewers
Preparation Time:
  30 Minutes
(note marinating time)
Cooking Time:
  5 Minutes

  1 lb. boneless chicken
    breast or tenderloin of
    beef or pork
  2 Tbsps. curry powder
  ½ tsp. salt
  1 Tbsp. ground coriander
  1 Tbsp. sugar
  1 cup coconut milk
    (see recipe page 216)
  ½ cup peanut oil
  1 Tbsp. rice wine vinegar

Peanut Sauce:
  ½ tsp. Tabasco
  1 Tbsp. curry powder
  2 Tbsps. sugar
  3 Tbsps. chunky peanut
    butter
  1 cup coconut milk

Cucumber Condiment:
  1 cup very thinly sliced
    English cucumber
  1 Tbsp. water
  2 tsps. rice wine vinegar
  ¼ tsp. Tabasco
  ½ tsp. salt
  1 Tbsp. chopped peanuts
    (garnish)

I learned to make satay at the Oriental Cooking School in Bangkok. It's a great party dish or first course and it's rare to find someone who doesn't like this Thai hors d'oeuvre.

Cut meat into strips 1 inch wide by 2 inches long by ³⁄₁₆ inch thick.

Thread the meat onto bamboo skewers so that no wood is visible except at the handle end. Do not crowd or ribbon the meat or it will not cook properly.

Mix the curry, salt, coriander and sugar together and coat the meat with this seasoning. Let the meat rest for 10 minutes.

Add the liquid ingredients to the meat, mix well and marinate at room temperature for 1 hour.

Barbecue the filled skewers until they are cooked through, turning only once.

Serve the satay sticks with Peanut Sauce and Cucumber Condiment.

Peanut Sauce:
Combine the ingredients in a pan and simmer over low heat until the sauce thickens.

Cucumber Condiment:
Combine ingredients, garnish with chopped peanuts and chill.

Spicy Orange Shrimp

This Chinese-inspired marinade is very tasty. I like to serve the grilled shrimp on a bed of arugula or baby lettuces that have been tossed in a bit of the marinade. I garnish the plate with a julienne of red and yellow peppers and then scatter sesame seeds on top of everything. You could also thread the shrimp on skewers with chunks of fruit or vegetables. Otherwise, the marinade makes a good dipping sauce if you wish to serve the shrimp chilled or at room temperature.

Combine all of the marinade ingredients in a small bowl and whisk to blend.

Add the shrimp, cover with plastic wrap and refrigerate at least 4 hours before cooking.

When ready to serve, heat your barbecue, adjusting the rack about two inches above the coals. Grill over a medium to high heat. The marinade is sweet, so it will burn if you are not careful. Shrimp cook quickly—5 to 7 minutes should be sufficient.

Serves 6
Preparation Time:
  15 Minutes
(note marinating time)
Cooking Time:
  7 Minutes

- ½ cup frozen orange juice concentrate
- ¼ cup peanut oil
- ¼ cup soy sauce
- 2 Tbsps. white wine
- 2 Tbsps. sweet hot mustard
- 2 tsps. sesame oil
- 2 tsps. Five-spice powder
- 1 clove garlic, minced
- 1 lb. large raw shrimp, peeled and deveined

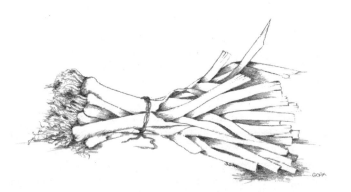

Spinach and Herb Gnocchi

Serves 8
Preparation Time:
 45 Minutes
(note refrigeration time)

½ lb. fresh spinach
   leaves, stemmed
1 cup arugula leaves
½ cup basil leaves
½ cup flat Italian parsley
3 scallions, including
   green tops
1 egg
1 cup whole-milk ricotta
½ cup freshly grated
   Parmesan
¼ tsp. nutmeg
¼ tsp. white pepper
½ tsp. salt
   Pinch of cayenne
   pepper
¼ cup flour
2 Tbsps. butter

Sauce:
2½ cups heavy cream
½ cup freshly grated
   Parmesan
   Salt, white pepper and
   nutmeg, to taste

Traditional gnocchi are made from potatoes and are often very heavy going. This version substitutes ricotta cheese and a small bit of flour for the starch. Spinach and herbs are added for flavor and texture. The result is a light and tasty, melt-in-your-mouth sensation. These gnocchi are fragile, so some care must be taken in the cooking. The dough, minus the flour, is also excellent as a ravioli filling.

Steam the spinach and arugula until wilted, about two minutes. Transfer to a colander or sieve and let cool. Meanwhile, purée the basil, parsley and scallions in a food processor.

When cool enough to handle, squeeze out all of the moisture from the spinach and arugula. This step is crucial: if there is residual water, the gnocchis will be too soft. Transfer these greens to the food processor and purée.

Add the remaining ingredients except the flour and butter, pulsing to blend.

Transfer the mixture to a bowl and stir in the flour, mixing just until combined. Refrigerate for 2 hours.

The easiest way to form the gnocchi is with a large pastry bag and a #16 round tip. Place a lightly floured sheet of parchment or waxed paper onto a counter, and pipe out a ribbon of dough, cutting it at 1-inch intervals. Let the gnocchis fall gently onto the paper, taking care to not let them touch one another. If a pastry bag is not available, you may form them by hand. Drop small spoonfuls onto a floured surface and roll the dough into small logs. Try to attain a uniform size and shape so the gnocchi will cook evenly.

To cook, bring a large pan of lightly salted water to a simmer. Using a large spoon, transfer half of the gnocchis to the water. Poach for 3 minutes in gently simmering water. Remove with a slotted spoon and cool on waxed paper; do not stack. Repeat with the remaining dough. It is important to keep the water at a gentle simmer; a rolling boil could cause the gnocchi to disintegrate.

To make the sauce, heat the cream slowly and reduce over medium heat for fifteen minutes, or until the cream thickens slightly. Stir in the Parmesan and season with the spices.

When ready to serve, heat 2 Tbsps. of butter in a large non-stick skillet. Add the gnocchis and lightly sauté to reheat, about three minutes. It is also possible to reheat them in a microwave oven.

Transfer the gnocchis to the warm sauce and cook another minute or two. If desired, transfer the pasta to a serving dish, cover with more Parmesan cheese and brown lightly under a broiler.

☆

Spinach Ravioli with Gorgonzola Sauce

Yield: 115 Raviolis
Preparation Time:
  15 Minutes
(note resting time)
Cooking Time:
  5 Minutes

Parmesan Pasta:
  2 cups semolina flour
  1 cup flour
  ¾ cup Parmesan cheese,
    grated to a powder
  ⅛ tsp. nutmeg
  5 extra-large eggs

Spinach Filling:
  2 cloves garlic, minced
  3 scallions, minced
  2 Tbsps. butter
  2 pkgs. frozen spinach,
    thawed
  4 oz. ricotta cheese
  ¼ cup grated Parmesan
    cheese
  Salt and fresh ground
  pepper
  Fresh ground nutmeg

Making homemade raviolis is a labor of love, as anyone who has done so will attest. When I wrote this recipe a decade ago, fresh pasta was not available in most supermarkets. It's a different story today. Dozens of shapes and fillings and flavors line refrigerator cases and certainly spinach ravioli is one of the more standard choices. So if you don't have a hankering to roll out a batch of fresh pasta, use a commercial brand and just make this sauce. The gorgonzola flavor is not overly assertive, so you may want to add a bit more if you are an aficionado. Or you could substitute asiago or Parmesan.

Place the flours, grated cheese and nutmeg in the bowl of a food processor. Pulse briefly to mix.

Add the eggs, one at a time, and process until the mixture forms a ball.

Turn the dough out onto a semolina-floured board and knead for 3 minutes. If the dough seems very sticky, add a bit more semolina. Conversely, add a few drops of olive oil if too dry. Let dough rest, covered with a towel, for 30 minutes.

Cut the dough into 6 pieces. Put one piece through the widest setting of your pasta machine. Fold the resulting strip of pasta into thirds and re-run through the machine at the same setting. Repeat one more time.

Set the pasta rollers one notch closer and run the pasta strip through. Tighten the rollers and re-roll. Keep narrowing the gap between the rollers until the pasta sheet is about ¹⁄₁₆ inch thick. On my Atlas machine I start at notch 1 and run the dough through to notch 5. You want the dough to be as thin as possible, yet still workable.

Place the pasta sheets on a semolina-dusted surface. Trim the edges of the strips to create 4-inch-wide pieces. Cut each strip into 16-inch lengths; anything longer is too difficult to handle. Let the pasta rest, covered with a towel for 30 minutes. The pasta should turn slightly leathery.

Hook the ravioli attachment to your machine. Spray the head with a no-stick cooking spray each time you run pasta through. Follow the manufacturer's directions for using your ravioli attachment. I use approximately ¼ cup of filling for each strip of pasta.

Place the ravioli sheets on paper-lined trays and, using a

ravioli wheel, crimp all 4 edges of each ravioli to seal.

Let the ravioli air dry for 30 minutes before cooking, or freeze on trays. When frozen, break up the raviolis and place in freezer bags.

Sauté the garlic and scallions in the butter over low heat for 5 minutes; set aside.

Squeeze out all of the liquid from the spinach—this is important.

Mix the spinach with the ricotta and Parmesan and add the sautéed garlic and scallions. Season to taste with salt, pepper and nutmeg.

Combine the garlic and cream in a heavy-bottomed pot and bring to a simmer. Cook over low heat until the cream thickens and reduces by half. Remove the garlic with a slotted spoon and discard. Add the cheeses and stir to melt. Season to taste with the spices.

Bring a large pot of water to a boil and add 1 tsp. salt and 1 Tbsp. oil. Add the raviolis and cook 2 minutes if fresh, 4 or 5 if frozen. Drain in a sieve or colander.

Toss the pasta with some of the Gorgonzola Sauce. Transfer the raviolis to individual plates and sprinkle with Parmesan and pine nuts. If you wish, gratinée the cheese under the broiler and then garnish with cherry tomatoes.

Gorgonzola Sauce:
  6 cloves garlic, crushed
  3 cups heavy cream
  ½ cup mascarpone cheese
  4 oz. imported gorgonzola cheese
  Salt, fresh ground pepper and ground nutmeg

  1 cup grated Parmesan cheese
  ⅓ cup toasted pine nuts
  Cherry tomatoes

★

Soups & Salads

Black Bean and Corn
   Salad

Caesar Salad

Café Salad

Chicken Stock

Chilled Cantaloupe Soup

Confit of Duck Salad

Fajitas Chicken Salad

German Potato Salad

Grilled Chicken Salad

Harvest Bisque

Lobster and Corn
   Chowder

New Potato Salad

Quahog Chowder

Red and Yellow
   Gazpacho

Roasted Pepper and Bean
   Salad Amandine

Roquefort and Squash
   Soup

Smoked Turkey Salad
   à la Waldorf

Tarragon Chicken and
   Wild Rice Salad

Thai Crab Soup

Tropical Chicken Salad

Zanzibar Chicken
   Banana Soup

Black Bean and Corn Salad

Few bean salads can rival this one for taste and appearance. The contrast of yellow corn, red tomatoes, green onions and herbs with the black beans results in a striking presentation. This salad keeps well under refrigeration.

Soak the beans in cold water overnight if possible. Drain and place in a large pot; cover with two inches of cold water.

Bring to a boil, then reduce the heat and simmer for 45 to 60 minutes. The beans should be tender but not mushy. If you did not soak the beans overnight, the cooking time will need to be increased.

Drain the beans and place in a bowl with the tomatoes, scallions, corn, cucumber and herbs.

Make a simple vinaigrette by whisking the olive oil into the salt and lemon juice. If you are in a hurry, substitute a prepared Italian-style dressing.

Add the vinaigrette to the bean mixture and stir gently to moisten. Serve the salad at room temperature for optimum flavor.

Serves 8
Preparation Time:
** 20 Minutes**
(note soaking time)
Cooking Time:
** One Hour**

  1 lb. dried black beans
  2 ripe tomatoes, diced
  ½ cup finely minced
    scallions
  1 cup cooked corn
    kernels, drained
  1 cucumber, peeled,
    seeded and diced
  ½ cup minced fresh
    parsley
  ⅓ cup minced fresh
    cilantro
  ½ cup olive oil
  2 tsps. salt
  ¼ cup fresh lemon juice

★

Caesar Salad

Serves 6
Preparation Time:
  30 Minutes
Cooking Time:
  15 Minutes

  5 **anchovies**
  3 **cloves garlic**
  1 **Tbsp. Dijon mustard**
  ½ **tsp. Worcestershire**
    sauce
    Juice of 1 lemon
  1 **egg**
  1 **cup vegetable or olive**
    oil
  ½ **cup butter**
  4 **slices firm white bread**
    or 8 slices French bread
  1 **head romaine lettuce**
  ½ **cup Parmesan cheese,**
    freshly grated
  6 **anchovies for garnish**
    Freshly cracked black
    pepper

If you like Caesar Salad, please try this recipe. Of all the recipes in this cookbook, this is the one that I receive the most feedback on. If I had a quarter for every time someone tells me "it's the best Caesar dressing I've ever tasted," I could retire. Really.

Place the anchovies and 2 cloves garlic in the bowl of a food processor or blender and blend to a paste. Add the mustard, Worcestershire sauce, lemon juice and egg and process to combine. Add the oil in a slow, steady stream, while the machine is running, to emulsify the dressing. Taste and adjust the seasoning if desired. If the dressing seems too thick, add 1 or 2 tsps. of water to thin.

Cut one garlic clove in half and rub both sides of the bread slices with the garlic. Cut the bread into bite-sized cubes. Melt the butter and sauté both halves of the garlic clove for 2 minutes over low to medium heat. Add the bread cubes and sauté until golden brown. Drain on paper towels and discard the garlic.

As an alternate method to sautéing, you may arrange the bread cubes on a sheet tray for baking. Simply pour the melted garlic butter over the bread and bake at 375° for 15 minutes or until the croutons are crisp and brown.

Tear the romaine lettuce leaves into bite-sized pieces and place in a large serving or salad bowl. Toss the lettuce with the Caesar dressing until all the leaves are coated. Add the freshly grated Parmesan cheese and the croutons and toss again. It is best to serve the salad immediately, as the dressing wilts the lettuce if it is left to sit. Garnish with the anchovies and freshly cracked black pepper.

Café Salad

This salad was a signature item on my menu at the Sconset Café, never waning in popularity over 15 years. Balsamic vinegar should be a staple in everyone's kitchen. The finest is made in Italy and derives its superior taste and aroma from aging in wood barrels, much like wine. Nowadays there is a wide range of balsamics on the market in all price ranges. Roquefort would substitute nicely for the Stilton cheese in this salad, as would walnuts for the pecans. Chunks of apple or pear also work well in lieu of the cherry tomatoes.

Serves 4
Preparation Time:
 20 Minutes
Cooking Time:
 5 Minutes

- 1 tsp. shallot, minced finely
- 1 tsp. Dijon mustard
- ½ tsp. salt
  Freshly cracked black pepper
- ¼ cup balsamic vinegar
- ¾ cup extra-virgin olive oil
- 8 leaves each Boston, Red Leaf and Butter lettuce
- 2 Tbsps. butter
- 1 cup pecan pieces, toasted
- 4 oz. Stilton cheese, crumbled
- 8 cherry tomatoes, halved (optional)

Whisk together the shallot, mustard, salt, pepper and balsamic vinegar in a deep, non-reactive bowl. Slowly add the olive oil in a steady stream, whisking constantly until the ingredients have emulsified. The dressing will separate upon standing; simply whisk again before using to recombine.

Wash each leaf of lettuce to remove sand or dirt. Dry with a towel or in a lettuce spinner, then crisp the lettuce in the refrigerator until serving time.

Melt the butter in a medium-sized skillet over low to medium heat and when bubbling, add the pecans. Sauté the nuts until golden brown and then drain on paper towels.

Dress the lettuce leaves with the balsamic vinaigrette and then arrange 2 leaves of each type of lettuce on 4 chilled salad plates. Evenly divide the pecans and Stilton between each plate. Garnish with the cherry tomatoes, if desired.

★

Chicken Stock

Yield: 5 cups
Preparation Time:
10 Minutes
Cooking Time:
3 Hours

- 1 **whole chicken,**
  including giblets and
  neck, about 4 lbs.
- 1 **large onion**
- 3 **leeks, cut into 4-inch**
  pieces
- 2 **carrots, cut into 4-inch**
  lengths
- 2 **celery stalks, halved**
- 10 **parsley stems**
- 2 **sprigs fresh thyme**
- 1 **bay leaf**
- 6 **whole black**
  peppercorns
- 2 **whole cloves**
- ½ **tsp. salt**

Flavorful, nutritious chicken stock is the backbone of any kitchen, home or commercial. The packaged, processed or canned stocks you find on your supermarket shelves have no basis of comparison to the superior product you can easily make at home. The extraordinarily high sodium content and the MSG additive make most commercial chicken stocks unattractive to me. If refrigeration space is at a premium, reduce the finished stock to a small amount of concentrate and freeze it in the compartments of an ice cube tray. When solid, transfer your "stock cubes" to plastic baggies. Each cube can be reconstituted with 1 cup of water to equal 1 cup of stock.

P lace the chicken, giblets and neck in a large stock pot and fill with lukewarm water to a level 1 inch above the contents. Bring the pot to a boil and skim the froth. Add the remaining ingredients and simmer the stock for about 1½ hours, skimming as needed. Then transfer the chicken to a carving board or platter and remove the meat and skin from the bones. Discard the skin but save the meat for future use.

Chop the chicken carcass and return it to the stock pot, adding more hot water, if necessary, to keep the contents covered. Simmer another 1½ hours, then strain the stock and cool. If you are not using the stock immediately, refrigerate or freeze it, as bacteria grows quickly in improperly stored stock.

Chicken stock may be stored, tightly covered, for 4 days in a refrigerator or frozen for 2 months. Always bring the stock to a full boil for 5 minutes before using.

Chilled Cantaloupe Soup

Purée the chunks of melon in a food processor or blender. Transfer to a deep bowl and add the lime juice, vermouth and preserved ginger with syrup. Stir well to combine. Taste and adjust flavors accordingly. If you feel the soup needs sweetening, add a few teaspoons of superfine sugar. Add the sour cream and the nutmeg and refrigerate the soup, covered, at least 4 hours. Serve in chilled bowls with mint leaves as garnish.

Serves 4
Preparation Time:
 10 Minutes
(note refrigeration time)

- **2 medium cantaloupes, coarsely chopped**
- **¼ cup lime juice**
- **½ cup sweet vermouth**
- **1½ Tbsps. preserved ginger, chopped fine, + 2 Tbsps. syrup**
- **⅓ cup sour cream, crème fraîche or heavy cream**
- **⅛ tsp. nutmeg**
  Fresh mint leaves for garnish

Confit of Duck Salad

Serves 4
Preparation Time:
30 Minutes

- 4 pieces confit of duck
  (see recipe page 125)
- 2 cups fresh spinach
  leaves, cut into ribbons
- 2 cups red leaf lettuce,
  cut into ribbons
- 1 cup Tangerine
  Vinaigrette (see recipe
  page 232)
- 2 tangerines
- ½ cup slivered almonds,
  toasted
- 12 cherry tomatoes,
  halved
- ½ cup diced English
  cucumber
- 2 Tbsps. sesame seeds,
  toasted

Here is an intriguing salad that partners the richness of confit of duck with the sweet-acid contrast of citrus. It relies upon an enticing combination of ingredients to create an unusual and memorable luncheon dish. If tangerines are out of season, use mineolas, blood oranges or even canned mandarins.

Discard the skin from the duck and wipe off all visible fat. Cut the meat into long strips.

Toss the spinach and lettuce chiffonades together in a bowl with enough dressing to moisten. Divide the greens between 4 plates.

Peel and section the tangerines.

Arrange the duck and tangerine slices on each plate.

Sprinkle the remaining ingredients over the salads and serve with additional dressing on the side.

Fajitas Chicken Salad

Fajitas *is a Spanish word meaning griddle or strip. Traditionally this dish is made with marinated skirt steak which is grilled with onions and wrapped up in a soft flour tortilla. My version is a radical departure from the authentic fajitas, but it is delicious, as thousands of satisfied customers have testified! The marinade is the key to this dish and you'll find it wonderful for most meats and seafood. Best of all, it makes a great dressing for the salad.*

You'll need a special double basket gadget to deep fry the tortillas, a variation of sorts on the French bird's nest implement. Williams Sonoma carries them as do many other kitchen shops. The shells are edible and they make the presentation of this salad extra special. If you don't want to bother with this step, arrange the chicken on a lettuce-lined platter, drizzle with marinade and serve the various condiments in small bowls.

Combine the juices, vinegar, oil, seasoning and garlic in a glass bowl and add the chicken. Cover with plastic wrap and refrigerate 24 hours or more before cooking.

Pour the chicken and marinade into a glass baking dish and bake, uncovered, for 20 minutes or until the chicken is cooked.

Allow the chicken to cool slightly in its marinade. When cool enough to handle, cut the meat into strips, discarding any skin. Save the marinade, but be sure to boil the marinade before using again or using as a dressing.

Fill each tortilla basket with shredded lettuce. Arrange the strips of chicken on top and add the scallions and tomatoes, apportioning between each basket.

If the marinade has cooled, reheat it briefly and pour enough into each tortilla shell to moisten the contents.

The salsa, sour cream and guacamole are condiments that may be served on the side so that your guests can help themselves.

Fajitas Seasoning:
Mix together in a small jar or container that has a lid and shake to combine.

Serves 6
Preparation Time:
   45 Minutes
(note marinating time)
Cooking Time:
   20 Minutes
Preheat oven to 350°

   2 **cups orange juice**
   ½ **cup fresh lime juice**
   ½ **cup red wine vinegar**
   1 **cup vegetable oil**
   2 **tsps. fajita seasoning (recipe follows)**
   2 **cloves garlic, minced**
   8 **boneless chicken breasts**
   6 **cups shredded head lettuce**
   ½ **cup scallions, minced**
   3 **tomatoes, diced Salsa**
   ¾ **cup sour cream Guacamole (see recipe page 222)**
   6 **flour tortilla shells, deep fried**

Fajitas Seasoning:
   ¾ **tsp. white pepper**
   ¾ **tsp. chili powder**
   ⅜ **tsp. garlic powder**
   3 **Tbsps. salt**
   ½ **tsp. cilantro**

German Potato Salad

Serves 6
Preparation Time:
  10 Minutes
Cooking Time:
  20 Minutes

  2 lbs. waxy boiling
    potatoes
  1 tsp. salt
  ½ lb. bacon
  2 Tbsps. white vinegar
  1 cup mayonnaise
  1 bunch scallions, finely
    minced
  ½ cup minced fresh
    parsley
    Fresh ground pepper
    Diced red onions,
    celery or pickles as
    optional additions

My grandmother was a natural cook and could always be found in her kitchen. She cooked without recipes, so sadly, her wonderful Austrian creations never became family treasures.

This potato salad recipe has, however, been firmly ensconced in my mother's repertoire for 50 years and is as good today as it was when Grammy made it.

Slice the potatoes about ⅛-inch thick. If your potatoes are very large, you might want to cut them in half before slicing. I usually use red-skinned potatoes and I don't peel them.

Place the potatoes in a pan and cover them with cold water. Add the salt and cook over high heat for 15 to 20 minutes or until tender.

Immediately drain the potatoes in a colander and let cool for about 10 minutes.

Sauté the bacon until it is crisp; drain on paper towels. Discard all but 1 Tbsp. of the bacon fat in the skillet.

Add the vinegar to the hot bacon fat in the skillet, stir to mix and then pour this mixture into a small bowl containing the mayonnaise. Stir to combine.

Place the potatoes in a large bowl. Crumble the bacon over the potatoes, sprinkle with the scallions and parsley and grind fresh pepper on top.

Gently mix the mayonnaise dressing into the potatoes. Season to taste with salt. Refrigerate until serving time.

Grilled Chicken Salad

Grilled chicken salads are a dime a dozen. What sets this one apart is an unusual vinaigrette made with cranberries, orange juice and walnut oil. The various components of the salad can be prepared a day ahead of time, allowing quick assembly just prior to serving.

Serves 4
Preparation Time:
  45 Minutes
Cooking Time:
  10 Minutes

- 1 cup walnut halves
- ¼ cup sugar
- 4 boneless, skinless chicken breasts, 8 oz. each
  Olive oil
  Salt and pepper
- 10 cups mixed baby greens, washed and dried
- 1 cup Cranberry Vinaigrette (see recipe page 219)
- 1 cup crumbled Stilton cheese

Place the walnuts in a large skillet and toast lightly over low heat for 5 minutes. The skillet must accommodate the walnuts in a single layer. Tend carefully as the nuts will burn very easily. When they are hot on both sides, sprinkle with the sugar, raise the heat to medium and continue cooking until the sugar melts and coats the nuts. Spread the walnuts on a plate to cool.

Lightly pound the chicken breasts between sheets of wax paper until they are an even thickness. Brush with olive oil and season with salt and pepper.

Grill the chicken on a hot barbecue and set aside to cool slightly. If you are grilling the chicken a day or two in advance of serving this salad, reheat for a minute in your microwave to warm the meat.

Place the lettuce in a large bowl and toss with ½ cup of the Cranberry Vinaigrette. Add more as needed. Divide the lettuce between four large plates.

Cut the chicken into attractive strips and arrange in a spoke pattern atop the lettuce. Garnish each plate with ¼ cup Stilton and ¼ cup walnuts. Drizzle a bit of vinaigrette over the chicken and serve.

Harvest Bisque

Serves 8
Preparation Time:
  One Hour

¼ cup butter
¾ cup yellow onion,
  minced
4 oz. mushrooms, sliced
1 lb. carrots, peeled and
  sliced
1 lb. parsnips, peeled
  and sliced
1 apple, peeled and
  sliced
3 cups chicken stock (see
  recipe page 70)
6 sprigs fresh thyme
1½ cups light cream
½ cup pure apple cider,
  unsweetened
¼ tsp. nutmeg
  Salt and fresh ground
  pepper

When summer days are only a memory, this soup will remind you of all the glories of autumn. Harvest Bisque is the essence of the season: it looks, tastes and smells like fall! For of you who have never tried parsnips, this is a great introduction to their unique flavor which marries perfectly with carrots. Serve this soup for a hearty lunch or in smaller portions as a starter course for a roast chicken dinner.

n a large skillet, melt the butter and add the onions and mushrooms. Sauté over medium heat until soft, about 10 minutes.

Put the onions and mushrooms, carrots, parsnips and apple into a large pot and add the chicken stock and thyme. Bring the contents to a boil, then lower the heat to a simmer, cover the pot and cook for 30 minutes or until the vegetables are soft. Add more stock if necessary to prevent burning.

Let the soup cool slightly and then remove and discard the woody stems of the thyme. Purée the soup until smooth in a food processor or blender.

Return the soup to the pot and add the cream, cider and nutmeg. Reheat slowly until the soup is warm, then season to taste with salt and pepper.

Thin the bisque to the desired consistency with either cream or cider, depending on your preference. The bisque should be fairly thick.

Lobster and Corn Chowder

The instructions for this recipe involve cooking a live lobster. If you wish to simplify the process by using canned or frozen lobster meat, the soup will not have the same flavor; most of the flavor of a lobster is in the shell, not the meat. An alternative would be to purchase a whole cooked lobster, in which case you would remove the meat and use the shells to impart flavor to the stock.

Melt the butter in a pan large enough to accommodate the lobster. When hot, add the celery, carrot and leek (and lobster shells if not using live lobster). Sauté over medium high heat for about 8 minutes, or until the vegetables soften.

Add the wine and water to the pan. When the liquid begins to boil, add the lobster, cover tightly and cook for 17 minutes.

Remove the lobster and set aside to cool. Reserve the cooking broth. Clean the lobster, removing tail, claw, knuckle and body meat; cut into bite-sized pieces and reserve.

Return the shells (but not the body cavity or brain sac) to the pan with the broth. Simmer, uncovered, for an additional 10 minutes to allow the shells to flavor the liquid.

Strain the broth into a saucepan, discarding the solids.

Add the creams and corn kernels to the stock and cook slowly until the soup is hot and corn is tender. Then add the lobster meat, cooking just long enough to heat through.

Season to taste with the salt and pepper. Divide between four bowls; sprinkle each with a dash of paprika and a pinch of parsley. Serve immediately.

Serves 4
Preparation Time:
 30 Minutes
Cooking Time:
 One Hour

- ¼ cup butter
- 2 stalks celery, diced fine
- 1 large carrot, diced fine
- 1 leek, sliced thin
- 1½ cups white wine
- 1½ cups water
- 2 lb. live lobster
- 2 cups heavy cream
- ½ cup half and half
- 1 cup corn kernels
   Salt, pepper and paprika
- 1 Tbsp. fresh minced parsley

☆

New Potato Salad

Serves 10
Preparation Time:
  25 Minutes
Cooking Time:
  30 Minutes

3½ lbs. new potatoes
 1 bunch scallions, white
    and green parts, finely
    minced
 ½ cup minced parsley
 ½ cup minced fresh dill
1½ cups Tarragon
    Vinaigrette (see recipe
    page 233)
 ½ cup mayonnaise
    Salt and fresh ground
    pepper

It seems to me that there are as many potato salads as there are cooks. Here is one more recipe for your repertoire. If you are in a hurry, use any bottled, Italian-style dressing in place of a homemade vinaigrette. This salad will keep for several days under refrigeration and the flavor intensifies with time.

Put 1 inch of water in a large pot, add the potatoes and cover tightly.

Steam the potatoes over high heat until they are just tender when pierced with a knife.

Drain the potatoes immediately. Let them cool just until they can be handled comfortably.

Cut the potatoes into uniform chunks and place in a large bowl. Toss the potatoes with the minced scallions, parsley and dill.

In a small bowl, whisk the mayonnaise with the Tarragon Vinaigrette and then pour the dressing over the potatoes and herbs, tossing to coat all surfaces. If the potatoes are still warm, they will absorb the dressing and the salad will be more flavorful.

Season to taste with salt and pepper.

Quahog Chowder

I made this chowder every day for more years than I care to remember. Whenever I tried to take it off the menu and serve something like gazpacho instead, there would be a storm of protest. There are as many versions of New England Clam (or Quahog) Chowder as there are cooks, but this one is tried and true and very good. If you like a full-flavored, creamy, chock-full-of-clams chowder, give this recipe a try.

Serves 8
Cooking Time:
  40 Minutes

- ½ lb. uncooked bacon, finely chopped
- 1 large onion, minced
- 1 carrot, very finely chopped
- ¾ cup minced celery
- 2 tsps. dried thyme
- 1 Tbsp. dried dill weed
- ½ tsp. white pepper
- ¼ cup flour
- 3 cups clam juice or fish stock
- ½ cup dry white wine
- 3 bay leaves
- 3 cans of chopped clams, with juice, 6.5 oz. each
- 3 cups diced potatoes, cooked until tender
- 1 cup heavy cream

I n a large, heavy-gauge stock pot, cook the bacon over medium-high heat until the fat is rendered and the bacon is crisp. Add the onion, carrot and celery and sauté until the vegetables are tender, about 8 minutes. Add the thyme, dill weed and pepper and sauté 2 minutes longer. Stir in the flour and cook, stirring constantly over low to medium heat for 4 to 6 minutes. Do not allow the flour to burn.

Heat the clam juice and wine with the bay leaves in a 2-quart, non-aluminum saucepan over high heat until boiling. Lower the heat and cook at a simmer for about 5 minutes, then gradually stir the broth into the base. Raise the heat under the stock pot to medium and cook the chowder for 10 minutes, stirring frequently. Add the clams and potatoes, roughly mashing about a half cup of the potatoes against the sides of the stock pot, and heat until the chowder is warmed through. At this point the chowder may be refrigerated for up to 3 days, loosely covered with plastic wrap.

To serve, add the heavy cream and allow the chowder to reheat to serving temperature, taking care not to let the mixture boil. Season to taste with salt, if necessary.

Red and Yellow Gazpacho

Serves 8
Preparation Time:
  One Hour
(note chilling time)

Yellow Gazpacho:
  6 **yellow tomatoes**
  2 **cucumbers, peeled and**
    seeded
  2 **yellow peppers, seeded**
  1 **bunch scallions, white**
    part only
  3 **cloves garlic, minced**
  4 **cups chicken stock (see**
    recipe page 70)
  1/3 **cup olive oil**
  1/4 **cup Champagne**
    vinegar or white wine
    vinegar
    Salt and white pepper

Red Gazpacho:
  6 **ripe red tomatoes**
  2 **cucumbers, peeled and**
    seeded
  2 **sweet red peppers,**
    seeded
  1 **green bell pepper,**
    seeded
  1 **bunch scallions**
  2 **cloves garlic, minced**
  1 **cup beef stock**
  3 **cups V-8 juice**
  1/3 **cup olive oil**
  1/4 **cup red wine vinegar**
    Salt, pepper and
    Tabasco
    Minced fresh parsley
    and sour cream,
    optional garnish

Gazpacho is enjoying a revival in popularity these days and I, for one, am delighted to see an old favorite back in fashion. This recipe is really two soups in one; either can stand on its own. The juxtaposition of the two colors in the same bowl is a very nice twist, however. Make the yellow and red gazpachos separately to keep the colors distinct. The procedure is identical for both soups.

Bring a large pot of water to a slow boil and add the yellow and red tomatoes in two separate batches. Cook for 1 minute and then remove the tomatoes with tongs to a bowl of ice water. When cool enough to handle, peel and discard the skins, seed and dice the tomatoes. Remember to keep the colors separate.

The cucumbers, peppers and scallions for each soup can be roughly puréed in a food processor or cut into small dice by hand. If you elect the food processor method (much faster), cut the vegetables into 1/2-inch chunks and process each vegetable separately to avoid over-processing.

Combine the chopped vegetables for each gazpacho in a bowl. Add the respective garlic, stocks, juice, olive oil and vinegars and stir to blend. Chill the soups, covered, for at least 1 hour before seasoning, then add salt and pepper to taste. In the case of the red gazpacho, also add Tabasco for zip. Often tomatoes need the addition of sugar to balance acidity and boost flavor; do not hesitate to add 1 or 2 tsps. to correct the taste.

Make sure the soups are completely chilled before serving. Carefully ladle 3/4 cup of the red gazpacho into a bowl. Tilt so the soup collects to one side and then add a matching amount of yellow gazpacho, taking care not to mix the two soups. Garnish with a dollop of sour cream and a sprinkling of minced fresh parsley, if desired.

Roasted Pepper and Bean Salad Amandine

This salad is visually stunning. Charring and peeling the peppers involves a fair bit of work, but the good news is that all components can be prepared several days ahead of serving. Don't add the vinaigrette in advance of serving time, however, or the vibrancy of the colors will be lost.

Preheat the broiler and place the peppers on a tray, close to the heat source. Alternately, place the peppers directly on a grill. Cook until blackened, turning the peppers so that all sides char. Cool the peppers until they are cool enough to handle.

Peel off the charred skin and rinse under cold water. Dry the peppers and then cut in half and core. Slice the peppers lengthwise into thin, even-sized strips.

Top and tail the beans to equal lengths.

Bring a pot of salted water to a boil and cook the beans for 2 minutes. The green beans should turn a vivid shade of green.

Drain and cool quickly by refreshing the beans under very cold water or in a bowl of water and ice. When cool, drain again.

Thinly slice the onion and place in a bowl. Add the beans and pepper strips to the bowl.

Place the vinegar in a small bowl and add the oil drop by drop, whisking constantly. Add the cumin and season to taste with salt and pepper.

Pour in the vinaigrette and toss well. Arrange the vegetables on a platter and sprinkle with the sliced almonds.

Serves 4
Preparation Time:
  30 Minutes
Cooking Time:
  12 Minutes

  2 **sweet red peppers**
  2 **yellow or orange peppers**
  ½ **lb. green beans**
  ½ **lb. yellow wax beans**
  1 **small red onion**
  ¼ **cup sliced almonds, toasted**

Vinaigrette
  3 **Tbsps. balsamic vinegar**
  ¼ **cup olive oil**
  ½ **tsp. cumin**
    Salt and pepper to taste

Roquefort and Summer Squash Soup

Serves 6
Preparation Time:
  15 Minutes
Cooking Time:
  30 Minutes

  1 **leek, sliced**
  ¼ **cup butter**
  3 **lbs. yellow summer**
    (crookneck) squash
  4 **cups chicken stock, hot**
    (see recipe page 70)
  1 **cup half and half**
  6 **oz. Roquefort cheese,**
    crumbled
    Salt and pepper to
    taste

Don't be put off by the combination of squash and bleu cheese—the Roquefort is subtle but intriguing. Use the imported French variety if you can find it; many of the domestic brands are very salty and harsh.

I n a 2 qt. saucepan, sauté the leeks in the butter until they soften, about 3 minutes.

Cut the squash into ¼-inch-thick slices. Transfer to the saucepan and add the chicken stock. Cook covered, over medium heat, until the squash is tender, about 20 minutes.

Purée the soup in batches in a food processor or blender. Return the purée to the stove. Add the half and half and reheat slowly. When the soup is warm, add the Roquefort and stir until it melts. Season to taste with salt and pepper and serve immediately.

☆

Smoked Turkey Salad à la Waldorf

The inspiration for this recipe is the classic Waldorf salad, which I find a bit too sweet for my taste. In my version, the smoked turkey adds protein and a complexity of flavor to a salad that is usually relegated to the status of a side dish. If you're looking for a light and unusual luncheon salad, this might be the perfect choice. It is best served on the day it is assembled, although it will certainly keep under refrigeration for several days. Chicken may be substituted, but a smoked meat such as ham is a better choice to maintain the balance of flavors.

Whisk the mayonnaise, crème fraîche, cider, nutmeg and salt in a small bowl until smooth.

Carefully fold in the whipped cream.

Mix the julienned turkey, apple, raisins, celery, walnuts, tarragon and poppy seeds in a large bowl.

Gently toss three-quarters of the dressing with the turkey mixture, adding the remaining dressing as needed.

Arrange the salad on a lettuce-lined platter or in a shallow bowl to serve.

Serves 4
Preparation Time:
  30 Minutes

  ½ cup mayonnaise
  ½ cup crème fraîche
    (see recipe page 220)
    or sour cream
  2 Tbsps. apple cider
  ¼ tsp. nutmeg
    Pinch of salt
  ½ cup sweetened
    whipped cream
  1 lb. smoked turkey
    breast, julienned
  1 Granny Smith apple,
    diced
  ½ cup golden raisins
  3 stalks celery, finely
    diced
  ½ cup walnut halves
  1 Tbsp. fresh tarragon,
    minced
  1 Tbsp. poppy seeds

Tarragon Chicken and Wild Rice Salad

Serves 6
Preparation Time:
  30 Minutes
(note refrigeration time)
Cooking Time:
  20 Minutes

- ⅓ **cup pineapple juice**
- ¼ **cup white wine or tarragon vinegar**
- ½ **tsp. sugar**
- ½ **tsp. salt**
  Fresh ground pepper to taste
- ½ **cup vegetable oil**
- 1 **cup wild and white rice blend**
- 1 **tsp. salt**
- 1 **Tbsp. butter**
- 3 **cups cooked chicken, cubed**
- ¼ **cup minced fresh tarragon**
- 1 **cup fresh pineapple cubes**
- ½ **cup minced scallions**
- ½ **cup finely diced celery**
- ½ **cup toasted slivered almonds**

Chicken and pineapple have always been a felicitous pairing. The addition of tarragon and wild rice creates a lovely luncheon salad that is perfect for a summer day. If you have leftover roast chicken or turkey on hand, this is an ideal way to use it; ham also partners beautifully with these ingredients.

Make a vinaigrette by combining the pineapple juice, vinegar, sugar, salt and pepper in a small bowl. Slowly whisk in the oil to emulsify the dressing. Set aside.

Cook the rice in a small saucepan with 1½ cups of water, the salt and butter. Bring to a boil and then lower the heat, cover and simmer for about 15 minutes or until all of the water has been absorbed. If the liquid has evaporated but the rice is still hard, let sit covered for another 10 minutes. Cool completely.

Combine the cooled rice, chicken, tarragon, pineapple, scallions and celery in a serving bowl. Add half of the vinaigrette and toss; add more dressing as required. Refrigerate the salad for several hours before serving to allow the flavors to develop and marry. Garnish with the almonds at serving time.

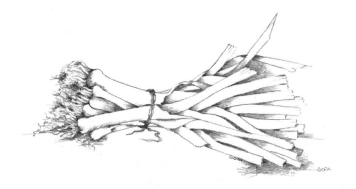

Thai Crab Soup

This delicate soup is a personal favorite. I'm so very fortunate to be able to spend part of my year on the Monterey Peninsula, where Dungeness crabs are plentiful during the winter. I'm always looking for ways to serve them, which is how this recipe evolved. The lemon grass is an essential ingredient and I don't recommend making this soup if it's not available in your area. (I'm a firm believer in asking produce managers to procure special items for me, and you might consider doing the same). As for the live Dungeness crab, cooking it in coconut milk does add subtle flavor to the soup base, but it is possible to eliminate this step and just add crab meat at the final stage. If live lobster is easier to find in your area, it will work equally well.

Combine the coconut milk, wine, lemon grass, ginger root and chili pepper in a large pot and bring to a boil. Add the crab and cover tightly. If you have one large crab, cook it for 20 minutes over medium-high heat; if you are using two, reduce cooking time to 15 minutes.

Remove the crab with tongs and place in a bowl to cool. Strain the coconut milk into a clean pot and discard the solids.

Wash off the crab and when cool enough to handle, remove the meat and set aside. The shells can be discarded unless you wish to save them for another recipe.

Gently reheat the soup base and when warm, add the basil, chives, lemon juice and crab meat. Cook several minutes to marry the flavors. Season with salt if desired.

Serves 4
Preparation Time:
 30 Minutes
Cooking Time:
 30 Minutes

- 3 **cans unsweetened coconut milk (about 40 oz.)**
- 1 **cup white wine**
- 4 **stalks lemon grass, roughly chopped**
- ¼ **cup minced or grated ginger root**
- 1 **dried hot chili pepper (optional)**
- 2½ **lbs. live Dungeness crab**
- ¼ **cup fresh minced basil**
- 2 **Tbsps. fresh snipped chives**
- 2 **Tbsps. fresh lemon juice**
  Salt to taste

☆

Tropical Chicken Salad

Serves 4
Preparation Time:
  30 Minutes
(note refrigeration time)

3½ cups diced cooked
    chicken
 ½ cup diced fresh
    pineapple
 1 mango, cut into small
    cubes
 ¼ cup finely diced celery
 ½ cup toasted pecan
    pieces or slivered
    almonds
 2 Tbsps. currants
 1 Tbsp. minced fresh
    parsley
 ⅓ cup mayonnaise
 ¼ cup plain nonfat
    yogurt
 1 Tbsp. curry powder
 ¼ cup mango chutney

The contrasting textures and flavors in this salad make it memorable. The crunch of nuts and celery are an interesting counterpoint to the soft, lusciously sweet mango and the tart, palate-tingling pineapple. The chutney adds a complex note of vinegar and sugar to enliven the dressing. Other ingredients can be added or substituted according to your whim. Papaya is ideal, apples and bananas work well and shrimp makes a nice change from chicken.

I n a large bowl mix the chicken with the pineapple, mango, celery, nuts, currants and parsley.
    Combine the remaining ingredients in a small bowl, blending thoroughly.
    Spoon half of the dressing into the chicken mixture and stir to combine. Do not add all of the mayonnaise mixture at once, in case this proves to be too much dressing. Usually after this salad sits for a while, a bit more dressing is needed, so don't discard any extra that you may have at this stage.
    Refrigerate the salad for at least an hour before serving to allow flavors to marry.

☆

Zanzibar Chicken-Banana Soup

This intriguing recipe has its root in Africa, where coconut and bananas are plentiful. You may think the recipe is bizarre, but I assure you that the blend of spices and textures is sublime. I had great difficulty getting customers to try this soup when it first appeared on my menus, but eventually it became one of my most popular items. Try it and I'm sure you'll see why!

Bring the stock to a boil and add the celery, coconut and spices. Cook for 10 minutes at a simmer.

Cut the chicken into bite-sized pieces and add to the pot along with the tomatoes. Cook on low heat for 8 minutes and then add the bananas; simmer for an additional few minutes and then serve immediately.

Serves 4 to 6
Preparation Time:
  20 Minutes
Cooking Time:
  30 Minutes

- 4 cups chicken stock (see recipe page 70)
- 1 cup celery, diced
- ½ cup shredded coconut
- 1 tsp. curry powder
- 1 tsp. salt (less if using canned stock)
- 1 tsp. minced garlic
- ½ tsp. white pepper Cayenne pepper to taste
- 4 boneless, skinless chicken breast halves
- 3 tomatoes, diced
- 2 bananas, just shy of ripe, diced

Fish & Seafood

Brazilian Seafood Stew

Délices de Nantucket

Honey-Lime Salmon

Javanese Shrimp
Skewers

Mixed Seafood Grill

Poached Striped Bass
with Champagne
Sauce

Salmon Pinwheels with
Watercress Hollandaise

Salmon with
Mediterranean Sauce

Shrimp Scampi

Snapper Grenobloise

Spicy Seafood Stew

Swordfish with Sauce
Choron

Tahitian Tuna

Tuna with Fennel-
Pepper Crust and
Ginger Beurre Blanc
Sauce

Brazilian Seafood Stew

Called vatapa *in Brazil, this stew partners fish and shrimp with coconut milk, tomatoes, peanuts and fresh ginger for a creamy, crunchy, spicy effect. Traditionally this dish would be made with* dende, *a red palm oil that is used in much of Brazilian cuisine. I've substituted olive oil and paprika here because* dende *is not readily available, at least where I live. The addition of bay scallops is not traditional but it doesn't really matter what manner of seafood you add—clams or lobster would be nice, too—because the essence of this stew lies in the wonderful complexity of flavors in the sauce.*

Serves 6
Cooking Time:
  1 Hour

- 2 Tbsps. olive oil
- 1 cup minced yellow onion
- 2 Tbsps. peeled, grated fresh ginger root
- 3 cloves garlic, minced
- 1 small hot chili, seeded and minced
- 1 Tbsp. sweet Hungarian paprika
- 1 Tbsp. fresh lemon juice
- 2 lbs. tomatoes, peeled & diced (or a 25 oz. can of diced, peeled plum tomatoes with juice)
- ¾ cup unsweetened coconut milk
- ¼ cup unsweetened shredded coconut
- ½ cup dry roasted peanuts
- 2 cups chicken or fish stock
  Salt to taste
- 6 Tbsps. butter
- ½ lb. bay scallops
- 12 oz. flounder, halibut or swordfish (or other white fish fillets)
- ½ lb. raw shrimp, peeled and deveined
- ¼ cup minced fresh cilantro or parsley (garnish)

Heat the oil in a heavy saucepan and add the onions, cooking over medium heat until soft and translucent. Add the ginger, garlic, chili pepper, paprika and lemon juice and cook until the mixture is heated through, about 3 minutes. Add half the diced tomatoes with some of the juice and the coconut milk. Cover and simmer until hot.

Meanwhile, grind the shredded coconut in a blender until it's coarse. Repeat with the peanuts, pulsing until the nuts are finely ground. Add both to the mixture in the pan and cook for several minutes.

Next, purée the sauce in a blender. Return the mixture to the pan and add the remaining diced tomatoes and the stock. Cover and simmer the sauce for about 15 minutes. If it seems too thin, remove the cover and reduce until it thickens a bit. Season to taste with salt and pepper and set aside, covered.

Heat 2 Tbsps. of the butter in a skillet and quickly sauté the bay scallops for two minutes; do not overcook. Remove with a slotted spoon and set aside.

Cut the fish into 1-inch cubes and sauté in 2 Tbsps. of butter until just barely cooked, about 5 minutes. Remove the fish from the skillet and add to the bay scallops. Use the remaining butter to sauté the shrimp, again taking care not to overcook. Add all the fish and pan juices to the sauce and gently simmer the stew for 5 minutes or until heated through. Taste and adjust seasoning as needed.

To serve, divide the stew between individual shallow bowls and garnish with a sprinkling of minced parsley or cilantro, peanuts and coconut. Serve with plain rice.

☆

Délices de Nantucket

Serves 6
Preparation Time:
 45 Minutes
Cooking Time:
 1 Hour

  6 **fresh artichokes**
 ¼ **cup lemon juice**
1½ **cups dry white wine**
  1 **lb. bay scallops**
  2 **Tbsps. butter**
  1 **cup mushrooms, sliced**
    Salt and white pepper
  2 **cups heavy cream**
  2 **Tbsps. Grand Marnier**
    or Cointreau

The sauce for the scallops is given a slight sweetness by the addition of Grand Marnier, a bit unorthodox maybe, but with delightful results. This is a great dish for a very special dinner, either as a first course or entrée.

Cut off the stem of artichokes level with the base. Begin at the bottom and work in a circular fashion around the globe of the artichoke. Remove several layers of leaves until the pale, inner leaves are reached. Cut off the top 2 inches of the artichoke and discard. Trim the artichoke bottom with a sharp paring knife to remove the fibrous outer skin. Rub the entire surface of the artichoke with lemon juice to prevent discoloration. Drop into a bowl of cold water acidulated with 2 Tbsps. of lemon juice while you prepare the remaining artichokes.

To cook, bring a large pot of salted water to a boil and add 1 Tbsp. of lemon juice. Drop the artichokes into simmering water and cook for 20 to 30 minutes or until the bottoms are tender. Drain upside down on a rack until cool enough to handle. Using a small spoon carefully scoop out the "choke" and discard. Cover the bottoms to keep them warm and set aside.

Remove the hard white muscle on the side of each scallop and discard. Meanwhile, bring the white wine to a simmer in a skillet and poach the scallops for 2 minutes. Transfer the scallops to a bowl and reduce the wine in the skillet to ¼ cup.

In a separate skillet melt the butter and when it bubbles add the mushroom slices. Sauté over medium heat until the mushrooms render their juices and become tender. Season with salt and white pepper.

Bring the heavy cream to a simmer in a medium saucepan and cook until it reduces by half. Add the Grand Marnier and the reserved wine and reduce another 10 minutes or until very thick. Stir in the mushrooms and the drained scallops, season to taste and remove from the heat.

Warm the artichoke bottoms, if necessary, either by steaming or briefly reheating in a 350° oven or a microwave. Place the artichokes on individual plates and spoon some scallop mixture into each bottom, allowing some to spill over the sides. Serve immediately.

Honey-Lime Salmon

A simple, intriguingly different marinade imparts sensational flavor to the fish.

Combine all the marinade ingredients in a small bowl, whisking to blend.

Place the salmon fillets in a glass, plastic or ceramic dish and coat with the marinade. Cover with plastic wrap and refrigerate for at least 2 hours or up to 24.

Grill the fillets over a hot fire on the barbecue or broil them, 4 to 6 inches from the heat source. It should take about 10 minutes to cook the salmon, but the cooking time will vary depending on the thickness of the fish and the intensity of your barbecue-broiler.

Extra marinade may be gently heated and used as a sauce.

Serves 4
Preparation Time:
  5 Minutes
Marination Time:
  2 Hours
Cooking Time:
  8 to 10 Minutes

  2 Tbsps. Dijon mustard
  1 Tbsp. olive oil
  1 Tbsp. honey
  2 Tbsps. dry sherry
  ¼ tsp. salt
    Rind and juice of
    1 lime
  2 tsps. dried tarragon
  4 salmon fillets, 6 oz.
    each

Javanese Shrimp Skewers

Serves 4
Preparation Time:
  45 Minutes
Marination Time:
  2 to 4 Hours
Cooking Time:
  12 Minutes

¼ cup peanut oil
¼ cup lemon juice
2 Tbsps. lime juice
⅛ cup low-sodium soy
  sauce
⅛ tsp. cayenne pepper
1 tsp. ground coriander
1¼ cups unsweetened
  coconut milk
1 Tbsp. minced garlic
1 Tbsp. grated lemon
  peel
1 Tbsp. sugar
½ tsp. salt

16 large raw shrimp,
  peeled and deveined
1 firm mango, cut into
  1-inch chunks
1 firm papaya, cut into
  1-inch chunks
1 red pepper, cut into
  1-inch squares
1 green pepper, cut into
  1-inch squares
½ pineapple, cut into
  1-inch chunks

Memories of a balmy night on an island in Malaysia inspired this dish, which is both easy to prepare and deliciously different—a perfect addition to your summer barbecue repertoire. The shrimp and fruit can be grilled on separate skewers or combined as directed in the recipe. Other firm fruits will also work, such as fresh coconut pieces, plums, nectarines or even chunks of green banana. Fish or chicken can be substituted for the shrimp. Try to cut the fruit into same-sized pieces so it will cook evenly and for an attractive presentation.

If you are using wooden rather than metal skewers, soak 8 of them in cold water for at least 1 hour.

Whisk the marinade ingredients together and then combine the shrimp and marinade in a glass or plastic container. Cover and refrigerate for 2 to 4 hours.

When you are ready to assemble the skewers, remove the shrimp from the marinade. As a rough guide, you should plan on using about 4 pieces of fruit, 3 squares of pepper and 2 shrimp per skewer. It will depend of course, on the length of the skewers.

Thread the shrimp by running the skewer through the thickest part of the shrimp first and then through the tail end so the shrimp forms a C-shape. Do not crowd the shrimp and fruit as that prevents even cooking.

Heat your grill to its highest setting and position the rack as close to the coals as possible. Grill the skewers for 3 to 6 minutes on each side. The cooking time will to vary widely depending on the size of the shrimp and the type of barbecue grill utilized. Keep checking so you don't overcook the shrimp.

Serve plain or with Peanut Sauce (page 60) over a bed of rice.

Mixed Seafood Grill

Here is a summertime variation on the English mixed grill theme. I have selected salmon, tuna and shrimp for their colors and textures, but don't feel compelled to stick with these choices.

Compound butters are a simple, make-ahead staple that are convenient to have on hand in the refrigerator or freezer. They jazz up vegetables and meat as well as fish, and are lower in calories than most sauces. These are some of my favorite combinations, but the possibilities are infinite, so let loose your imagination.

Combine the marinade ingredients in a glass bowl and add the shrimp. Marinate for 2 hours, then remove the shrimp and thread on skewers. Grill over a medium-high flame for 1½ to 2 minutes per side.

Grill the salmon and tuna over hot coals for 3 to 4 minutes per side or until cooked to your preference. Grilling times will vary according to the thickness of your fish and the temperature of your barbecue.

Place a piece of tuna, salmon and three shrimp on each of 4 warm plates and top with the appropriate compound butter.

The Wasabe Butter (for tuna):
Mash the butter with the wasabe and lemon juice until blended. Roll the butter into a cylinder, wrap in plastic and refrigerate until solid. Cut into slices to serve.

The Lime-Ginger Butter (for salmon):
Mix the butter with the ginger, lime juice and rind until smooth. Roll into a cylinder, wrap and refrigerate until chilled. Cut into slices to serve.

The Dilled Lemon Butter (for shrimp):
Mix all of the ingredients until smooth. Roll the butter into a cylinder, wrap in plastic wrap and refrigerate until solid. Cut into slices to serve.

Serves 4
Preparation Time:
  30 Minutes
Marination Time:
  2 Hours
Cooking Time:
  10 Minutes

½ cup white wine
½ cup olive oil
½ cup + 1 tsp. lemon juice
1 tsp. salt
2 cloves garlic, minced
  Grated rind of 1 lemon
12 large shrimp, peeled and deveined
4 salmon fillets, 3 oz. ea.
4 tuna steaks, 3 oz. each
  Compound Butters

Wasabe Butter:
½ cup salted butter
1 tsp. wasabe (powdered horseradish)
6 drops lemon juice

Lime-Ginger Butter:
½ cup salted butter
  2-inch piece ginger root, peeled and grated
1 tsp. lime juice
  Grated rind of 1 lime

Dilled Lemon Butter:
½ cup salted butter
2 tsps. lemon juice
1 clove garlic, minced
  Grated rind of 1 lemon
2 Tbsps. finely minced dill

Poached Striped Bass with Champagne Sauce

Serves 4
Preparation Time:
  25 Minutes
Cooking Time:
  25 Minutes
Preheat oven to 400°

Parchment paper
4 fresh striped bass
  fillets, about 6 oz. each
1 Tbsp. butter, softened
1 Tbsp. shallot, minced
¾ cup dry white wine or
  champagne
1 cup fish stock
3 Tbsps. shallots, minced
⅓ cup champagne
  vinegar
¼ cup champagne
2 Tbsps. heavy cream
  Salt and white pepper
1 cup unsalted butter,
  cut into 16 pieces
¼ cup each julienned
  carrots, celery and
  zucchini, blanched

Striped bass is one of the most prized fishes in the Atlantic. For many years the species was seriously endangered and it's only after years of protection that commercial fishing has now resumed on a limited basis. In this recipe I recommend poaching, as I find grilling too heavy-handed for the delicacy of striped bass. The champagne butter sauce is a perfect light and elegant foil for the subtle sweetness of this fish. If striped bass is not available in your area, snapper, sole, flounder or any other delicate fillet may be substituted.

Cut a piece of parchment paper to fit a large, ovenproof skillet. Butter one side of the paper and set aside. Butter the skillet and sprinkle with the 1 Tbsp. of shallots. Arrange the bass fillets, seasoned with salt and pepper, in one layer and add the white wine and fish stock. Cover with the parchment paper, buttered side down, and bring the liquid just to a simmer on the stovetop. Next, place the skillet in 400° oven and poach the fish for 7 to 9 minutes. Transfer the fish with a slotted spatula to a plate and cover with foil to keep it warm. Reserve the poaching liquid.

Combine the remaining shallots, the vinegar and champagne in a heavy-bottomed saucepan. Add ¼ cup of the poaching liquid to the pan and cook over medium-high heat until the liquid is reduced to 2 Tbsps. Add the heavy cream and season with salt and pepper.

Reduce again to 2 Tbsps. of liquid. Reduce the flame to low and whisk in 2 pieces of butter. When the butter is just incorporated, whisk in another piece and continue this without interruption until you have used all of the butter. Do not allow the sauce to become too hot or it will break. The sauce should be thick and emulsified.

Arrange the striped bass fillets on warm plates. Sprinkle with the julienned vegetables, making sure you have reheated them briefly in boiling water. Top with champagne sauce and serve immediately.

★

Salmon Pinwheels with Watercress Hollandaise

Instead of mundane salmon fillets or steaks, this recipe proposes slicing the fish into long, thin strips, which are then coiled into pinwheels. Partnered with an elegant sauce, this dish makes quite a statement at the dining table.

Cut the salmon lengthwise into four long 1-inch-wide strips. Coil each strip into a pinwheel and secure the loose end with a toothpick.

Butter a skillet large enough to accommodate the pinwheels. Sprinkle with the shallots and arrange the fish, seasoned with salt and pepper, in a single layer. Add the wine and fish stock; bring to a simmer over medium heat. Cover with a piece of buttered parchment or waxed paper and poach the salmon for 15 to 20 minutes, or until cooked.

Meanwhile, make the hollandaise sauce by combining the shallots, wine and vinegar in a small pan. Chop one cup of watercress (stems included) and add to the pan. Reserve the remaining cress.

Simmer these ingredients over low heat until about 2 Tbsps. of liquid remain. Strain the reduction into a stainless steel bowl, pressing hard on the solids to extract all the liquid. Discard solids.

Add the egg yolks and lemon juice to the reduction and place the bowl over a double boiler or directly onto your stove burner (medium setting). Heat the yolk mixture, whisking constantly until it thickens and becomes hot to the touch. The double boiler method is safer but infinitely slower. If you use the direct heat method, you must move the bowl on and off the burner periodically to avoid scrambling the eggs. The object here is to cook the egg yolks as much as possible without curdling them. It takes some practice to know how far to go, so if you're hesitant, experiment with egg yolks and lemon juice so as not to waste the watercress reduction.

When the yolks have thickened, remove the bowl from the heat and add one piece of butter. Whisk until it melts into the sauce. Add another piece and continue in this manner until you've used it all. It will be necessary to return the bowl to the burner or the double boiler as you proceed with this step

Serves 4
Preparation Time:
  30 Minutes
Cooking Time:
  20 Minutes

- 1 **side fresh Atlantic salmon, boned and skinned**
- 1 **Tbsp. butter**
- 2 **Tbsps. minced shallots**
  Salt and pepper
- 1½ **cups dry white wine**
- 2 **cups fish stock or clam juice**
  Parchment or waxed paper
- 1 **large shallot, finely minced**
- ½ **cup dry white wine**
- ½ **cup champagne vinegar or white wine vinegar**
- 1 **bunch watercress**
- 4 **egg yolks**
- 1 **Tbsp. lemon juice**
- ¾ **cup butter, cut into pieces**
  Salt and white pepper

☆

because adding the butter cools down the yolks. Again, if you elect to use the direct heat method, move the bowl on and off the heat to keep the temperature from spiking.

Taste the sauce and add salt and pepper as required. Reserve 4 nice sprigs of watercress for a garnish and chop the remaining leaves, discarding the stems. Add some or all of the minced cress to the hollandaise.

To serve, remove the salmon from the poaching liquid and arrange on warm plates. Top with some of the hollandaise and garnish with the reserved watercress sprigs.

☆

Salmon with Mediterranean Sauce

This easy-to-prepare and healthy sauce is a celebration of the vibrant flavors and colors of the Mediterranean region. It is delightful with any full-flavored, firm fish such as tuna, halibut, swordfish or snapper.

Combine the garlic, tomatoes, artichoke hearts, capers, olives, lemon rind, olive oil, basil and parsley in a large bowl and toss to combine. Add the salt, pepper and sugar and stir again.

Heat your barbecue to its highest setting, with the grill rack positioned as close to the heat source as possible. Brush the salmon with olive oil and grill two minutes on one side. With a wide spatula, turn the fillets 90° degrees and cook a further two minutes. This will give you nice grill marks. Next, flip the fish and finish cooking. The grilling time will vary widely, depending on the thickness of the fish, your preference for doneness and the intensity of heat of the barbecue.

While the fish is cooking, transfer the sauce to a large skillet and heat gently to a simmer. Add the balsamic vinegar, butter and wine to the sauce and simmer the mixture until it is warmed through. Taste and adjust seasonings as required. If your tomatoes are lackluster, you may need to balance the acidity with a bit more sugar.

Arrange the salmon on warm plates and top with about ½ cup of sauce per fillet.

Serves 8
Preparation Time:
  30 Minutes
Cooking Time:
  15 Minutes

  4 cloves garlic, minced
  6 ripe tomatoes, diced
  8 artichoke hearts, quartered (8.5 oz. water pack)
  3 Tbsps. capers
  25 Calamata olives, pitted and chopped
  1 Tbsp. grated lemon rind
  ½ cup extra virgin olive oil
  1 cup fresh basil leaves, snipped into ribbons
  ½ cup fresh minced parsley
  1 tsp. salt
  1 tsp. fresh ground pepper
  1 Tbsp. sugar (or as needed)
  8 fresh salmon fillets, 6 oz. each
  2 Tbsps. balsamic vinegar
  2 Tbsps. butter
  ¾ cup white wine

Shrimp Scampi

Serves 4
Preparation Time:
 25 Minutes
Cooking Time:
 1 Hour

20 large raw shrimp,
   shell-on

Shrimp Stock:
   Shrimp shells
 1 cup chicken stock
 1 cup white wine
 1 bay leaf
 1 tsp. black peppercorns
 12 parsley stems
 1 clove garlic
 1 shallot, sliced

Sauce:
 ¼ cup unsalted butter
 1 Tbsp. minced garlic
 2 shallots, minced
 ¾ cup shrimp stock (see
   below)
   Juice of 1 lemon
 ¼ cup veal stock (see
   recipe page 235)
 2 tsps. Dijon mustard
 2 Tbsps. minced parsley

For years I would order shrimp scampi whenever I went out to eat, trying to relive a memorable meal I'd enjoyed years before in Italy. Invariably I'd be disappointed as I encountered a succession of tough, fishy, garlicky shrimp that had nothing in common with the dish I remembered so fondly. Finally, I decided to experiment myself, seeking a complexity of flavors that seemed to be lacking in so many versions I'd tried. In my recipe, the use of both shrimp and veal stocks, in addition to the traditional lemon, garlic and butter, creates a rich and silky sauce reminiscent of what I tasted in Italy. I recommend the use of homemade chicken stock or a high quality product such as Perfect Additions or More Than Gourmet's Jus de Poulet. Canned stocks are high in sodium and when reduced, the salt is overpowering.

Peel and devein the shrimp, reserving the shells. Combine all of the stock ingredients in a large pot. Bring to a simmer over medium heat and cook for 30 minutes. Strain the stock and discard the solids.

Place the liquid in a small pan and reduce the stock to ¾ cup.

Melt the butter in a large skillet and over low heat, sauté the garlic and shallots until they are soft. Be careful not to burn the garlic or it will turn bitter.

Add the shrimp, the lemon juice and both stocks and cook the shrimp over medium-high heat for about 4 minutes. Do not overcook.

Remove the shrimp from the skillet with a slotted spoon and set aside. Add the Dijon mustard to the sauce in the skillet, raise the heat to high and reduce the sauce to concentrate the flavor and to thicken slightly.

Return the shrimp to the pan to reheat briefly, sprinkle with the minced parsley and serve.

Snapper Grenobloise

Any thin fish fillets will work well in this recipe. The classic French presentation includes a garnish of tiny croutons, which I like to make if time permits.

Serves 4
Preparation Time:
  15 Minutes
Cooking Time:
  10 Minutes

  2 lemons
¼ cup flour
  Salt and pepper
  4 red snapper fillets, boned and skinned, about 6 oz. each
⅓ cup butter
  1 Tbsp. lemon juice
  2 Tbsps. dry white wine
  2 Tbsps. capers
  2 Tbsps. minced fresh parsley
½ cup tiny croutons (optional garnish)

The 2 lemons need to be segmented. To do this, cut off both ends of the lemon so that it will sit solidly on a cutting board. Using a sharp paring knife trim the rind and pith in strips, starting at the top of the lemon and following the downward curve of the fruit. Once you've removed the rind you should be able to free the individual lemon segments by slicing carefully along each side of the membranes. Set aside.

Season the flour with salt and pepper and place the mixture in a shallow pan. Dip the fish fillets into the flour, shaking off the excess.

Heat half of butter in a large, non-stick skillet and when it sizzles, add the fillets. Sauté over moderate heat for 3 minutes on one side and then carefully flip the fish with a spatula and cook for an additional 2 or 3 minutes. Remove the fish to a warm serving platter and cover with aluminum foil while you quickly finish the sauce.

Add the remaining butter to the skillet and lightly brown. Add the lemon juice, wine, capers and parsley and cook over high heat for about a minute to thoroughly warm the mixture. Pour this sauce over the fish fillets and garnish the platter with the reserved lemon segments and a scattering of croutons, if desired. Serve immediately.

Spicy Seafood Stew

Serves 4
Preparation Time:
  30 Minutes
Cooking Time:
  30 Minutes

  3 Tbsps. olive oil
 ½ cup finely minced
    shallots
 ¼ cup finely minced
    scallions
 ¼ cup finely diced celery
  2 cloves garlic, minced
  1 Tbsp. flour
 ⅔ cup white wine
    28 oz. can peeled
    Italian plum tomatoes
  2 bay leaves
 ¼ tsp. salt
    Fresh ground pepper
  6 drops Tabasco sauce
  2 dried hot chili peppers
  1 tsp. Worcestershire
    sauce
  1 cup clam juice
 16 large raw shrimp,
    peeled and deveined
  2 Tbsps. fresh minced
    tarragon
 12 fresh oysters with their
    liquor, shelled
  8 oz. crab meat or
    lobster, cooked
  2 Tbsps. fresh minced
    parsley

This is one of my favorite recipes—a full-flavored melange of shellfish in a light, slightly spicy sauce. It is delicious over rice or pasta, which is how I usually serve it.

Heat the olive oil in a large saucepan and sauté the shallots, scallions and celery over medium heat until they soften, about 5 minutes. Add the garlic and flour and cook another 2 minutes, stirring constantly. Pour in the wine and reduce the heat to low.

Chop the tomatoes and add to the saucepan, along with the strained can juices. Season with the bay leaves, salt, pepper, Tabasco, chilis, Worcestershire and clam juice. Simmer for 15 minutes.

Add the shrimp and tarragon and cook for 5 minutes, or until the shrimp are just barely cooked. Add the oysters, any accumulated oyster liquor, and the crab, and heat through, about 2 minutes. If the stew becomes too dry, add more clam juice or water to thin.

Discard the bay leaves and chili peppers. Serve the stew in shallow bowls over shell pasta or rice; sprinkle with parsley for garnish.

Swordfish with Sauce Choron

Béarnaise Sauce is a great favorite of mine for partnering with swordfish or beef. Sauce Choron is a derivative of béarnaise, distinguished from it by the addition of tomato. My version is a very pretty color and is enlivened by the addition of fresh and sun-dried tomatoes. This recipe makes a substantial amount of sauce. If you have some left over, be sure to save it in the refrigerator or freezer. Although it won't re-emulsify, it's a delicious flavor enhancer for vegetables. Toss a tablespoon or two with your vegetables in place of butter just before serving.

Combine the vinegar, wine, shallot, herbs and seasonings in a small pot and reduce over low heat to about 2 Tbsps. of liquid. Pour the reduction into a double boiler and cool slightly. Add the egg yolks and return to medium heat. Whisk constantly until the yolks thicken, then remove from the heat and add a piece of butter, whisking constantly. When the butter is absorbed, add another piece, and so on. Do not rush this stage or your sauce will not thicken properly.

Whisk in the tomato paste. Discard any liquid that has accumulated in the minced tomatoes, then add the tomatoes to the sauce along with the sun-dried tomatoes. Correct the seasoning as required. The sauce will hold for several hours if kept in a warm thermos.

Broil or grill the swordfish steaks; do not overcook.

Serve on warm plates and spoon a generous dollop of Sauce Choron on top of the steaks. If you notice that the butter begins to melt out of the sauce when it hits the hot fish, do not be alarmed—this is normal.

Serves 6
Preparation Time:
  15 Minutes
Cooking Time:
  30 Minutes

- ¼ cup tarragon vinegar
- ¼ cup dry white wine
- 2 Tbsps. minced shallot
- 1 Tbsp. minced fresh tarragon
- 1 tsp. chervil
- ¼ tsp. salt
- ¼ tsp. white pepper
- 4 egg yolks
- 1 cup unsalted butter, cut into 16 pieces
- 1 Tbsp. tomato paste
- 2 tomatoes, peeled, seeded and very finely minced
- 8 sun-dried tomatoes, finely diced
  Salt and pepper
- 6 fresh swordfish steaks, 8-oz. each

Tahitian Tuna

Serves 4
Preparation Time:
  30 Minutes
Marination Time:
  2 to 3 Hours
Cooking Time:
  6 Minutes

Marinade:
  1 cup low-sodium soy
    sauce
  3 cloves garlic, minced
  4 -inch piece of ginger
    root, peeled and
    grated
  ¼ cup vegetable oil
  ¼ cup sake
  1 Tbsp. brown sugar
  4 fresh tuna steaks, 8 oz.
    each

Tropical Fruit Salsa:
  1 cup diced pineapple
  1 cup diced mango
  ½ cup diced papaya
  ½ cup diced sweet red
    pepper
  3 Tbsps. minced
    scallions
  ¼ cup passion fruit juice
    and seeds
  1 Tbsp. finely diced
    jalapeño pepper
  1 Tbsp. minced fresh
    cilantro
  1 Tbsp. olive oil
    Salt to taste

With year-round availability of fresh tuna, it's opportune to have several preparation methods in your repertoire. Here is a light, low fat and low calorie presentation that always draws compliments. The marinade is something of a standard in Oriental cuisine and works successfully with other fish and meats. The Tropical Fruit Salsa is a nice counterpoint to this preparation, but if you're pressed for time, the fish is flavorful enough to stand on its own without a sauce or condiment.

Combine the marinade ingredients and pour into a shallow glass baking dish or plastic container. Add the tuna to the marinade and refrigerate, loosely covered with plastic wrap, for 2 to 3 hours. Turn the fish occasionally so that all surfaces of the tuna are bathed in the marinade.

For an attractive salsa, take the time to neatly dice all components, aiming for uniformity of size and shape.

Combine the ingredients and refrigerate for several hours or overnight to allow flavors to develop. Let the salsa sit at room temperature for one hour before serving or warm gently in a saucepan.

Shortly before cooking the fish, remove the tuna from the marinade and let it sit at room temperature for 30 minutes. Discard the marinade.

Heat your grill to its highest setting and position the rack as close to the coals as possible. Arrange the tuna on the grill and cook for 2 minutes on one side. Then carefully move each tuna steak one-quarter turn. Cook an additional 2 minutes to create cross-hatch grill marks, then flip the fish and finish grilling. Tuna is succulent and tender when it is served medium rare.

Plate the tuna and garnish with the Tropical Fruit Salsa, which can be served warm or at room temperature.

☆

Tuna with Fennel-Pepper Crust and Ginger Beurre Blanc Sauce

East meets West in this recipe. I've taken the classic French butter sauce and given it a Japanese twist with the addition of ginger root, rice wine vinegar and pickled ginger. The result is a silken, mellow sauce that contrasts nicely with the piquant liveliness of spice-crusted tuna.

Serves 6
Preparation Time:
  20 Minutes
Cooking Time:
  20 Minutes

G rind the fennel, coriander and peppercorns with a mortar and pestle or in a spice grinder until fine.
    Dip the tuna in the spice mixture, coating both sides lightly.

Heat the oil in a non-stick skillet until hot. Sauté the tuna over medium heat to desired degree of doneness.

To make the Ginger Beurre Blanc Sauce, combine the shallots, vinegars, wine, ginger root and peppercorns in a small pan and reduce over medium heat to 3 tablespoons.

Strain the reduction into a clean pan, pressing hard on the solids to extract the liquid. Over low heat add one tablespoon of butter and whisk constantly until melted. Add another piece and continue in this manner until you've used all the butter. Don't let the sauce get too hot or it will liquefy.

Add the julienned pickled ginger and season to taste. Top the tuna with some of the sauce and serve immediately.

- ¼ cup fennel seeds
- 3 Tbsps. coriander seeds
- 2 Tbsps. white peppercorns
- 6 fresh tuna steaks, 6-oz. each
  Olive oil
- 1 Tbsp. minced shallots
- ½ cup white wine vinegar
- ¼ cup rice wine vinegar
- ¾ cup white wine
- ¼ cup grated fresh ginger root
- 8 black peppercorns
- 10 Tbsps. cold butter, cut into 8 pieces
- 1 Tbsp. pickled ginger, julienned

★

Meat

Beef Stroganoff

Bobotie

Chiles Rellenos

Chili for a Crowd

Cured Pork Chops with
Maple Glaze

Everybody Loves This
Curry

Hoisin Pork

Lamb Provençal

Orange-Skewered Pork

Pork and Cranberry
Sandwich

Pork with Ginger-
Cranberry Sauce

Tenderloin of Beef with
Shiitake Cognac Sauce

Veal Chops with
Tarragon Glaze

Veal Française

Beef Stroganoff

I like to serve this classic dish over simple buttered noodles, but it's also good with mashed potatoes. After experimenting with many different cuts of meat, I recommend chuck because it's tender and very flavorful. If you like an intense mushroom flavor, shiitakes would be a good substitute for white mushrooms.

Season the meat with the salt and pepper. Heat the oil in a heavy Dutch kettle and when hot, add the meat cubes. Sauté over high heat for about 5 minutes, turning the meat to brown all sides. Remove the meat with a slotted spoon to a bowl and set aside.

Add the onions to the oil in the pan and cook until soft, about 7 minutes. Add the flour and cook, stirring constantly, to lightly brown the flour and cook off the raw taste. Next add the mustard, wine and stock and bring to a simmer. Add the thyme, bay leaves and paprika, then cover the pan. Reduce the heat to low and simmer the casserole for 2 hours.

Cut the mushrooms into quarters. Heat the butter in a skillet and sauté the mushrooms for 5 to 7 minutes or until golden. Set aside.

When about 2 hours have passed, add the mushrooms to the kettle. Cook 15 minutes and then add the sour cream. Watching carefully, simmer the stroganoff just until it is hot. If you let the mixture boil, you run the risk of curdling the sour cream. Taste and adjust seasonings as desired.

Serves 6
Preparation Time:
  45 Minutes
Cooking Time:
  2½ Hours

- 3 lbs. beef chuck, cut into 1-inch cubes
- 2 tsp. salt
  Fresh ground pepper
- ¼ cup olive oil
- 1½ cups minced yellow onion
- ¼ cup flour
- 2 tsps. Dijon mustard
- 2 cups red wine
- 4 cups rich beef or veal stock
- 2 tsps. dried thyme
- 2 bay leaves
- 2 Tbsps. sweet paprika
- 12 oz. white or brown mushrooms
- ¼ cup butter
- 1½ cups sour cream

Bobotie

Serves 6
Preparation Time:
   45 Minutes
(note refrigeration time)
Cooking Time:
   45 Minutes
Preheat oven to 375°

   ¼ cup vegetable oil
1½ cups minced yellow
   onion
   1 lb. ground beef
   ½ lb. ground lamb
   6 cloves minced garlic
   ¾ cup apricot jam
   ¾ cup golden raisins
   ½ cup dried apricots,
   chopped
   3 Tbsps. lemon juice
   2 Tbsps. curry powder,
   or to taste
   1 tsp. cayenne pepper
1½ tsps. salt
   ½ cup light cream
   ¾ cup fresh (soft) bread
   crumbs

   6 eggs
   2 cups milk
   ½ tsp. salt
   ¼ tsp. white pepper
   ¼ tsp. nutmeg

Bobotie is a classic South African dish that exemplifies Malay cuisine, a blending of Dutch, Indonesian and British influences. It is both delicious and different, a nice change from the usual ground beef casserole. Traditionally it would be served with yellow rice (plain white rice colored with turmeric), Malay sweet potatoes (see recipe, page 154) and spiced peaches.

Heat the oil in a large skillet and sauté the onion until soft and translucent, about 10 minutes. Add the beef, lamb and garlic and cook over medium heat, stirring frequently. When the meat is mostly cooked, add the jam, raisins, apricots and lemon juice. Next add the spices, adjusting the seasoning to your preference.

Stir in the cream and the bread crumbs and cook an additional 5 minutes or until almost all of the liquid has evaporated. Transfer the mixture to a large casserole dish or baking pan and refrigerate at least 4 hours before continuing.

In a bowl whisk the eggs with the milk and seasonings. Pour this custard over the chilled casserole and bake in the middle of a 375° oven until the custard is set and the bobotie is hot, about 45 minutes.

Chili for a Crowd

Chili is a cold-weather dish and I can always count on this recipe as a crowd pleaser after a football game or a day of skiing. I personally cannot stand kidney beans, thus you will not find any in this version. By all means add them, and anything else you like, with abandon. As a matter of interest, I have made this chili with chicken instead of beef, and it was equally delicious.

Heat the oil in a large pot until hot. Add the onions, both peppers and the celery and cook over moderate heat for 5 minutes, stirring frequently.

Next add the garlic and cook another 2 minutes; take care not to burn the garlic here.

Chop the meat into bite-sized chunks, or if you prefer, coarsely grind in a food processor. If you elect the latter method, use the pulse button to avoid over-processing. Add the meat to the pot and cook briskly until it browns, about 5 minutes.

Add the remaining ingredients (except the cheese and sour cream) and bring the chili to a simmer. Reduce the heat to low and cook, uncovered, for about three hours, stirring and tasting often. Season with salt to taste when the chili has finished cooking.

Serve in individual bowls and top with cheese and sour cream, if desired.

Serves 10
Preparation Time:
  45 Minutes
Cooking Time:
  3 Hours

- ¼ cup vegetable oil
- 1 large yellow onion, finely diced
- 1 green bell pepper, diced
- 2 pickled jalapeño peppers, seeded and diced
- 1 stalk celery, diced
- 2 cloves garlic, minced
- 3 lbs. boneless beef (any cut)
- 28 oz. can peeled Italian tomatoes, diced
- 6 oz. tomato paste
- 8 oz. tomato sauce
- 2 Tbsps. cayenne pepper (or more to taste)
- 2 Tbsps. chili powder
- 4 oz. diced green chilies (canned is fine)
- 1 tsp. cumin
- 1 bay leaf
- 12 oz. beer
  Salt, to taste
  Grated Monterey Jack or cheddar cheese, optional
  Sour cream, optional

Chiles Rellenos

Serves 4
Preparation Time:
  2 Hours
Cooking Time:
  60 to 90 Minutes

Rellenos:
  8 to 10 medium
    Anaheim chilies
    (always best to have a
    few extras for errors or
    big appetites)
  1 lb. plus, grated
    cheddar and jack
    cheeses
  1 package egg-roll
    wrappers
  1 Tbsp. cornstarch

  Peanut oil

My good friend Sally Martinek from Tempe, Arizona, is a talented and creative chef. She and an old friend, Tom Ryall, love cooking and recipe experimentation. Years ago they devised this sophisticated, 'dress-up' version of a Mexican favorite. Knowing that I'm not a fan of Mexican cuisine, they were eager to prepare this for me, certain I would be won over. I was!

Sally and Tom always use fresh chilies, which they roast for the stuffed rellenos part of the recipe. This step is very time-consuming, but they feel it's absolutely worth the effort as canned chilies are just not as good, although they work fine for the pork sauce preparation. They like to garnish the rellenos with chopped avocado and sour cream, especially if a particular batch of Anaheim peppers is hot.

Grill the chilies on a hot barbecue or broil on the top shelf of your broiler, turning the peppers frequently as the skins begin to char. Set aside and let cool completely. When you can comfortably handle the peppers, gently peel off the blackened skins. Carefully make a slit along one side of the pepper, leaving the stem attached. Gently scrape out the seeds while trying to maul the chili as little as possible. Fill each chili with some of the grated cheese. Do not overstuff or you will have problems later on. Press the slit edges back together so the chili somewhat resembles its fresh appearance.

Place an egg-roll wrapper on the diagonal on a clean work surface (it should look like a diamond). Mix the cornstarch with 2 Tbsps. of water and keep it handy. Fold the top corner of the wrapper down just slightly and position the stem end of the chili on this folded edge. Fold the opposite corner of the wrapper (bottom point) over the tip of the chili. Next, roll up the pepper in the egg-roll skin, liberally applying the cornstarch paste to seal the wrapper. Line a baking tray with waxed paper and transfer the rellenos, as they are assembled, to this tray. You may refrigerate up to six hours before cooking.

Using a large sauté pan or high-sided cast iron skillet, sauté the bacon over medium high heat until crisp. Remove the bacon with a slotted spoon and set aside. Reserve the fat in the pan.

Add the onion to the bacon drippings and sauté until soft and translucent, about 7 minutes. Add the garlic and red pepper flakes and sauté another minute or two, taking care not to burn the garlic. Remove the onion mixture from the skillet with a slotted spoon, trying to leave as much of the fat in the pan as possible.

Mix the flour, cumin and ground peppers in a large plastic baggie. Add the pork cubes, shaking to coat all surfaces of the meat. Brown the pork in the fat, adding a bit of oil or butter if you don't have enough bacon drippings.

Peel off the papery husks from the tomatillos and wash them thoroughly. Remove the cores and then purée the tomatillos in a food processor until smooth.

Next combine the onion mixture, browned pork, chopped green chilies, bacon and the tomatillo purée. Simmer until heated through and then add the hot chicken stock. Simmer for 30 minutes to an hour so the sauce thickens and the flavors marry. Add the tomato paste and cilantro then season to taste with salt and pepper.

To cook the rellenos, heat about half an inch of peanut oil in a large skillet to 370°. A heavy electric skillet is useful for this step. Add the wrapped and stuffed chilies, taking care not to crowd them or they might stick together. Fry until browned on all surfaces, about 2 to 4 minutes. Drain on paper towels, then arrange on a plate with some of the green chili pork sauce.

Green Chili Pork Sauce:
- ½ lb. bacon, chopped
- 1 cup minced yellow onion
- 5 cloves garlic, minced or mashed to a paste
- 1 tsp. red pepper flakes
- ¾ cup flour
- 2 Tbsps. ground cumin
  Fresh ground pepper
- ½ tsp. cayenne pepper
- 2 lbs. pork tenderloin, cut into 1-inch cubes
- 12 fresh tomatillos
- 27 oz. can chopped green chilies (or 3 lbs. fresh: roasted, peeled, seeded and chopped)
- 1½ qts. chicken stock, heated
- 2 Tbsps. tomato paste
- ½ cup minced fresh cilantro
  Salt and pepper to taste

Cured Pork Chops with Maple Glaze

Serves 4
Preparation Time:
   10 Minutes
Marination Time:
   48 Hours
Cooking Time:
   15 to 20 Minutes

   4 **center-cut pork chops,**
      at least 1 inch thick
 ½ **cup pure maple syrup**
 ¼ **cup sugar**
 ½ **cup Kosher salt**
 ½ **cup sugar**
   2 **qts. cold water**
 ¼ **cup pure maple syrup**

I've always had difficulty getting enthusiastic about pork chops. This probably stems from childhood years when every Thursday was pork chop night. And what I remember is thin, dry, tough cutlets that had been cooked for hours. No sauce or condiment could redeem them for me. As a result, for decades I avoided cooking pork chops, favoring roasts and boneless tenderloin on my menus. Recently, however, I discovered that immersion in a simple brine transforms pork chops, rendering them moist and juicy.

L iberally brush all surfaces of the pork chops with the maple syrup. Sprinkle each with a tablespoon of sugar. Cover loosely with plastic wrap and refrigerate 24 hours.

The next day, mix the Kosher salt and ½ cup of sugar with the water, stirring to dissolve.

Place the chops in a non-reactive container that is large enough to accommodate the meat in a single layer. Pour the brine over the chops, making sure they are totally immersed.

Refrigerate for another 24 hours. Several hours before serving, discard the brine and cover the chops with cold water. Soak for 10 minutes, then change the water and soak again for 15 minutes.

Dry the chops thoroughly with paper towels and arrange on a plate in a single layer. Brush the remaining maple syrup over both sides of the meat and let sit at room temperature for at least 2 hours before cooking. If the meat absorbs all the maple syrup during this interval, add more.

Heat your grill to high and arrange the rack as close to the fire as possible. Grill the chops 7 to 10 minutes per side. The cooking time will vary, depending on the temperature and thickness of the chops as well as the intensity of the fire. Remember that pork does not have to be well-done to be safe to eat; use an instant-reading thermometer to ensure that the internal temperature is at least 140°.

☆

Everybody Loves This Curry

With curries there seem to be as many recipes as there are cooks; as a result there are few right or wrong ways to prepare this dish. The addition of coconut milk and apple is not standard, but I love the subtle hint of sweetness that these ingredients impart. I use low-fat coconut milk, which eliminates more than half the fat and calories.

Serves 4
Preparation Time:
  30 Minutes
Cooking Time:
  45 Minutes

¼ **cup vegetable oil**
1 **medium yellow onion, diced or thinly sliced**
1½ **tsps. ground cinnamon**
1 **tsp. ground turmeric**
2 **tsps. ground cumin**
2 **tsps. ground coriander**
1 **tsp. ground cardamom**
¼ **tsp. ground cloves**
½ **tsp. cayenne pepper**
½ **tsp. fresh ground pepper**
½ **tsp. ground fenugreek**
1 **bay leaf**
2 **tsps. salt**
  2-inch piece fresh ginger root, peeled and grated
4 **large garlic cloves, minced**
1 **cup chopped tomatoes**
1 **apple, peeled and grated**
1½ **lbs. top sirloin (or lamb, chicken or raw shrimp)**
1 **cup coconut milk**
  Fresh or frozen peas, peeled and diced potatoes, cubed zucchini or cubed eggplant
1 **lb. fresh spinach, washed and cut into**

I n a large, non-stick skillet or saucepan, heat the oil until hot. Add the onion and dry spices to the pan and sauté over medium-high heat until the onion is tender, about 5 minutes.

Stir in the ginger root, garlic, tomatoes and apple. If you are using lamb, beef or bone-in chicken pieces, add these now and cook over high heat, stirring frequently for 10 to 15 minutes. Note that if you are making a shrimp or boneless chicken curry, the fish or meat will be added at a later stage to avoid overcooking.

The most critical step in the successful creation of your curry occurs at this point. You must cook the mixture until the liquid evaporates and the oil begins to bubble out and turn orange. Depending on the size of your pan and the temperature of your stove and ingredients, this step will take anywhere from 7 to 15 minutes. If you have not added any meat at this stage, the cooking will take less time. Do not rush this process, as the flavor of the curry is dependent on proper frying of the spices. When the oil separates, forming small pools, and the ingredients begin to sizzle, the spices have been cooked to perfection.

Next add the coconut milk and 1 cup of water. If you are making a boneless chicken curry or are including potatoes or eggplant in your dish, add these items now. Basically you want to incorporate your selection of ingredients in an order which corresponds to their cooking time so that nothing gets mushy. Peas and zucchini and spinach cook quickly, so such vegetables need to be added just a few minutes before serving. The same holds true for shrimp, which require only 3 minutes of cooking time.

For beef or lamb curry you will need to cover your pan and simmer the ingredients over low heat for about 20 minutes. For boneless chicken 15 minutes will be adequate.

Just before serving add the cilantro, if desired. Season to

★

1-inch wide ribbons
½ **cup chopped fresh**
    cilantro (optional)
    Salt to taste

taste. Serve with Basmati Pilaf (see recipe, p. 143) and pop-padums (a thin Indian bread made with lentil flour.)

Hoisin Pork

Boneless pork tenderloins are extremely versatile and easy to cook. Just about anything you can do with chicken, you can do with pork. If the meat is trimmed, pork loins are very low in calories and fat. Here, a simple marinade using hoisin sauce—a Chinese condiment made from fermented soy beans—adds intriguing flavor and a lovely caramel glaze to the meat. The pork doesn't require any further embellishing, but I like to serve it with a Thai peanut sauce.

Serves 4
Preparation Time:
  10 Minutes
Marination Time:
  8 Hours
Cooking Time:
  20 Minutes

- ½ **cup hoisin sauce**
- 1 **Tbsp. water**
- 2 **Tbsps. rice wine vinegar**
- 2 **Tbsps. fresh lime juice**
- 2 **cloves garlic, minced**
- ¼ **cup vegetable oil**
- 2 **lbs. boneless pork tenderloin**

Combine the marinade ingredients, blending well. Place the pork tenderloin in a small dish (a bread loaf pan works well) and cover with the marinade. Seal with plastic wrap and refrigerate for 8 hours or overnight.

When ready to cook, remove the pork from the marinade and grill over a hot barbecue for 15 to 20 minutes. If you have a microwave, it is helpful to first warm the meat on high heat for 1 or 2 minutes, just long enough to bring it to room temperature. This will aid in grilling the meat so the outside does not char while waiting for the interior to cook. Discard the marinade because it contains raw pork juice.

Cut into ½-inch-thick slices and serve with Peanut Sauce (see recipe page 60).

Lamb Provençal

Serves 4
Preparation Time:
  10 Minutes
Marination Time:
  4 Hours
Cooking Time:
  15 Minutes

Marinade:
  1 **cup red wine**
1½ **cups olive oil**
  2 **Tbsps. minced garlic**
  2 **Tbsps. herbs de**
    Provençe
  1 **tsp. salt**

  4 **boneless lamb**
    tenderloins
½ **cup Dijon mustard**
    Fresh rosemary sprigs

This was a perennially popular dish in my restaurant—so much in demand that I never took it off the menu, although it changed daily. Boneless lamb tenderloins are a specialty item. Ask your butcher to prepare these for you to save the time and waste involved in deboning racks of lamb. This dish benefits from a very flavorful marinade, so a sauce is redundant. Setting the rosemary alight is a dramatic touch and will imbue your dining room with a perfume redolent of Provence.

Mix the marinade ingredients and pour into a non-reactive pan or container.

Trim the lamb, removing any fat or silverskin.

Rub the tenderloins with the mustard and then place the meat in the marinade. Cover and refrigerate for at least 4 hours or up to 2 days.

Grill or broil the lamb to the desired degree of doneness. If you bring the meat to room temperature before cooking, it will take less time.

Slice the lamb on a slight diagonal and arrange on a platter.

Set the rosemary afire and place on top of the sliced lamb. Serve immediately.

Orange-Skewered Pork

Over the years, I've been asked frequently to name my "best" or "favorite" recipes. This is on my Top Ten list. Nothing could be simpler than plopping a piece of meat in a marinade, then setting it on the barbecue. It's the marinade, by the way, that makes this pork so sublime.

Grind the cinnamon stick, fennel and peppercorns to a powder in a mortar or spice grinder. Combine the spices with the orange juice, mustard, honey, vinegar and orange peel and pour into a glass baking dish.

Cut the pork into 1-inch chunks and thread onto skewers. Place the skewers into the marinade, turning to coat all surfaces. Cover loosely with plastic wrap and refrigerate for at least 6 hours or up to 2 days. Rotate the pork to expose all surfaces to the marinade.

Remove the skewers from the marinade and grill them for 6 to 10 minutes. The grilling time will vary depending on the size of the pork chunks, the intensity of the fire and the distance between the grill and the flames. Remember that trichinae are killed at an internal temperature of 137° and that pork can be served slightly pink if you like it moist.

Serves 6
Preparation Time:
  30 Minutes
(note marination time)
Cooking Time:
  6-10 Minutes

4-inch cinnamon stick
  2 Tbsps. fennel seeds
  ½ tsp. whole black peppercorns
  1 cup orange juice
  ½ cup Dijon mustard
  ¼ cup honey
  1 Tbsp. balsamic vinegar
  Grated peel of 2 oranges
2½ to 3 lbs. boneless pork tenderloin

☆

Pork and Cranberry Sandwich

Serves 4
Preparation Time:
  25 minutes
Cooking Time:
  3 minutes

  12 **oz. boneless pork**
     tenderloin
  ¼ **cup Dijon mustard**
  ½ **cup cornmeal**
   2 **to 3 Tbsps. vegetable**
     oil
   4 **fresh sandwich rolls**
  ¼ **cup Cranberry**
     Chutney
     (recipe page 217)
     Lettuce

Pork sandwiches are a staple in the Midwest, but I can't say that I've ever seen them on a menu in New England or California. I once had a surplus of pork tenderloins, which led to some experimentation, and this is the result. The pork is pounded thin, coated with a spicy mustard (there are so many wonderful ones from which to choose), and finished with a crispy corn crust. I don't know what they'd think in Iowa, but the cranberry chutney is a tasty, albeit a Yankee, addition.

T rim any fat or silverskin from the tenderloin. Cut the meat into one-inch-thick slices. Gently pound the pork between 2 sheets of waxed paper, flattening the meat to a ⅛-inch thickness.

Brush both sides of the pork pieces with mustard. Dip the meat into the cornmeal, patting firmly to make sure the coating adheres.

Heat the oil until it is hot in a large, non-stick skillet. Sauté the pork in batches if necessary. Cook 2 minutes on one side, then turn and cook another minute to finish.

Drain the pork on a paper towels, then assemble the sandwiches. Spread one tablespoon of chutney on the top half of each roll, arrange a bed of lettuce and top with the pork. Serve immediately.

Pork with Ginger-Cranberry Sauce

In an era of consciousness about healthy eating, tenderloin of pork is a good ally. Often advertised as the "other white meat", it is extremely low in both fat and calories. It's a versatile meat that benefits from all manner of flavorful marinades and is tender and juicy if not overcooked. If ginger is not to your liking, substitute a teaspoon of grated orange zest. Sun-dried cherries also work well in this recipe.

Place the pork tenderloin into a large zip-lock plastic bag or in a non-reactive pan. Combine the cranberry juice, port, sugar, ginger and cardamom and add to the bag. Seal tightly and refrigerate at least 12 hours, turning the bag occasionally to distribute the liquid.

Remove the meat from the bag and set on a platter. Allow the pork to come to room temperature.

Pour the marinade into a saucepan or skillet and add the veal stock and sun-dried cranberries. Bring to a boil and cook until the liquid has reduced by half.

Make a slurry by mixing the cornstarch with 2 Tbsps. of water. Stir into the sauce and cook gently for about 2 minutes or until the sauce thickens slightly.

Meanwhile, heat your barbecue and when it is hot, grill the pork tenderloin until it reaches an internal temperature of at least 140°. This should take between 15 and 25 minutes depending on the thickness of your meat and the intensity of the fire.

Cut the meat into half-inch-thick slices and serve with the ginger-cranberry sauce.

Serves 6
Preparation Time:
  10 minutes
(note marinating time)
Cooking Time:
  30 minutes

- 2 to 2½ lbs. pork tenderloin, trimmed
- 1 cup cranberry juice
- 1 cup tawny port
- 3 Tbsps. dark brown sugar
- 2 Tbsps. grated fresh ginger root
- ¼ tsp. ground cardamom
- 1 cup concentrated veal stock (see recipe page 235)
- 1 cup sun-dried cranberries
- 1 Tbsp. cornstarch or arrowroot

Tenderloin of Beef with Shiitake Cognac Sauce

Serves 6
Preparation Time:
5 Minutes
(note sitting time)
Cooking Time:
15 Minutes
Preheat oven to 450°

2 lbs. tenderloin of beef,
  fully trimmed
  Salt and freshly
  ground pepper to taste
6 oz. shiitake
  mushrooms
1 Tbsp. butter
1 shallot, minced
1 Tbsp. fresh minced
  tarragon
⅓ cup dry white
  vermouth
1 Tbsp. sherry wine
  vinegar
½ cup cognac
1 cup concentrated beef
  or veal stock
3 Tbsps. butter
1 Tbsp. cognac

As is so often true of memorable sauces, homemade stock is the backbone of this recipe. If you're going to splurge on tenderloin, shiitakes and cognac, your own stock or a quality commercial product such as Perfect Additions or More Than Gourmet demi glace is a prerequisite.

Pat the tenderloin dry with paper towels and then liberally season with salt and fresh ground pepper. Allow the meat to sit at room temperature for at least 1 hour before cooking.

Remove the stems from the mushrooms and finely mince them.

Melt the butter in a medium-sized skillet and sauté the shallots, tarragon and mushroom stems over moderate heat for 5 minutes. Add the vermouth and vinegar and cook until the liquid is absorbed. Add the Cognac and reduce again to about ¼ cup liquid. Add the stock and strain the sauce through a fine sieve into a clean skillet. Press hard on the solids to extract all of the liquid. Discard the solids.

Heat the sauce and then season to taste. If your stock is not sufficiently concentrated in flavor, you will need to reduce the mixture. Note that this sauce does not thicken.

Rub the tenderloin with a bit of olive oil and place it in a baking dish just large enough to accommodate it comfortably. Roast at 450° in the center of the oven for 15-20 minutes for rare meat. Use an instant-reading thermometer to check the cooking progress. Remember that the beef will continue to cook after it is removed from the oven, so stop baking a few degrees shy of what is ideal for your tastes.

While the beef is cooking, slice the shiitakes and sauté them in 3 Tbsps. of butter. When the mushrooms soften add the remaining cognac and continue cooking for 3 to 5 minutes.

Let the tenderloin rest for at least 10 minutes before slicing. Just before serving, cut the meat into thick slices. Arrange attractively on a platter, scatter with the sautéed shiitakes, and top with the sauce.

Veal Chops with Tarragon Glaze

If you have a reputable butcher, veal chops can be a nice departure from the more routine veal scallops. I prefer loin chops cut no more than 1-inch thick because I find these the most tender and juicy and also the easiest to cook properly. If the veal is not a pale pink but is on the red side, you might consider a brief marination period to assure a tender chop. The tarragon glaze suggested here is really delicious, but veal stock is the foundation of the sauce: substitute a compound butter or serve the chops plain if veal stock is not lurking in your freezer. The Sambuca is optional but adds an intriguing hint of sweetness to the sauce.

P at the veal chops dry with paper towels and then liberally season with salt and pepper. Leave at room temperature for 1 hour before cooking.

Melt the butter in a skillet and sauté the shallots and ¼ cup of the tarragon for 2 to 3 minutes over low heat, taking care not to brown the shallots.

Add the vermouth, raise the heat to medium and cook until the liquid reduces to 2 Tbsps. Add the veal stock and cook until the stock is hot.

Strain the sauce through a fine sieve and discard the solids. Return the sauce to a medium heat, add the Sambuca and the remaining tarragon and reduce to a concentrated glaze. You should have about ½ cup of sauce. Season to taste with salt and pepper.

To cook the chops, heat the clarified butter in your largest skillet until it is hot. Add the meat and reduce the heat to medium. Sauté for 5 minutes and then turn the veal. Continue to cook for another 4 minutes for medium-rare.

Serve the chops on heated plates and top with tarragon glaze.

Veal Chop Marinade (optional):

Combine these ingredients and pour over the veal chops. Marinate for one hour at room temperature and then proceed with the recipe, starting with sautéing the shallots and tarragon.

Serves 4
Preparation Time:
10 Minutes
(note sitting or
marination time)
Cooking Time:
15 Minutes

- 4 loin veal chops, cut
  1-inch thick
  Salt and pepper
- 2 Tbsps. butter
- 2 Tbsps. minced shallots
- ½ cup minced fresh
  tarragon
- ¾ cup dry white
  vermouth
- 1 cup veal stock
- 2 tsps. Sambuca liqueur
- 2 Tbsps. clarified butter

Veal Chop Marinade (optional):
- ⅓ cup olive oil
- ⅓ cup dry white
  vermouth
  Salt and pepper
- 1 tsp. dried tarragon
- ½ tsp. tarragon vinegar

★

Veal Française

Serves 4
Preparation Time:
  10 Minutes
Cooking Time:
  4 Minutes

  4 **veal loin medallions,**
    no more than ½-inch
    thick, about 5 oz. each
    Salt and white pepper
  ¼ **cup flour**
  1 **egg, beaten with 1 tsp.**
    water
  ¾ **cup fresh Parmesan**
    cheese, very finely
    grated
  6 **Tbsps. clarified butter**
  2 **Tbsps. fresh parsley,**
    minced
  1 **lemon, cut in wedges**

This delectable veal preparation is the invention of Richard Young, an Australian chef, restaurateur and culinary professor who worked for me on Nantucket many, many years ago. It's a snap to make and if you don't believe in eating veal, it's almost as good with chicken or turkey breasts.

T enderize the veal by pounding it gently until it's about ¼-inch thick. Season the meat with salt and pepper then dip both sides of the veal in the flour, shaking off any excess. Next, dip the medallions in the beaten egg, making sure to moisten all surfaces. Transfer the veal to a plate containing the Parmesan cheese and coat the slices, pressing lightly to ensure that the cheese adheres.

Meanwhile, heat the clarified butter in a large non-stick skillet until it is very hot. Add the veal medallions and sauté about 2 minutes on each side, making sure not to crowd the pan. Do not overcook or the veal will be tough.

Transfer to warmed plates and garnish with minced parsley and the lemon wedges.

Poultry

Chicken Dockside

Chicken Madagascar

Confit of Duck with
Lemon-Caramel Sauce

Crispy Pesto Chicken

Grilled Chicken Prego

Roasted Cornish Game
Hens

Thai Stir Fry Chicken

Chicken Dockside

Serves 6
Preparation Time:
 One Hour
Cooking Time:
 25 Minutes

  3 carrots, julienned
  2 celery stalks, julienned
  2 leeks, white part only,
    julienned
  1 Tbsp. minced fresh
    parsley
  1 Tbsp. minced fresh
    tarragon
  6 Tbsps. butter, softened
  6 chicken breasts halves,
    boneless and skinless,
    8 oz. each
    Salt and white pepper
7½ cups chicken stock
  ¼ cup dry white wine or
    vermouth
  ¾ cup crème fraîche
  ¼ tsp. white pepper
  1 Tbsp. minced fresh
    parsley
  1 Tbsp. minced fresh
    tarragon

Years ago I devised this recipe to be the signature dish of the restaurant that carried my name. Most of the preparation can be done in advance, however, which is the saving grace of this recipe. The chicken rolls can be refrigerated for two days before cooking or frozen for a month. I like to serve the chicken with Basmati Pilaf (see recipe page 143) and an elegant vegetable like asparagus or haricots verts.

In a medium-sized pot of boiling water, blanch the julienned carrots for 1 minute. Add the celery to the carrots and boil for an additional 45 seconds. Next, add the leeks and blanch another 30 seconds. Drain the vegetables and rinse under cold water until cool. Drain again and pat dry. Divide the vegetables in half and set aside in 2 separate bowls. Mix the parsley and tarragon with the butter to make a paste. Set aside.

Trim the chicken breasts of fat and tendons. Lightly pound each breast between sheets of waxed paper to enlarge and thin slightly. Season the breasts with salt and pepper.

Cut 6 pieces of plastic wrap approximately 16 × 12 inches and set aside. Place some of the julienned vegetables on one of the long sides of a chicken breast. Arrange the vegetables in a neat group to facilitate rolling. Place a piece of herb butter on top of the vegetables and then roll the breast tightly, starting from the end with the vegetable stuffing. Transfer the chicken to one of the pieces of plastic wrap and center it on the long edge (16") of the plastic. Then, simultaneously twist both ends of the plastic wrap in the same direction to tighten the wrappings. Knot each end as close to the chicken as possible. Repeat with each chicken breast.

Bring 6 cups of chicken stock to a slow boil. Add the chicken "rolls" and poach, uncovered, for 15 minutes. Turn off the heat and let the chicken remain in the stock while you prepare the sauce. If the chicken is frozen, you may cook it in its solid state, but the cooking time will increase to 35 to 45 minutes, depending on the size and number of the chicken breasts.

Boil the remaining chicken stock in a large skillet over high heat until it is reduced by one-half. Add the wine and cook for 3 minutes. Lower the heat and add the crème fraîche and white pepper. Cook slowly for about 5 minutes or until the sauce has thickened. Add the reserved julienned vegetables and 1 Tbsp. each of parsley and tarragon; taste and adjust seasonings. Leave the skillet with the sauce on a very low flame while you attend to the chicken "rolls".

Remove the plastic wrap from the chicken breasts and drain any accumulated juices. Cut each chicken roll crosswise into 5 or 6 pieces. Overlap the pieces on warmed, individual serving plates and top with the sauce.

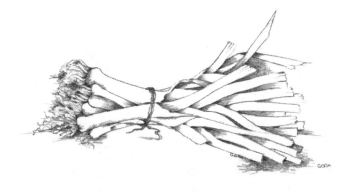

Chicken Madagascar

Serves 4
Preparation Time:
  15 Minutes
Cooking Time:
  20 Minutes

- 4 boneless, skinless chicken breasts, 8 oz. each
  Salt and pepper
- 3 Tbsps. flour
- 2 Tbsps. butter
- 1 Tbsp. oil
- 1 cup apple cider or fresh apple juice
- ¼ cup Calvados or apple brandy
- 1 cup chicken stock
- 2 Tbsps. curry powder
- 1 cup heavy cream
- 2 Tbsps. mango chutney
- 1 cup fresh pineapple, julienned

France meets India in the Indian Ocean on the islands of Madagascar, Mauritius and Réunion. This recipe borrows inspiration from both Chicken Normandy and Chicken Curry, to delicious effect. Turkey or pork will work equally well.

Flatten the chicken breasts slightly so they will cook evenly. Season with salt and pepper and then dust lightly with flour, shaking off the excess.

Melt the butter and the oil in a large skillet and when hot, add the chicken breasts. Sauté for 2 minutes on each side and then remove from the pan. The chicken will not be totally cooked at this stage. Reserve, tented with aluminum foil.

Add the cider and Calvados to the skillet and reduce the liquid by half.

Mix the chicken stock and curry powder; add to the skillet along with the cream, chutney and pineapple strips. When the sauce begins to thicken, return the chicken to the pan and simmer gently for 3 or 4 minutes to finish cooking the meat.

For an attractive presentation, neatly slice each breast into strips and reassemble on a plate. Top with some of the sauce and serve with rice.

Confit of Duck
with Lemon-Caramel Sauce

Confit of duck or goose is a traditional dish of southwestern France that predates refrigeration. The technique of seasoning, slow cooking and storing in fat preserves the duck and, at the same time, transforms the meat into a delightful, melt-in-your-mouth taste sensation.

The recipe that follows is not difficult, although it is time consuming. Confit may be eaten as soon as it is cooked, but it improves with age. Store up to 3 months in the refrigerator. Whenever you remove some of the meat, simply reheat the dwindling contents of your container (fat and meat) and reseal.

Serves 4
Preparation Time:
  45 Minutes
(note marinating time)
Cooking Time:
  2 Hours

  2 **Long Island ducklings**
  1 **tsp. allspice**
  ¼ **tsp. ground cloves**
  ¾ **tsp. ground cardamom**
  ¼ **tsp. ground ginger**
  ¾ **tsp. ground nutmeg**
  2 **bay leaves, crumbled**
  1 **tsp. dried thyme**
  1 **tsp. ground pepper**
  1 **tsp. ground cinnamon**
  1 **tsp. ground coriander**
  8 **cloves garlic, peeled**
  2 **Tbsps. Kosher salt**
  4 **lbs. vegetable lard (not shortening)**

With a sharp knife remove the breasts and legs from the 2 ducks, leaving the skin intact.

Cut all the skin and fat off the duck carcasses with scissors. Discard the carcasses (or save for stock) and put the skin and fat in a pan with ¾ cup water. Cook at a simmer for about 1 hour until all the fat has been rendered. Remove any bits of skin and reserve the fat for the cooking stage.

In a bowl, mix together all the spices—allspice through coriander.

Rub garlic all over the breast and leg pieces. Then lightly dip the meat in the spice mix, shaking off any excess. Arrange the pieces in a single layer in a shallow pan. Sprinkle with the salt and surround with the remaining garlic cloves. Cover loosely with plastic wrap and refrigerate 24 to 36 hours.

Pat the duck dry with paper towels. Separate the legs and breasts and place in separate baking dishes, scattering the garlic cloves. Do not overlap the pieces or the meat will not cook evenly.

Melt the lard and add the reserved rendered fat to it. Divide between the two baking pans, adding enough fat to completely cover the meat.

Place the meat in a cold oven set at 275°. Cook the breasts for 1½ hours and the legs for 2 hours, or until the meat is tender.

Place the duck in a container with tight-fitting lid and pour the fat over the meat, covering with at least a 1-inch layer. Let cool completely and then cover and refrigerate.

★

To remove the duck from the fat, either reheat the entire container slowly or just dig in and pull out the pieces that you need. Heat a large skillet until it is very hot and then add the pieces of confit to the pan. The fat that clings to the meat will be sufficient for browning. Sauté the duck over medium-high heat until the meat is browned and warmed through. This should take about 7 minutes or you may broil the duck.

Serve with Lemon-Caramel Sauce (see recipe page 224).

☆

Crispy Pesto Chicken

This is my husband's favorite chicken dinner. It's a snap to prepare and very tasty, too.

Mix the ricotta, pesto and the Parmesan in a small bowl. Season with fresh ground pepper to taste.

Carefully slide your fingers under the skin of the breast, separating it from the flesh to form a pocket. Leave the skin attached along one side and at one end so the stuffing will be enclosed. Push the cheese and pesto mixture into the pockets you have created.

Brush the surface of the chicken with the olive oil. Place the breasts in a small baking dish and roast for 40 minutes at 375°.

Remove the pan from the oven and brush the surface of the chicken with the remaining ¼ cup of pesto. Return to the oven for an additional 15 minutes.

Let the chicken rest for 5 minutes at room temperature before serving.

Serves 2
Preparation Time:
  15 Minutes
Cooking Time:
  One Hour
Preheat oven to 375°

⅓ cup ricotta cheese
⅓ cup pesto
¼ cup grated Parmesan cheese
  Fresh ground pepper
2 chicken breast halves with bones and skin
2 Tbsps. olive oil
¼ cup pesto

Grilled Chicken Prego

Serves 4
Preparation Time:
  30 Minutes
(note marination time)
Cooking Time:
  5 Minutes

  3 **cloves garlic, minced**
     Juice of 3 lemons
  ¾ **cup olive oil**
  ½ **tsp. salt**
  ¼ **tsp. white pepper**
  2 **tsps. tarragon**
  8 **chicken breast halves,**
     boned and skinned

The marinade imparts a terrific flavor to the chicken, which grills in a flash because you have flattened the breasts into paillards. Try topping the grilled chicken with a dollop of Basil Butter (see recipe page 153).

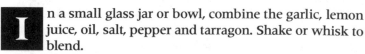 n a small glass jar or bowl, combine the garlic, lemon juice, oil, salt, pepper and tarragon. Shake or whisk to blend.

Pound each breast between sheets of waxed paper with a meat tenderizer or rolling pin. The object is to flatten the chicken to a uniform thickness so it cooks quickly and evenly. The breasts should be about ¼- to ⅜-inch thick and they will become quite large. Place the paillards in a shallow glass pan and pour the marinade over them. Refrigerate, loosely covered with plastic wrap, for 4 hours minimum, turning the chicken occasionally. The chicken can remain in the marinade for up to 2 days.

Heat your barbecue to a medium-hot fire. Set the grill about 2 inches from the flame and arrange the chicken paillards, spacing so they do not touch. Grill for 2 minutes, then turn the breasts and grill 1 to 2 minutes more on the other side. The secret is to not overcook the chicken. If your paillards are very thin, decrease the total cooking time to 3 minutes. Serve immediately.

☆

Roasted Cornish Game Hens

In a small skillet sauté the shallots and garlic in the butter over low heat until they have softened, about 5 minutes.

Squeeze all the moisture out of the spinach and put the spinach in a bowl. Add the sautéed shallot mixture, the cheeses, minced basil, salt, Worcestershire, cayenne, egg and pine nuts to the spinach. Stir to thoroughly combine all of the ingredients.

Wash the hens, removing any giblets, and pat dry with paper towels, inside and out. Rub the cavity of the birds with the halved lemon, squeezing some of the juice into each hen. Place a lemon half and 2 basil leaves into each bird.

Starting at the main cavity end of the hen, very carefully slide your fingers under the skin of the breast on either side of the breast bone. Leave the skin attached at the neck end (shoulder) of the bird. You want to loosen the skin from the flesh without tearing it. Do not detach the skin from the breast bone, as you want to maintain a pocket on either side of it. You should be able to wiggle your fingers under the skin of the legs to loosen it, also.

Gently fill the pockets you have created over the legs and breasts with the spinach stuffing. You should be able to use almost all of the stuffing. Truss the game hens or neatly tie them with twine.

Rub the birds with olive oil and liberally sprinkle with salt and pepper. Arrange the hens on a rack in a roasting pan and place in the oven at 425°.

After 30 minutes baste the birds and lower the oven temperature to 400°. Roast another 15 minutes, and remove the birds from the oven.

Let the hens rest for 15 minutes then transfer from the rack to a platter and remove the string or twine. Serve the birds whole for maximum impact.

Serves 2
Preparation Time:
  30 Minutes
Cooking Time:
  45 Minutes
Preheat oven to 425°

- 2 shallots, minced
- 3 cloves garlic, minced
- 1 Tbsp. butter
- 10 oz. frozen chopped spinach, thawed
- 8 oz. ricotta cheese
- 1/4 cup grated Parmesan cheese
- 1/4 cup grated romano cheese
- 10 basil leaves, minced
- 1/8 tsp. salt
- 1 tsp. Worcestershire sauce
  Pinch of cayenne pepper
- 1 egg
- 1/4 cup toasted pine nuts
- 2 Cornish game hens
- 1 lemon, halved
- 4 basil leaves
- 1 clove garlic
- 1/4 cup olive oil
  Salt and pepper

★

Thai Stir Fry Chicken

Serves 4
Preparation Time:
  30 Minutes
Cooking Time:
  10 Minutes

  ½ lb. asparagus
  1 sweet red pepper
  ¼ cup peanut oil
  3 Tbsps. chicken stock
  4 chicken breasts, boned
    and skinned
  2 Tbsps. peanut or hot
    chili oil
    2-inch piece of fresh
    ginger, peeled and
    grated
  4 cloves garlic, minced
  4 scallions, minced
  1 Tbsp. soy sauce
  ½ tsp. Tabasco
  3 Tbsps. chunky peanut
    butter
  1 cup coconut milk
    (unsweetened)
  ¼ cup toasted sesame
    seeds

This recipe is very quick to cook once you have the preparatory work completed. It is not spicy or fiery hot, so if you like that kind of thing, use hot chili oil and increase the Tabasco. Asparagus and sweet red pepper are totally unorthodox, of course, but the colors are lovely and these items add a nice crunch. Serve with jasmine or plain boiled rice.

Cut the asparagus into 2-inch pieces and slice the pepper into ¼-inch-thick strips. If the asparagus spears are thick, peel the stalks with a vegetable parer or knife.

Heat 2 Tbsps. of oil in a large skillet and when it is hot add the asparagus and stir fry over medium-high heat for 2 minutes. Add the chicken stock, cover the skillet and continue to cook until the liquid evaporates. Add the red pepper strips and stir fry for another 3 minutes. Remove the pan from the heat and set aside.

Cut the chicken into evenly sized strips.

Heat the remaining oil in your largest skillet or in a wok and sauté the ginger and garlic. Add the chicken and scallions and cook 2 minutes. Add the soy, Tabasco, peanut butter and coconut milk and cook over medium heat until the sauce has thickened, about 4 minutes. If the sauce becomes too hot it will separate a bit. If this occurs, simply add another Tbsp. or two of coconut milk to the skillet.

Add the asparagus-pepper medley to the pan and cook another minute to heat through. Transfer the chicken to a serving platter and sprinkle with sesame seeds.

Pasta

Arugula Ravioli with
Salsa Fresca

Fettuccine with Shrimp
and Scallops

Grilled Vegetable
Lasagna

Linguine Floridiana

Pasta di Mare

Shells with Artichokes
and Prosciutto

Wild Mushroom Risotto

Ziti with Eggplant and
Tomato

Arugula Ravioli with Salsa Fresca

Serves 4
Yield: About 40 Ravioli
Preparation Time:
  15 Minutes (note resting time for sauce)
Cooking Time:
  5 Minutes

  8 **cups fresh arugula leaves (no stems)**
  1 **cup ricotta cheese**
  ⅔ **cup mascarpone cheese**
  ½ **cup fresh grated Parmesan**
  1¼ **tsps. salt**
  ½ **tsp. fresh ground pepper**
  1 **recipe Ravioli Dough (see recipe page 231)**

Salsa Fresca:
  5 **cups diced ripe tomatoes**
  ½ **cup extra virgin olive oil**
  ¾ **tsp. lemon oil (optional)**
      Zest of 1 lemon
  5 **Tbsps. fresh minced basil**
  5 **cloves garlic, minced**
      Salt and pepper to taste
  ½ **cup white wine**

      Shaved Parmesan (garnish)
      Fresh basil leaves (garnish)

Arugula is one of those greens that has been rediscovered in the '90's. The suggested sauce is low-calorie and a snap to prepare; its fresh, vibrant taste makes this dish memorable.

Wash the arugula and steam with 2 Tbsps. of water in a large skillet until wilted, about 2 minutes. Transfer to a sieve, refresh with cold water and let drain. When cool enough to handle, squeeze all of the moisture from the arugula with your hands. Purée in a food processor or blender. Add the 3 cheeses and the salt and pepper to the processor and pulse to blend.

Form the ravioli as directed. Transfer the ravioli to a cornmeal- or semolina-dusted tray; separate with wax paper if layering. The pasta can be frozen for up to 3 months at this point or refrigerated several hours before cooking.

For the Salsa Fresca, combine all of the ingredients except the white wine in a bowl and stir thoroughly to blend. It is advisable to prepare the sauce several hours before serving to allow the flavors to marry.

Cook the ravioli in a large quantity of salted, simmering water until tender. While the pasta is cooking, transfer the sauce to a skillet, add the ½ cup of white wine and cook over high heat for 4 minutes.

Divide the ravioli and Salsa Fresca between 4 plates, garnish with basil leaves and a scattering of shaved Parmesan. Serve immediately.

☆

Fettuccine with Shrimp and Scallops

At home I've gotten into the habit of saving scraps of tomatoes, carrots, other mild vegetables, chicken, etc., and freezing them in small baggies. When I wish to make this broth, I simply clean house, supplementing what's in my freezer as necessary. Truffle oil is an expensive, but oh, so, wonderful item available in well-stocked gourmet shops. It's not essential to the dish, but it does add a subtle, earthy element to the broth.

Combine the celery, carrots, leek, tomatoes, parsley, peppercorns, fish, stock, water and 1 cup wine in a large pot and bring to a simmer.

Shell the shrimp and remove the small side muscle from each scallop. Add these muscles and the shrimp shells to the stock pot.

De-stem the shiitake mushrooms; slice the caps and set aside. Finely mince the stems and add to the broth. Cook the broth slowly, uncovered, for several hours. You want the ingredients to release their flavors and the liquid to reduce by about half. Strain into a clean pan; discard the solids. The broth can be frozen for several months.

Cook the fettuccine according to the package directions.

While the pasta is cooking, heat the olive oil in a large skillet until hot. Add the shiitake mushrooms and the shallots and sauté for 3 or 4 minutes, stirring constantly. Add the shrimp, red and yellow tomatoes, sugar snap peas, the ½ cup of wine and 1 cup of hot broth. Cook over high heat for 2 minutes and then add the scallops and basil. Cook for 3 minutes, adding more broth if the liquid evaporates. Avoid overcooking the seafood. Remove from the stove and stir in the truffle oil.

Drain the pasta and divide between six bowls. Likewise, divide the seafood sauté and then add 1 cup of hot broth to each bowl. Sprinkle with grated Parmesan and serve immediately.

Serves 6
Preparation Time:
 45 Minutes
Cooking Time:
 3 Hours

- 2 stalks celery, sliced
- 4 carrots, sliced
- 1 leek, sliced
- 3 ripe tomatoes, diced
- 12 fresh parsley stems
- 12 whole peppercorns
- 7 cups chicken or vegetable stock
- 6 cups water
- 1 cup white wine
- 1 lb. U16-20 shrimp, raw, shells on
- 1 lb. fresh scallops
- 12 oz. fresh shiitake mushrooms
- 1 lb. spinach fettuccine
- 3 Tbsps. olive oil
- ¼ cup minced shallots
- 2 ripe red tomatoes, neatly diced
- 2 ripe yellow tomatoes, neatly diced
- 1 cup sugar snap peas, stringed
- ½ cup white wine
- ½ cup fresh basil, cut into ribbons
- 2 Tbsps. truffle oil
- 1 cup Parmesan cheese

Grilled Vegetable Lasagna

Serves 10
Preparation Time:
  2 Hours
Cooking Time:
  One Hour
Preheat oven to 375°

  3 **eggplants**
  6 **zucchini**
  1 **cup olive oil**
    Salt and pepper
  2 **sweet red peppers**
 24 **oz. skim-milk ricotta**
    cheese
  2 **eggs**
1¼ **cups grated Asiago or**
    Parmesan cheese
 ¼ **cup fresh minced basil**
 ¼ **cup fresh minced**
    parsley
 ½ **box lasagna noodles**
  4 **cups flavorful**
    spaghetti sauce
 ⅔ **cup pesto**
 ¾ **lb. mozzarella cheese,**
    shredded

This creative lasagna has always elicited rave reviews, even from meat-eaters! The most tedious step is the grilling of the vegetables as these need constant attention. Once this is accomplished, however, the actual assembly is quick.

Cut the eggplants lengthwise into ¼-inch thick slices. Cut the zucchini lengthwise into ⅛-inch thick slices. Arrange the vegetables on a baking tray and liberally brush both sides with the olive oil. Season lightly with salt and pepper. Grill the eggplant and zucchini on a hot barbecue until they are just tender, about 7 minutes. Do not overcook. Set aside to cool.

Place the peppers directly on the grill and cook until the skin chars, turning frequently. Transfer the peppers to a paper bag, seal tightly and let steam for 5 minutes. When cool enough to handle, peel, seed and stem. Cut the peppers into long, 1-inch-wide strips.

Combine the ricotta, eggs, ¾ cup of Asiago cheese, herbs and ½ tsp. each salt and pepper.

Cook the lasagna noodles according to package directions. Do not undercook; the pasta will not finish cooking in the oven.

Brush a 9x13x3-inch baking pan with some of the spaghetti sauce. Place a single layer of cooked noodles in the pan. Top with a layer of eggplant. Spread half of the ricotta mixture on the eggplant and sprinkle with ⅓ of the mozzarella. Top with a layer of noodles.

Spoon a thin coating of spaghetti sauce onto the pasta and cover with the zucchini slices and red pepper strips. Spread the remaining ricotta over the vegetables and top with half of the remaining mozzarella.

Arrange another layer of noodles and cover with the rest of the eggplant. Brush with the pesto and then sprinkle with the remaining mozzarella. Cover with a final layer of noodles.

Spoon some of the spaghetti sauce over the pasta and top with ½ cup of Asiago cheese.

Bake at 375° for 1 hour. Let the lasagna sit for at least 15 minutes before cutting. Serve with the remaining sauce.

★

Linguine Floridiana

This is a truly luscious pasta preparation. The underlying citrus flavor marries beautifully with the seafood and adds a subtle nuance to this dish.

Serves 6
Preparation Time:
  30 Minutes
Cooking Time:
  15 Minutes

- **1 lb. raw shrimp, shells-on (16 to 20 shrimp)**
- **1 cup white wine or champagne**
- **2 shallots, minced**
- **2 oranges**
- **1 lemon**
- **½ cup white wine or champagne**
- **3 cups heavy cream**
- **1 Tbsp. Grand Marnier or orange liqueur**
- **⅛ tsp. salt**
- **1 lb. linguine**
- **1 Tbsp. butter**
- **1 clove garlic, minced**
- **⅓ cup white wine**
- **1 lb. bay scallops, muscles removed**
- **16 cherry tomatoes, halved**
- **2 Tbsps. minced fresh parsley**

Peel and devein the shrimp, reserving the shells. Place the shells in a small pan and add 1 cup of wine. Cook over medium-high heat until all but 1 Tbsp. of liquid has evaporated. Transfer the shells and liquid to the bowl of a food processor and purée until pulverized. Place the purée in a large skillet and set aside temporarily.

Combine the shallots, the juice and grated rind of 1 orange the juice and grated rind of ½ lemon and the ½ cup of wine in a small pan. Simmer over medium-low heat until the liquid reduces to 1 Tbsp. Add this mixture and the heavy cream to the shrimp shells in the skillet. Cook over low heat for 10 minutes, stirring frequently.

Strain the cream through a sturdy mesh sieve into a clean bowl, pressing hard on the solids to extract all the liquid. Discard the shells and return the cream to the skillet. Add the liqueur, salt and the grated rinds of the remaining orange and half-lemon to the cream sauce. Simmer until the sauce reduces by about ⅓. You want the sauce to thicken enough to coat the back of a spoon.

Cook the linguine according to package directions.

Melt the butter in a large skillet and sauté the garlic, taking care not to burn it. Add the wine and heat until boiling. Add the shrimp and cook for 3 minutes. Add the scallops and cook another 2 minutes.

Mix the seafood with the sauce; drain the linguine. Combine everything in a large bowl and garnish with cherry tomatoes and parsley.

Pasta di Mare

Serves 4
Preparation Time:
15 Minutes
Cooking Time:
40 Minutes

1½ **cups dry white wine or**
   vermouth
20 **medium shrimp, raw,**
   with shells
¾ **lb. bay scallops**
2 **Tbsps. butter**
1 **clove garlic, minced**
2 **cups heavy cream**
3 **Tbsps. fresh grated**
   Parmesan cheese
12 **artichoke bottoms,**
   quartered
1 **lb. fresh spinach**
   fettuccine
2 **oz. fresh spinach**
   leaves, cut in ribbons
   Salt and pepper

A rich and elegant pasta dish that is quick and easy to prepare. Lobster or crab also work well in this recipe.

In a non-aluminum skillet or saucepan bring the wine to a simmer. Add the shrimp and poach 1 minute. Add the scallops and poach with the shrimp for another 1½ minutes. Do not overcook the seafood. Transfer the shrimp and scallops to a bowl and reduce the wine to ¼ cup. Set aside. Peel and devein the shrimp when cool; reserve the shrimp shells for the sauce.

Melt the butter in a small saucepan over medium heat and sauté the shrimp shells for about 5 minutes. Add the garlic and cook another 2 minutes but do not allow the garlic to brown. Add the heavy cream and cook over medium-high heat until reduced in volume by half. Strain the sauce and discard the shrimp shells. Return the sauce to the pan and add the wine-poaching liquid and the Parmesan cheese. Cook over medium heat for another 5 to 7 minutes or until thickened. Remove from the stove and add the artichoke bottoms.

Cook the fettuccine according to package directions or until it's al dente. Drain and then return it to the pot. Add the spinach ribbons and toss the mixture well. Next add the shellfish and the cream sauce and stir to combine. Season with salt and pepper to taste and reheat if necessary. Serve immediately on warm plates.

Shells with Artichokes and Prosciutto

This is one of the best pasta dishes I've ever eaten but it's not for dieters. A recipe for homemade mascarpone on page 225, but the commercial variety is preferable for this dish if it's available in your area. The sauce can be made without the cheese—just reduce the heavy cream by half so it thickens nicely. For an even more sublime effect, substitute fresh artichoke hearts or bottoms for the canned variety and use pancetta (Italian bacon) instead of the prosciutto.

Serves 6
Preparation Time:
  15 Minutes
Cooking Time:
  30 Minutes

  3 cups heavy cream
  4 cloves garlic, unpeeled
  7 oz. Mascarpone cheese
  2 egg yolks
  6 Tbsps. butter
  2 cans of artichoke
    hearts in water, 12 oz.
    each, drained
  ¼ lb. prosciutto, diced
  1 lb. medium pasta
    shells
1½ cups fresh grated
    Parmesan cheese
    Salt and fresh ground
    pepper

Place the heavy cream in a large, heavy-bottomed pan and set over low heat.

Put the garlic cloves in a small pot of water and bring to a boil. Drain and peel the cloves of garlic when cool enough to handle. Slice the cloves in half and add to the reducing cream.

Mix the mascarpone cheese with the egg yolks in a small bowl and set aside.

Melt the butter in a large skillet and add the artichoke hearts and prosciutto. Sauté over medium heat for several minutes until these items are heated through. Set aside.

When the cream has reduced and thickened slightly, remove from the heat, discard the garlic and cool briefly. Whisk in the mascarpone-egg mixture and return pan to a very low flame to reheat the sauce gently. Do not allow the sauce to boil.

Add the artichokes and prosciutto to the sauce and season to taste.

Cook the shells in plenty of boiling, salted water until they are al dente. Drain thoroughly so residual water doesn't dilute the sauce.

Toss the shells with the warm sauce and divide the pasta between 6 plates. Sprinkle with Parmesan and serve immediately.

Wild Mushroom Risotto

Serves 4
Preparation Time:
  15 Minutes
Cooking Time:
  One Hour

8 oz. fresh shiitake
  mushrooms
¾ cup butter
¼ cup cognac
1½ cups veal stock
1½ cups chicken stock
¾ cup finely diced onion
1 cup Arborio rice
¾ cup white wine
½ cup grated Parmesan
  cheese
  Salt and pepper to
  taste

Is there anyone who doesn't like risotto? Judging from its international popularity, this is surely the dish of the decade. Made from an Italian rice called Arborio, risotto is a hearty medley of rice and stock with anything from artichokes to zucchini thrown in. Because the rice is basically bland, what you add in the way of herbs, stock, meat, seafood, vegetables or cheese will determine the direction of your risotto. My version is earthy and makes a toothsome, satisfying supper. Other wild mushrooms can be used, alone or in combination with the shiitakes. The flavors of this risotto are subtle, so be sure to use the best stock, wine and Parmesan you can find.

Remove the stems from the mushrooms and cut into a fine dice; reserve. Slice the caps and sauté in ¼ cup of the butter for about five minutes or until they begin exuding juice. Add the cognac and ½ cup of veal stock and cook until the mushrooms are soft and tender. Set aside.

In a saucepan combine the remaining veal stock with the chicken stock, add the reserved mushroom stems and simmer for 15 minutes. Strain and discard the solids.

Meanwhile, melt the remaining butter in a heavy-bottomed saucepan and sauté the onion until it is soft and translucent, about 8 minutes. Add the rice and cook over medium heat for two minutes, stirring frequently.

Next add ½ cup of the hot stock to the rice and cook until it is absorbed. The trick to a successful risotto is slow cooking, frequent stirring and small additions of liquid. Whenever the liquid is absorbed, add another ½ cup of stock.. After about 10 minutes of cooking, add the wine, then continue on with stock additions once it's absorbed. Generally it takes about 30 minutes until the rice is tender.

When tender, add the cheese and reserved mushrooms; season to taste. Add a bit more stock (or water) if the dish seems dry—it is meant to be creamy and loose.

Ziti with Eggplant and Tomato

If you like eggplant, you will like this dish (and if you don't, use zucchini). There is a myriad of tasty possibilities here: add olives, anchovies, roasted peppers, crumbled Italian sausage or different herbs, for example. If your tomatoes are not great, add other zesty items to compensate.

S alt the eggplant and let it drain in a sieve or colander for 30 minutes to decrease its bitterness. Pat dry with paper towels before cooking.

Place the garlic cloves in 1 inch of water and bring to a slow boil. Boil for 5 minutes, then drain and allow the cloves to cool. Discard the tough skin and mash the cloves slightly.

Heat the olive oil in a large, heavy-bottomed skillet until hot. Sauté the eggplant in small batches until just tender and golden. Set aside, covered, while you finish the recipe.

Add the garlic, fresh and sun-dried tomatoes and the chicken stock to the skillet. Sauté over high heat for 3 to 4 minutes. Stir in the basil and the reserved eggplant and remove from the heat. Cover and keep warm.

Cook the ziti in boiling, salted water until it's al dente, then drain well.

Toss the pasta with the sautéed vegetables, rewarming in a skillet if necessary. Sprinkle with Parmesan and fresh ground pepper to serve.

Serves 4
Preparation Time:
  45 Minutes
Cooking Time:
  30 Minutes

- 1 **eggplant, unpeeled, cut into $1/3 \times 1$-inch sticks**
- 6 **cloves garlic, unpeeled**
- 1 **cup olive oil, approximate**
- 3 **ripe tomatoes, peeled, seeded and diced**
- 12 **sun-dried tomatoes, cut into thin strips**
- 16 **yellow cherry tomatoes, halved (low acid)**
- $1/2$ **cup chicken stock**
- 1 **cup fresh basil, cut into ribbons**
- $1/2$ **lb. ziti or other small tubular pasta**
- $1/2$ **cup fresh grated Parmesan or asiago cheese**
  Fresh ground pepper

Vegetables & Accompaniments

Applesauce

Artichoke Ragout

Basmati Pilaf

Boursin Potatoes

Braised Fennel

Buttermilk Mashed
Potatoes

Carrots in Dilled Cream

Cheesy Potatoes

Creamy Polenta

Creamy Swiss Chard

Fried Green Tomatoes

Garlic Potato Gratin

Grilled Zucchini with
Basil Butter

Malay Sweet Potatoes

Mascarpone Mashed
Potatoes

New England Corn
Pudding

Oven Roasted Vegetables

Potato-Parsnip Pancakes

Spaghetti Squash
Parmesan

Spicy Roasted New
Potatoes

Wild Rice

Applesauce

Cut each unpeeled apple into 3 or 4 chunks.
Place the apples in a pan with the water, cover tightly and cook for 10 minutes or until the apples are soft.

Purée in a food mill or pass through a sieve; discard the skins.

Add the sugar and spices and stir to dissolve.

Yield: 3 cups
Preparation Time:
  5 Minutes
Cooking Time:
  10 Minutes

  6 **Macintosh apples,**
    unpeeled, cored
  $\frac{1}{2}$ **cup water**
  $\frac{1}{3}$ **cup sugar**
  $\frac{1}{4}$ **tsp. cinnamon**
  $\frac{1}{8}$ **tsp. nutmeg**

Artichoke Ragout

Serves 4
Preparation Time:
  10 Minutes
Cooking Time:
  40 Minutes

  2 **large artichokes**
  1 **lemon, juiced**
  1 **tsp. salt**
  ½ **cup Italian dressing**
  ½ **cup grated Parmesan**
    cheese

This is a delicious artichoke preparation, but it is messy to eat. Artichoke leaves need to be picked up with your fingers, so don't serve this vegetable at a fancy dinner party. Steamed artichokes will keep for days in the refrigerator and if you have some of the broiled quarters left over, they will reheat nicely in the microwave.

Remove the stems from the artichokes and discard. Cut off the top half of the artichokes and discard. Snip off the tips of the remaining artichoke leaves beginning at the base and working your way around the artichoke. Wash the artichokes and rub them with the lemon juice.

Bring 2 inches of water to a boil, add the salt, the artichokes and any remaining lemon juice. Cover the pan and cook for 25 to 30 minutes or until the tip of a knife easily pierces the bottom of the artichokes.

Remove from the pan with tongs and drain the artichokes upside down until cool. Remove the fuzzy chokes with a small spoon and discard. Using a serrated knife, cut each artichoke into quarters.

Place the sections in a baking dish that will accommodate them snugly. Gently spread the leaves apart, fanning them out as much as possible.

Pour the dressing over the artichokes, sprinkle with the cheese and broil 4 inches below the flame for 10 minutes or until golden. Serve hot or warm.

Basmati Pilaf

Basmati rice recently has become popular in the United States and is readily available in most markets. A staple of Indian cuisine, it's the classic accompaniment to curry. If you are not familiar with basmati, I recommend you give it a try. It's sold in white or brown form. I prefer the latter as it is more nutritious and retains a distinctive, nutty flavor that I quite like. As a matter of fact, I have come to prefer basmati to converted rice and use it almost exclusively.

The pilaf technique of cooking rice, as opposed to simple boiling, works well with basmati. Onion is sautéed in butter, the rice is added and stirred for two minutes to heat the kernels, then hot chicken stock is poured in. I have not suggested adding any herbs or spices, fruits or nuts. Rather, this is a basic recipe and all manner of flavorings may be added at your discretion.

Serve 6
Preparation Time:
  10 minutes
Cooking Time:
  30 minutes

  4 **Tbsps. butter**
  1 **cup finely minced**
     yellow onion
1½ **cups brown basmati**
     rice
  3 **cups chicken stock, hot**
  1 **tsp. salt (omit if using**
     canned chicken stock)

Heat the butter in a 2 qt. saucepan and when hot, add the onion. Sauté onions for 4 or 5 minutes over medium high heat, or until soft.

Contrary to what the package directions may read, do not soak the rice before cooking. This creates a soggy finished product. Instead, add the raw rice to the skillet and stir with a wooden spoon for 2 minutes to coat and heat the kernels.

Add the chicken stock and optional salt to the rice. Cover the pan with a tight-fitting lid. Reduce the heat to low and cook for 20 minutes. Check the rice; if the water has not been absorbed, return to the heat and cook another 5 minutes. Then allow the rice to sit, covered, for an additional 10 minutes. Fluff with a fork to serve.

Boursin Potatoes

Serves 8
Preparation Time:
  10 minutes
Baking Time:
  45 minutes
Preheat oven to 350°

   2 lbs. red-skinned new
     potatoes
   1 cup heavy cream
  12 oz. Boursin or Rondele
     herb & garlic cheese

Here is a speedy but novel potato dish that is simply and sinfully divine. I usually make it with Boursin or Rondele "light" cheese, which lessens the calorie count but not the flavor. It is a fine accompaniment to grilled steak or lamb and is rich enough to eliminate the need for any sauces. This dish reheats well in a microwave.

Wash the potatoes and cut them into ⅛-inch-thick slices. It is not necessary to peel them. Layer half the potatoes in a 7 × 11-inch baking pan.

Meanwhile, combine the cream and the cheese in a small pot and heat slowly until blended. Pour half this mixture over the potatoes in the pan. Cover with remaining potatoes and cream.

Bake uncovered in the middle of a 350° oven for 45 to 50 minutes or until golden brown and bubbly.

Braised Fennel

This recipe is so simple that it hardly qualifies as a recipe. Nonetheless, fennel is a misunderstood vegetable that seems to enjoy little popularity in this country, so here's a perfect introduction. A fall-winter vegetable similar in shape and color to celery, fennel is popular in Italian cooking, where it is known as finocchio. Raw, it adds appeal to salads with its distinctive licorice flavor, which admittedly not everyone enjoys. Braised in chicken stock, however, the anise flavor is much more subtle—merely a mysterious nuance.

Serves 6
Preparation Time:
   10 Minutes
Cooking Time:
   15 Minutes

   3 fennel bulbs
   2 cups light chicken
      stock

Wash the fennel bulbs, discarding any bruised or discolored outer leaves. Chop off the celery-like stalks and save for another use (I like them minced and added to tuna salad).

Cut the bulbs through the root end in half or into 4 wedges, depending on the size of the bulbs. You want the wedges to stay together, so you must include some of the root end (core) on each piece, otherwise the fennel will separate into onion-like layers. If the root end is dirty or discolored, trim it with a paring knife.

Bring the chicken stock to a simmer in a skillet large enough to accommodate the fennel in a single layer. Immerse the fennel, cover and cook gently for 10 to 15 minutes or until just tender. Drain and serve with a soupçon of butter.

Buttermilk Mashed Potatoes

Serves 8
Preparation Time:
15 Minutes
Cooking Time:
30 Minutes

3 lbs. small red-skinned
  new potatoes
  Salt
¾ cup buttermilk
¼ cup butter
  Salt and pepper to
  taste

Made with small, red-skinned new potatoes and flavored with the tang of buttermilk, this recipe gives a new definition to mashed potatoes. I choose not to peel the potatoes, preferring the color and texture lent by the skins.

Scrub the potatoes and cut into 1-inch cubes. Bring a pot of water to a boil, add 1 tsp. of salt and the potatoes. Cover and cook until tender, about 30 minutes. Drain the potatoes and mash roughly.

Add the buttermilk and butter and mash or stir until well blended. Season to taste.

Carrots in Dilled Cream

A heavenly but caloric approach to that everyday standby—the carrot. This is an elegant vegetable dish that will dress up a plain roast or piece of fish quite nicely. Once you've got the carrots julienned, the rest is a snap!

Melt the butter in a large skillet and add the carrots, sugar, salt and pepper. Sauté over medium heat for 3 minutes, stirring constantly. Add the chicken stock, cover the pan and reduce the heat to low. Simmer the carrots for about 5 minutes or until they are just barely tender.

Uncover the skillet, raise the heat to medium high and cook until the stock is reduced. Add the crème fraîche and allow the mixture to boil until the sauce thickens. Just before serving stir in the fresh dill.

Serves 6
Preparation Time:
  25 Minutes
Cooking Time:
  15 Minutes

- 3 Tbsps. unsalted butter
- 1 lb. carrots, peeled and julienned
- ½ tsp. sugar
  Pinch of salt
  Pinch of white pepper
- ½ cup chicken stock
- ⅔ cup crème fraîche (see recipe page 220)
- 2 Tbsps. fresh minced dill

Cheesy Potatoes

Serves 4
Preparation Time:
  20 Minutes
Baking Time:
  60 Minutes
Preheat oven to 375°

  1 **cup grated Cheddar
    cheese**
  1 **cup grated Swiss or
    Gruyère cheese**
  6 **large baking potatoes,
    peeled and thinly
    sliced**
  1 **cup chicken stock,
    heated**
  ½ **cup freshly grated
    Parmesan cheese
    Fresh ground black
    pepper**

A simple side dish that is flavorful and much lower in calories than most versions of scalloped potatoes.

Mix the cheddar and Swiss cheeses together in a small bowl.

Grease a large baking pan or casserole and layer half of the sliced potatoes in it. Season with pepper and cover with half of the cheese mixture. Top the casserole with the remaining potatoes, season, and then sprinkle with the rest of the cheese mixture. Pour the hot chicken stock into the pan and spread the Parmesan cheese on top of the dish.

Bake at 375° for 1 hour or until the potatoes are tender and golden.

★

Creamy Polenta

Cornmeal mush? I don't think so! Polenta is an ancient Italian dish that's become a popular substitute for potatoes or rice in trendy restaurants. My version is downright decadent: cream constitutes half the liquid and a liberal dose of cheese boosts the flavor of an otherwise bland dish.

Combine the chicken stock and cream in a large saucepan and bring to a boil. Slowly add the polenta flour to the liquid, stirring constantly. It is helpful to use a sieve for this step to reduce the likelihood of lumps. Reduce the heat and cook, stirring constantly, until the liquid has been absorbed and the polenta is smooth.

Add the butter and cheese and cook over low heat for another few minutes. Season to taste with salt and pepper. Serve immediately.

Serves 8
Preparation Time:
 5 Minutes
Cooking Time:
 15 Minutes

- 2 **cups chicken stock, preferably homemade**
- 2 **cups half and half**
- 2 **cups coarse polenta flour or yellow cornmeal**
- ¼ **cup butter**
- 1 **cup grated Parmesan cheese**
  Salt and fresh ground pepper to taste

Creamy Swiss Chard

Serves 6
Preparation Time:
   20 Minutes
Cooking Time:
   10 Minutes

   3 **shallots, finely minced**
   2 **Tbsps. butter**
   1 **lb. Swiss chard**
   ½ **cup heavy cream**
      Salt and fresh ground
      pepper
      Fresh ground nutmeg
   ½ **cup grated Parmesan**
      cheese

Tired of the same old vegetables? Ready for something new? Then try this elegant yet easy to prepare recipe. Swiss chard is a member of the beet family and is available during the long winter months.

Sauté the shallots in the butter in a very large frying pan until soft, about 3 minutes.
   Wash the chard and remove the thick white stems. Cut the leaves crosswise into 1-inch strips. Add the Swiss chard to the shallots and sauté over medium heat until the chard wilts, about 1 minute.

   Add the heavy cream, raise the heat to medium-high and continue to cook, stirring frequently, until the cream reduces and thickens. Season to taste with salt, pepper and nutmeg. Stir in the Parmesan and serve immediately.

Fried Green Tomatoes

In Africa we always have lots of green tomatoes, so I devised this recipe to make use of them when ripe specimens are in short supply. I serve them at breakfast or brunch and people are always surprised at how much they like them.

Slice the green tomatoes ¼-inch thick and soak in buttermilk for 15 minutes.

Mix the dry ingredients and pour into a shallow dish or plate.

Pour a thin film of oil into a heavy skillet and heat until hot but not smoking. Dip the tomatoes into the cornmeal mixture, coating both sides. Fry in batches until golden; don't crowd the pan. Serve immediately or hold in a warm oven for up to 30 minutes.

Serves 6
Preparation Time:
   15 Minutes
Cooking Time:
   10 Minutes

- **3 green tomatoes**
- **¾ cup buttermilk**
- **½ cup cornmeal**
- **¼ cup flour**
- **2 tsps. sugar**
- **½ tsp. salt**
- **¼ tsp. white pepper**
   Pinch of cayenne
   (or more to taste)
- **½ cup vegetable oil**

☆

Garlic Potato Gratin

Serves 6
Preparation Time:
  15 Minutes
Cooking Time:
  One Hour
Preheat oven to 350°

  8 potatoes, scrubbed
  6 cloves garlic, peeled
  2 cups heavy cream
  ½ tsp. salt
  ¼ tsp. fresh ground
     pepper
  ¼ tsp. nutmeg

A sinfully rich potato preparation that I find absolutely irresistible. These potatoes make a superb accompaniment to steak or lamb, but should definitely not be considered by those attempting to diet. If you have leftovers, they can be reheated in a microwave.

Cut the potatoes into thin slices and place in a heavy-bottomed pan.

Combine the garlic, cream and spices in a small saucepan and bring the mixture to a simmer. Cook over low heat for 10 minutes.

Pour the cream and garlic into the pot with the potato slices and cook over medium heat for 10 minutes.

Transfer the contents of the pot to a baking dish and bake at 350° for 40 minutes, or until the potatoes are tender.

Grilled Zucchini with Basil Butter

Zucchini grills beautifully and here it's enhanced by the flavor of fresh basil and garlic.

Cut the zucchini in half lengthwise. Place in a shallow baking pan that can accommodate them in a single layer and toss with olive oil and pepper. Let marinate at room temperature for about 30 minutes or longer.

Meanwhile, make the basil butter by mixing the butter, garlic, lemon juice, optional salt and basil leaves in a small bowl. Keep at room temperature.

Heat your grill and cook the zucchini over a medium fire until they are tender, about 10 minutes. As the zucchini gets hot, baste it with some of the basil butter. Remove from the grill and spread a bit of basil butter on each spear. Serve immediately.

Serves 6
Preparation Time:
  5 Minutes
Marination Time:
  30 Minutes
Cooking Time:
  10 Minutes

  6 **small to medium zucchini**
  ½ **cup olive oil**
     Fresh ground pepper
  ½ **cup butter, softened**
  2 **cloves garlic, minced**
  1 **Tbsp. lemon juice**
  ½ **tsp. salt (delete if using salted butter)**
  10 **fresh basil leaves, snipped into small pieces**

Malay Sweet Potatoes

Serves 6
Preparation Time:
  15 minutes
Baking Time: 45 minutes
Preheat oven to 350°

  4 **sweet potatoes, peeled**
  4 **Tbsps. butter**
  3 **Tbsps. dark brown**
    sugar
  ¾ **cup fresh orange juice**
  4 **cardamom pods,**
    crushed, or ½ tsp.
    ground cardamom

Where I live in Africa, sweet potatoes are a staple vegetable, available most of the year, unlike so many other vegetables. Out of necessity, I've learned to take a more creative approach to this humble tuber, hitherto only encountered at my table on Thanksgiving. The inspiration for this recipe is the fascinating Malay cuisine of South Africa, where sweet and fruity side dishes are traditionally served with grilled meats and stews.

Cut the sweet potatoes into ½-inch slices and arrange them in a baking pan or ovenproof casserole dish.

Melt the butter in a small saucepan and add the brown sugar, orange juice and cardamom. Heat to boiling, then pour the mixture over the sweet potatoes.

Cover the pan with aluminum foil and bake at 350° for 30 minutes. Remove the foil and bake another 10 minutes. Then drain any excess juice into a small pan and reduce over high heat until the mixture turns syrupy.

Pour the sauce over the sweet potatoes and return the pan to the oven for another 5 or 10 minutes to glaze.

Mascarpone Mashed Potatoes

Sarah Leah Chase, noted cookbook author and columnist, is a friend of mine on Nantucket Island. As spokesperson for the Butterball Turkey Talk-Line, she was asked to devise some do-ahead recipes for Thanksgiving. This is one of her creations and I guarantee that mashed potatoes never tasted so good.

Serves 8
Preparation Time:
 30 Minutes
(note refrigeration time)
Cooking Time:
 One Hour
Preheat oven to 350°

- 3 lbs. Yukon Gold potatoes, peeled and cut into chunks
- 12 oz. mascarpone cheese, at room temperature
- 2 Tbsps. butter, at room temperature
- ¾ cup finely minced chives or scallions
  Salt and freshly ground pepper
- 1 cup freshly grated Parmesan cheese
- 1 tsp. sweet Hungarian paprika
- ¼ tsp. ground nutmeg

F ill a large pot with enough water to come up to the bottom of a round steamer insert. Arrange the potatoes on top of the steamer, cover the pot and steam over medium-high heat until tender, about 20 to 30 minutes.

Pass the potatoes through a food mill into a large mixing bowl. Using a hand-held mixer, beat in the mascarpone and butter until fully incorporated and fluffy. Add the chives and season the potatoes with salt and pepper to taste.

Transfer the mixture to a buttered, shallow 2-qt. baking dish. Sprinkle the Parmesan cheese over the top and then dust lightly with the paprika and nutmeg. Cover the dish with plastic wrap and refrigerate for at least 8 and up to 48 hours before baking.

When ready to cook the potatoes, bring them to room temperature and preheat the oven to 350°. Bake the potatoes until puffed and light golden brown on top, 30 to 40 minutes. Serve hot.

New England Corn Pudding

Serves 6
Preparation Time:
  15 Minutes
Cooking Time:
  30 Minutes
Preheat oven to 350°

 3 **whole eggs**
 3 **egg whites**
 3 **cups corn kernels**
    fresh, or frozen and
    thawed
 2 **Tbsps. flour**
 1 **Tbsp. minced fresh**
    parsley
 2 **tsps. sugar (less if corn**
    is freshly picked)
 ½ **tsp. salt**
    Pinch of cayenne
    pepper
 1 **cup heavy cream**
 ¾ **cup buttermilk**

Corn pudding is an American classic that never goes out of style. My version includes buttermilk to cut the richness of the custard. The secret is to watch the cooking time carefully and remove the pudding from the oven before it sets up totally.

Mix the eggs and whites together with a whisk in a medium bowl. Add the remaining ingredients and blend thoroughly. Pour the mixture into a generously buttered 2-qt. baking dish.

Set the dish in a roasting pan and add enough hot water to come halfway up the sides of the pudding. Bake at 350° for 25 minutes and then open oven to check for doneness. It is likely that the pudding will need another 5 or 10 minutes of cooking, but be sure to undercook it slightly, as it will finish setting up once it has been removed from the oven.

Oven Roasted Vegetables

Cut the eggplants into ¾-inch cubes; it is not necessary to peel the skin. Place in a colander or strainer, sprinkle with salt and let drain for 30 minutes. This will help exude any bitter juices. Pat the cubes with a towel to dry. Brush the eggplant with olive oil and transfer to a large baking dish or tray.

Wash and dry the peppers, then cut into squares. Brush with oil and season with salt and pepper. Add the peppers to the pan with the eggplant.

Wash and dry the summer squash and zucchini; cut in half lengthwise. Brush with olive oil, season and then slice crosswise into 1-inch chunks. Place the squashes in a separate baking pan.

Place the eggplant-pepper mixture in the oven and bake at 350° for 10 minutes. At the end of that time, add the second pan with the squashes and bake an additional 15 minutes. The vegetables are done when they are just tender; do not overcook. To serve, toss everything together in a large bowl or arrange on a platter.

Serves 8
Preparation Time:
  30 Minutes
Cooking Time:
  25 Minutes
Preheat oven to 350°

  2 **small eggplants**
  1 **yellow pepper**
  1 **sweet red pepper**
  3 **small summer squash**
  3 **small zucchini**
  1 **cup olive oil**
    Coarse salt and freshly
    ground pepper

Potato-Parsnip Pancakes

Yield: 12 pancakes
Preparation Time:
  20 Minutes
Cooking Time:
  5 Minutes

  3 **parsnips, peeled**
  3 **baking potatoes,**
    peeled
  ½ **cup yellow onion,**
    finely minced
  ½ **cup flour**
  ¼ **tsp. baking powder**
  ½ **tsp. salt**
  ¼ **tsp. fresh ground**
    pepper
  ⅛ **tsp. nutmeg**
  2 **eggs, beaten**
  ½ **cup vegetable oil or**
    bacon fat

Potato pancakes and applesauce was my favorite dinner when I was a child. In the days before the advent of food processors, however, grating the potatoes was a tedious chore, so we only had this meal as a special treat. Now, thanks to modern equipment I can whip up a batch of potato pancakes in a matter of minutes, any day of the week. This recipe combines potatoes and parsnips—a delicious partnering. My applesauce recipe is a perfect accompaniment to the pancakes. Try these with a roast chicken some night or serve alone as a simple dinner. The batter discolors quickly due to oxidation, so it should be made just prior to cooking.

Shred the parsnips and potatoes with a grater or in a food processor with the grating disc.

Mix the parsnips and potatoes in a large bowl with the onion.

Combine the flour, baking powder, salt, pepper and nutmeg in a small bowl and sprinkle over the vegetable mixture, stirring to mix. Pour in the eggs and mix well.

Heat a skillet, preferably non-stick, with some of the oil or fat until it is very hot.

Spoon some of the batter into the pan and spread it in a thin layer. Cook over medium-high heat for about 3 minutes or until the bottom of the pancake has become brown and crispy. Flip to the other side and cook an additional 2 or 3 minutes.

Repeat with the remaining batter. Use two skillets if you are doing large quantities. Keep the cooked pancakes warm in a 250° oven, if necessary.

Serve with hot applesauce.

☆

Spaghetti Squash Parmesan

Often called dieters' pasta, this unique yellow squash separates into thin strands hat resemble spaghetti when cooked. Unadorned, it is rather bland, but here is a version that is quick and tasty. Asiago cheese is a great substitute for the Parmesan if you can find it in your neighborhood.

Serves 6
Preparation Time:
  15 Minutes
Cooking Time:
  45 Minutes

  1 **large spaghetti squash**
  4 **Tbsps. butter**
  1 **clove garlic, minced**
  ¾ **to 1 cup Parmesan
     cheese freshly grated
     Salt and freshly
     ground pepper to taste**

T here are several methods you may use to cook a spaghetti squash. If you have a pot with a cover that is large enough to hold the squash, either boil or steam it until it is tender and soft. This will usually take 30 to 45 minutes, a bit less if you elect to steam it. Otherwise, place the squash on a baking tray and in a 350° oven bake it for 1¼ hours or until it is easily pierced with a fork. Cut the squash in half length-wise and then let it cool before you attempt to elicit its strands.

When cool enough to handle, scrape the pumpkin-like seeds and gooey fibrous matter from the center of the squash with a spoon and discard. Be careful not to scrape away too much of the real squash here. Then, using the spoon, scrape the "spaghetti" lengthwise from the sides of the squash shell and place in a bowl, separating and fluffing the strands with your fingers.

Melt the butter in a large, no-stick skillet and sauté the garlic over low heat for 2 minutes. Add the squash and cook over medium heat until the strands are heated through, stirring frequently. Add the Parmesan cheese and stir to coat the "spaghetti." Season with salt and pepper and serve immediately.

☆

Spicy Roasted New Potatoes

Serves 8
Preparation Time:
 10 Minutes
Cooking Time:
 40 Minutes
Preheat oven to 375°

16 small red new
    potatoes
½ tsp. garlic powder
½ tsp. Hungarian hot
    paprika
½ tsp. salt
¼ tsp. fresh ground
    pepper
 1 Tbsp. Worcestershire
    sauce
⅓ cup olive oil

Wash the potatoes and then blot dry. Cut into halves, quarters or eighths, depending on their size.

Place the potatoes in a baking pan and sprinkle with the garlic powder, paprika, salt and pepper.

Mix the Worcestershire sauce with the olive oil and drizzle this mixture over the potatoes. Toss to make sure that all surfaces of the potatoes are covered with the oil.

Bake in the lower half of a 375° oven for 35 to 40 minutes or until browned and tender.

☆

Wild Rice

This recipe was given to me by my good friend Sally, from Tempe, Arizona. It's the best wild rice dish I've ever tasted and it's a wonderful accompaniment to roast duck. Thanks, Sally!

Sauté the scallions and mushrooms in the butter in a large skillet over medium-high heat for 5 minutes. Add the rice and nuts and continue cooking for 2 minutes, stirring constantly.

Add the hot stock and lower the heat to maintain a simmer.

Cover the pan and cook for 45 minutes, stirring occasionally.

Serves 4
Preparation Time:
  10 Minutes
Cooking Time:
  55 Minutes

  3 **scallions, minced**
1½ **cups mushrooms,**
    sliced
  ¼ **cup unsalted butter**
  4 **oz. wild rice**
  ½ **cup slivered almonds**
    or pecans
  2 **cups chicken stock, hot**

Dessert

Almond Macaroon Cake

Bananas à la Foster

Bête Noire

Brioche Bread Pudding

Cape Brandy Pudding

Caramel Fudge Brownies

Caramel Ice Cream

Carrot Cake

Coeur à la Crème

Cranberry-Apple Pie

Creamy Ginger
  Cheesecake

Crème Brûlée

Decadent Truffle Cake

Floating Island

French Silk Pie

Fresh Fig Tart

Fresh Peach Pie

Frozen Passion Fruit Pie

Fruit Cake

Ginger Crinkle Cookies

Ginger Ice Cream

Gingerbread

Grand Marnier Cake

Italian Chocolate Torte

Luscious Lemon Mousse

Malva Pudding

Mango Shortcake

Peach Coffee Cake

Persimmon Pudding
  Cake

Pumpkin-Date Tea
  Bread

Roasted Banana Cream

Sour Cream Pound Cake

Stem Ginger Pear Cakes

Sticky Toffee Pudding

Sun-Dried Cherry and
  Peach Crumble

Tiramisù

Treacle Steamed Pudding

Tropical Rice Pudding

Tropical Trifle

Volcano Cakes

Warm Gratin of Fruits

Whipped Amaretto Pie

White Chocolate Bread
  Pudding

White Chocolate Custard
  Cake

White Chocolate Tartufi

Almond Macaroon Cake

A very light but distinctly almond-flavored concoction that resembles an angel-food cake. I like it plain, but a berry coulis or chocolate sauce would not be unwelcome.

Grease and flour a 10-inch tube pan.

Using an electric mixer cream the shortening, butter and sugar. Beat in the egg yolks, one at a time, until the mixture is light and fluffy.

Add the almond extract and liqueur.

On low speed, add the flour and milk alternately in 3 additions and mix until combined. Add the coconut and mix just to blend.

In another clean, grease-free bowl, beat the egg whites until foamy and then add the pinch of salt and continue beating until stiff. Lighten the cake batter with one-third of the egg whites and then fold in the remainder, taking care not to deflate the mixture.

Pour the batter into the prepared pan and bake at 300° for 2 hours. Cool in the pan for 10 minutes and then turn out onto a wire cake rack to finish cooling.

Serves 10
Preparation Time:
15 Minutes
Baking Time:
2 Hours
Preheat oven to 300°

- 1 **cup shortening**
- ½ **cup unsalted butter, softened**
- 3 **cups sugar**
- 6 **eggs, separated**
- 1 **Tbsp. almond extract**
- ¼ **cup Amaretto liqueur**
- 3 **cups flour, sifted**
- 1 **cup milk**
- 1 **cup shredded coconut**
  Pinch of salt

★

Bananas à la Foster

Serves 4
Preparation Time:
  5 Minutes
Cooking Time:
  5 Minutes

  3 Tbsps. butter
  ½ cup brown sugar
  ½ tsp. cinnamon
  ¼ cup orange juice
  1 Tbsp. lemon juice
  2 Tbsps. cognac or
     brandy
  2 Tbsps. dark rum
  2 Tbsps. banana liqueur
  4 ripe bananas,
     quartered lengthwise
  1 qt. vanilla ice cream

An old-fashioned dessert that may have gone out of style but still tastes unbelievably great. I make this at our bush camp in Zambia where we cook over an open fire without benefit of electricity. The cook makes the most amazing paper-thin crêpes, while I whip together this "spirited" banana concoction. He always gives me a wide berth when it comes time to ignite the liquors, ever since the night when, in the darkness, I accidentally poured the alcohol into the fire instead of the skillet. As he is fond of recounting with great hilarity: "The fire went whoosh and Madame Pam, she flew through the night backwards!"

In a medium-sized skillet melt the butter and the brown sugar. Add the cinnamon, orange juice and lemon juice and heat over a medium-high flame until bubbling. Add the cognac, rum and banana liqueur and heat for an additional one minute. Then, standing well back from the pan and with your face averted, flambé the syrup, shaking the pan until the flames die out. Add the bananas and sauté over low heat for 2 to 3 minutes.

Place one or two scoops of ice cream in each of four chilled bowls. Arrange the banana spears in the dishes and then pour the syrup over the ice cream, dividing evenly. Serve immediately.

Bête Noire

*Whenever I want to make an extra special dessert for a true
chocolate devotee, I bake Bête Noire, which translates from the
French as black beast. There is absolutely no flour or other starch
in this recipe, so technique is all-important. As you might surmise,
the cake is intensely chocolate, very dense and not particularly
sweet. The white chocolate sauce is a perfect foil from both a visual
and sweetness standpoint.*

Butter a 9-inch round cake pan and line with buttered
parchment.

Combine the water and 1 cup of the sugar in a pan
and bring to a boil. Boil for 2 minutes. Remove from the heat
and add the chocolates, stirring until melted.

Cut the butter into small pieces and add to the chocolate,
one piece at a time, waiting until each is melted before adding
the next. It will take about 10 minutes to incorporate all of the
butter.

With an electric mixer, beat the eggs with the remaining
⅓ cup of sugar for 5 full minutes. Then add the chocolate mixture and whisk gently until it is just combined. Do not overmix
or you will deflate the cake.

Pour the batter into the prepared pan. Set the cake in a
water bath bake at 350° for 25 to 30 minutes or until the cake
is just set. Cool on a rack for 10 minutes and then invert onto
a cake platter.

Scald the cream in a small saucepan. Remove from the
stove and add the white chocolate, stirring until melted and
smooth. Add in the liqueur of your choice.

To serve, cut the cake into wedges, wiping the knife blade
after each cut. Place the cake atop a pool of sauce; garnish with
whipped cream and white chocolate curls.

Serves 10
Preparation Time:
  30 Minutes
Baking Time:
  30 Minutes
Preheat oven to 350°

½ cup water
1⅓ cups sugar
8 oz. unsweetened
  chocolate, chopped
4 oz. bittersweet
  chocolate, chopped
1 cup unsalted butter,
  softened
5 large eggs, room
  temperature
½ cup heavy cream
5 oz. white chocolate,
  chopped
¼ cup Licor 43, Amaretto
  or Drambuie

Brioche Bread Pudding

Serves 6
Preparation: 30 Minutes
(note refrigeration time)
Baking Time:
   20 Minutes
Preheat oven to 350°

½ cup golden raisins
⅓ cup Grand Marnier
6 pieces brioche, ½-inch
   thick (see recipe
   page 213)
¼ cup unsalted butter,
   melted
2¾ cups half and half
2 vanilla beans, split
2 eggs
3 egg yolks
1 cup sugar
   Whipped cream and
   nutmeg for garnish

I think this is one of the best desserts in this cookbook, which is saying a lot considering that I'm not really a bread pudding fan. However, the brioche and the Grand Marnier in this recipe elevate this pudding above the realm of the ordinary and conspire to create an extraordinary taste sensation. Because of the addition of liqueur, this is not a dessert most children will like. Adults, on the other hand, may well become addicted, like me!

lace the raisins in a small bowl and cover with the Grand Marnier. Allow to soak for 15 minutes or longer to plump.

Arrange the brioche slices on a baking sheet and brush both sides with melted butter. Bake at 350° until the bread turns lightly golden, then remove and cool.

In a heavy-bottomed pot, bring the half and half and vanilla beans to a simmer. Carefully remove the beans and with a knife, scrape out the tiny black seeds. Add these to the cream and discard the pods.

Whisk the eggs, yolks and sugar in a bowl. Pour the hot cream slowly into the bowl, whisking to mix.

Butter an 8- or 9-inch glass baking pan. Remove the raisins from the liquor with a slotted spoon and scatter the fruit on the bottom of the pan. Add the Grand Marnier to the custard.

Arrange the brioche slices, cutting to fit as required. Some overlapping of the pieces is acceptable. Carefully pour in the custard.

Bake the pudding in a bain-marie or water bath for approximately 20 minutes or until the custard has set. Cool completely on a wire rack. Then cover with plastic wrap and refrigerate overnight, allowing the flavors to marry. If you can't wait, eat it warm!

To serve, cut into squares and reheat in a microwave oven (1 minute per slice) before garnishing with whipped cream and nutmeg.

☆

Cape Brandy Pudding

This classic South African dessert capitalizes on a moist texture and a rich, intoxicating flavor. It is a cake rather than a pudding by American definition. Overseas, pudding is often used as a generic term for dessert. Be sure to choose a good quality brandy, because it does make a difference in the taste of the cake.

Butter a 7 × 11-inch baking pan and set aside. Place the dates and pecans in a mixing bowl and add the boiling water. Stir in the baking soda and salt and let sit until cool.

Cream the butter with the brown sugar and then beat in the eggs, vanilla and allspice. Use an electric mixer if you have one to get the batter light and fluffy. Sift the flour with the baking powder and then sift again, this time over the butter-sugar mixture. Mix well and then fold in the date-nut mixture.

Pour the batter into the prepared pan and bake at 350° for 30 to 40 minutes, or until the cake is firm to the touch and begins to pull away from the sides of the pan.

While the cake is baking, prepare the sauce by boiling the sugar, water and butter until the mixture turns syrupy. Remove from the heat and cool for 10 minutes before adding the brandy and the vanilla. Pour the sauce over the hot cake and allow it to soak in thoroughly. Serve warm with a dollop of whipped cream.

Serves 8
Preparation Time:
   30 Minutes
Baking Time:
   45 Minutes
Preheat oven to 350°

   1 cup chopped, pitted
      dates
   ¾ cup chopped pecans
      (optional)
   1 cup boiling water
   1 tsp. baking soda
   ¼ tsp. salt
   ¼ cup butter, softened
   ½ cup dark brown sugar,
      packed
   2 large eggs
   1 tsp. pure vanilla
   1 tsp. allspice
1⅛ cups flour
   4 tsps. baking powder
   1 cup sugar
   ¾ cup water
   1 Tbsp. butter
   ¼ cup brandy, or more to
      taste
   1 tsp. pure vanilla
   1 cup whipped cream,
      garnish

☆

Caramel Fudge Brownies

Yield: 12-16
Preparation Time:
  30 Minutes
Baking Time:
  20-25 Minutes
Preheat oven to 350°

14 oz. package of
  caramels
1/3 cup evaporated milk
1 box devil's-food cake
  mix
3/4 cup butter, melted
1/3 cup evaporated milk
1 1/2 cups chocolate chips

Every pastry chef I've worked with over the years has contributed one or two special recipes to my repertoire. This one comes from Leslie Head and with it she has fostered a legion of caramel brownie addicts across America. The brownies are simple to make, once you've unwrapped the candies, that is. Wonderfully sticky and sweet, they won't last long if left unguarded! If you want to really indulge, serve the brownies with vanilla ice cream and hot fudge sauce.

In a heavy saucepan, combine the caramels and the 1/3 cup evaporated milk. Cook over low heat, stirring until the candies are melted.

Grease a 9 × 13-inch pan. In a large bowl, combine the cake mix, butter and the remaining 1/3 cup evaporated milk. Stir until the dough begins to mass together. Press two-thirds of the mixture into the bottom of the prepared pan. Bake for 6 minutes at 350°.

Remove the pan from the oven and spread the chocolate chips and then the caramel on top of the partially baked brownie layer. Next, piece on the remainder of the chocolate dough mixture over the caramel. Return the pan to the oven and bake for an additional 15 to 18 minutes.

Cool and cut into squares.

Caramel Ice Cream

I n a heavy-bottomed saucepan, combine the sugar and water for the caramel and stir over medium heat until sugar is dissolved. Raise the heat to high, cover the pot and bring the syrup to a boil. When boiling, remove the cover and continue cooking the syrup until it becomes a medium caramel color. Do not stir the mixture at any time. When the correct color is achieved, remove the saucepan from the heat immediately.

In a separate saucepan, bring the heavy cream to a boil. Pour it into the hot caramel, stirring constantly until the caramel has dissolved.

The Ice Cream Custard:
Place the egg yolks and sugar in a bowl and beat with an electric mixer until the mixture forms a ribbon, approximately 5 minutes. Slowly add the caramel to it, beating at low speed. Return this mixture to a saucepan, and over low heat, cook the custard until it thickens. This process takes about 10 minutes and should be watched constantly as the mixture must not boil. The custard should coat the back of a wooden spoon so that if you draw your finger across the surface, the line will hold its shape. When the custard is cooked, remove from the heat and transfer the mixture to a clean bowl. Add the milk and vanilla and then refrigerate the custard until it is completely chilled.

Transfer the mixture to an ice cream maker and freeze according to the manufacturer's directions.

Yield: 1 Quart
Preparation Time:
  10 Minutes
(note refrigeration time)
Cooking Time:
  15 Minutes

  1 cup sugar
  ¼ cup water
  2 cups heavy cream
  6 egg yolks
  ½ cup sugar
1¼ cups milk
  1 Tbsp. vanilla

☆

Carrot Cake

Serves 10
Preparation Time:
  45 Minutes
Baking Time:
  45 Minutes
Preheat to 325°

  4 eggs
1½ cups vegetable oil
  2 cups flour
  2 cups sugar
  1 tsp. salt
  1 Tbsp. cinnamon
  2 tsps. baking powder
  2 tsps. baking soda
  3 cups raw carrot, grated
  1 cup pecans or walnuts,
    chopped

Cream Cheese Frosting:
  1 cup unsalted butter,
    softened
  1 cup cream cheese,
    room temperature
  1 lb. confectioners' sugar,
    sifted
  1 Tbsp. pure vanilla
    extract
  ¾ cup pecans or walnuts
    (optional)

The perennially popular carrot cake never seems to go out of vogue. I've been making this recipe for two decades and it's still one of the best versions around. It will stay moist and fresh for about a week if tightly wrapped in plastic and foil; it also freezes well.

Whisk the eggs with the vegetable oil until combined. Set aside.

Sift the flour, sugar, salt, cinnamon, baking powder and soda into a large bowl. Add the egg-oil mixture to the dry ingredients and stir to combine. Add the carrots and nuts to the batter.

Pour the batter into two heavily greased and floured 8-inch cake pans.

Bake for 45 minutes at 325° or until the center is set and the cake begins to pull away from the edges of the pan. Cool completely on a wire rack before unmolding.

Cream Cheese Frosting:
Mix the butter and cream cheese in a bowl until smooth. Gradually add the confectioners' sugar, beating to combine. Stir in the vanilla extract.

Place one cooled cake layer on a plate and spread with frosting. Top with the second layer and frost the sides and top of the cake. Sprinkle the cake with nuts if desired.

★

Coeur à la Crème

For a beautiful, chic and unusual dessert, try your hand at my version of coeur à la crème. The porcelain, heart-shaped molds are a prerequisite for this recipe: if you don't mind the initial investment, you will have them for a lifetime. Pair any fruit sauce with the coeurs. At my restaurant we always used two sauces on the same plate for a more dramatic presentation.

L ine 8 4-ounce coeur à la crème molds with a double layer of dampened cheesecloth, allowing the edges of the cheesecloth to extend beyond the sides of the molds. You want enough excess cloth to totally enclose the filling.

Beat the cream cheese with ½ cup of heavy cream and the powdered sugar until it is fluffy. Add the melted white chocolate and beat until smooth.

Whip the remaining 1 cup of heavy cream until stiff and then fold into the cream cheese mixture. Spoon ½ cup of the filling into each mold, smooth the surface and then fold the cheesecloth over the top to cover the filling. Refrigerate the molds on a baking tray overnight.

Reserve 8 perfect strawberries for garnish and purée the remainder.

Strain the purée through a sieve and add the eau-de-vie and lemon juice. Taste and add sugar to desired sweetness.

Starting just below the stem end of the reserved strawberries, make 4 or 5 thin cuts down the length of each strawberry, taking care not to detach any of the slices you are creating. Gently push against the strawberries to fan the cut sections.

To serve, spread a pool of berry sauce on 8 dessert plates. Carefully unmold the coeurs, removing the cheesecloth. Center the desserts on each plate. Garnish with a fanned strawberry and a mint leaf.

Serves 8
Preparation Time:
  40 Minutes
(note refrigeration time)
Special Needs:
  Cheesecloth and heart-shaped molds

  8 oz. cream cheese,
    softened
1½ cups heavy cream
  ¾ cup powdered sugar
  3 oz. white chocolate,
    melted
  1 pint fresh strawberries
  2 Tbsps. fraise eau-de-vie or strawberry
    liqueur
  1 tsp. lemon juice
    Sugar to taste
  8 mint leaves

Cranberry-Apple Pie

Serves 8
Preparation Time:
  40 Minutes
Baking Time:
  50 Minutes
Preheat oven to 375°

  1 **9-inch pie shell,**
    unbaked
  1 **egg white**
  ¼ **cup ginger cookie**
    crumbs
  8 **oz. fresh or frozen**
    cranberries, coarsely
    chopped
  4 **tart apples, peeled and**
    thinly sliced
  ½ **cup golden raisins**
  1 **cup sugar**
  2 **Tbsps. flour**
  1 **Tbsp. cornstarch**
  ¼ **tsp. nutmeg**
    Grated peel of 1 lemon

Streusel:
  ½ **cup walnuts, chopped**
  ¾ **cup oatmeal (not**
    instant)
  ⅓ **cup flour**
  ⅓ **cup brown sugar,**
    packed
  6 **Tbsps. unsalted butter,**
    cut into 6 pieces
  ½ **tsp. cinnamon**
  ¼ **tsp. nutmeg**

A delicious pie that is perfect for the holiday season. Cranberries are very tart, which is part of the appeal, and this pie is not overly sweet as a result. Pears would work nicely in this recipe, either in addition to, or in place of, the apples.

Brush the bottom and sides of your pie shell with the egg white to seal the crust. Place the pie plate in the refrigerator, uncovered, for about 30 minutes to dry the egg white. When dry, sprinkle the cookie crumbs over the crust.

Toss the cranberries, apples and raisins in a large bowl. Add the sugar, flour, cornstarch and nutmeg and mix thoroughly. Add the grated lemon peel.

Place the walnuts, oatmeal, flour, brown sugar and butter in a small bowl. Using 2 knives, cut in the butter until it resembles coarse meal. This may be done in a food processor. Mix in the cinnamon and nutmeg.

Fill the pie shell with the fruit mixture and pour the streusel on top. Do not pack down the topping. Bake on a cookie sheet at 375° for 50 minutes. Cool completely on a wire rack before serving. Vanilla ice cream complements this pie wonderfully.

Creamy Ginger Cheesecake

A light and luscious cheesecake with a subtle but distinct ginger flavor. This is not as sweet as many cheesecakes, but as its name implies, it is very creamy. If you are an avid ginger fan, you might garnish the top of the cake with finely chopped crystallized ginger just before serving.

Finely crush the ginger snaps and mix with the sugar, butter and ground ginger. Grease a 9-inch spring-form pan and press the cookie mixture onto the bottom and halfway up the sides of the pan.

In a large mixing bowl, beat the cream cheese until smooth. Very gradually add the sour cream and heavy cream, beating until smooth. Add the sugar, eggs, ground and crystallized ginger and blend well. Pour into the prepared pan and bake at 350° for 30 to 40 minutes or until the center is set. Do not over bake.

Cool on a wire rack and then refrigerate the cake at least 4 hours before serving.

Serves 8
Preparation Time:
  20 Minutes
(note refrigeration time)
Baking Time:
  40 Minutes
Preheat oven to 325°

1¼ **cups ginger snaps**
  ⅓ **cup granulated sugar**
  6 **Tbsps. butter, melted**
  2 **tsps. ground ginger**
  1 **cup cream cheese, very**
    soft
  1 **cup sour cream, room**
    temperature
  1 **cup heavy cream,**
    room temperature
  ¾ **cup granulated sugar**
  4 **eggs, room**
    temperature
  1 **Tbsp. ground ginger**
  8 **large pieces of**
    crystallized ginger,
    very finely chopped or
    grated
  2 **tsps. ground ginger**

☆

Crème Brûlée

Serves 8
Preparation Time:
  30 Minutes
(note refrigeration time)
Cooking Time:
  30 Minutes
Preheat oven to 325°

1½ **cups milk**
2½ **cups heavy cream**
 2 **vanilla beans**
⅔ **cup sugar**
⅛ **tsp. salt**
 6 **egg yolks**
¼ **cup sugar (for topping)**

There is something of a cult among crème brûlée fans these days. My version is very light and creamy and is intensely vanilla-scented. It's one of the easiest desserts to assemble and the custards, without topping, can be made several days ahead of serving. My favorite technique and by far the quickest method is a household propane torch available in any hardware shop for about $12. Keep the flame moving in a circular motion over the top of the custards so the sugar melts evenly and does not burn.

Place the milk and cream in a medium-sized saucepan. Slit the vanilla beans in half lengthwise and scrape the seeds into the cream mixture. Add the vanilla bean pods and over low heat bring the mixture to the start of a simmer. Turn off the heat, cover the saucepan and let the cream steep for 15 minutes.

Remove the cover from the pan and begin reheating the cream over medium heat. Add the ⅔ cup sugar and the salt and stir until dissolved.

Whisk the egg yolks in a large bowl and very slowly pour the hot cream into the yolks, whisking constantly but not vigorously. Strain the custard.

Portion the custard between eight ramekins and place the dishes in a water bath.

Tightly cover the pan with aluminum foil and bake at 350° for 25 minutes. The custard should be just set and should wiggle when shaken.

Cool on a wire rack for 15 minutes, then refrigerate the ramekins, uncovered, for 1 hour. When cool, cover with plastic wrap and refrigerate for 2 hours or overnight.

Shortly before serving spread about 2 tsps. of sugar evenly across the surface of each custard. Place the ramekins in a metal baking pan and caramelize the sugar topping with a propane torch. The sugar should melt and turn a dark amber color very quickly. Be careful not to overcook and burn the sugar.

Serve the crème brûlée within 10 minutes so the topping remains crunchy.

Decadent Truffle Cake

Redolent with raspberry eau-de-vie and decorated with a glistening crown of berries, this dessert makes a statement! The recipe is quite involved but it can be completed in stages over a span of several days. Be certain to read the recipe in its entirety before beginning, as each step requires its own time frame before the final assembly. Feel free to improvise with other flavors such as orange, rum, apricot or hazelnut. The cake and filling are a luscious foil for whatever flavors and fruits you wish to pair.

Melt the chocolate with the 5 Tbsps. butter in the top of a double boiler. Let cool slightly and then add the framboise.

Beat the egg yolks with the sugar until the mixture is thick and fluffy, about 3 minutes on high speed.

Beat the egg whites in a clean bowl until foamy. Add the salt and continue beating until stiff and shiny.

Fold the chocolate into the yolks. Lighten the batter with some of the egg whites and then fold in the remainder.

Grease two 9-inch springform pans. Cut 2 rounds of parchment, place in the pans and butter again. Divide the batter between the 2 pans and bake at 350° for 15 to 20 minutes. Cool completely on wire racks.

Slowly heat the crème fraîche, heavy cream and ¾ cup butter until the mixture begins to simmer. Remove from the heat and let cool for 5 minutes.

Whisk the egg yolks in a small bowl. Add ¾ cup of the crème fraîche mixture, blend well and stir into the crème fraîche in the pan.

Chop the chocolate in a food processor and with the machine running, pour in the crème fraîche mixture. Process until smooth. Transfer the chocolate truffle filling to a mixing bowl, blend in the framboise and chill for 90 minutes or until the mixture thickens.

Melt the jam with the water over low heat. Strain through a fine sieve, discarding the seeds. Stir in the framboise.

Release the cakes from the sides of the springform pans. Invert onto cardboard rounds, peel off the paper and the metal pan bottoms.

Return one cake layer to the bottom of a springform pan and reassemble the sides. Brush the cake with half of the rasp-

Serves 12
Preparation Time:
 1½ Hours
(note refrigeration time)
Cooking Time:
 20 Minutes
Preheat oven to 350°

 8 oz. bittersweet
  chocolate, chopped
 5 Tbsps. unsalted butter
 1 Tbsp. framboise or
  raspberry brandy
 5 eggs, separated
 ½ cup sugar
 ⅛ tsp. salt
 ¾ cup crème fraîche (see
  recipe page 220)
 ¾ cup heavy cream
 ¾ cup unsalted butter
 2 egg yolks
 14 oz. bittersweet
  chocolate, chopped
 ¼ cup framboise or
  raspberry brandy
 ¼ cup raspberry jam
 1 tsp. water
 1 Tbsp. framboise or
  raspberry brandy
 1 cup sugar
 ½ cup water
 1 pt. fresh raspberries
 8 oz. bittersweet
  chocolate, chopped
 3 Tbsps. water

★

Raspberry Purée:

12 oz. fresh or frozen
  raspberries,
  unsweetened
1 Tbsp. water
¼ cup sugar
1 Tbsp. framboise or
  raspberry brandy

berry glaze. Invert the remaining cake layer onto yet another cardboard round so that it is right-side up. Brush with the raspberry glaze and freeze until it is solid.

Whip the truffle filling with a whisk to homogenize it a bit. Scoop the filling onto the cake in the springform pan and spread it evenly.

Place the frozen cake layer atop the filling, glazed-side down. Remove the cardboard round. Gently press the cake against the filling to remove air pockets. Cover with plastic wrap and refrigerate the cake until it is very firm.

Combine the sugar and water in a small pan and slowly bring the syrup to a boil, stirring to dissolve the sugar.

Spread a piece of waxed paper on a tray. Using a toothpick, dip each raspberry into the sugar syrup and place on the paper to dry.

Make the chocolate glaze by melting the chocolate with the water in the top of a double boiler.

Remove the springform pan from the cake. Smooth the sides with a warm cake spatula. Place the cake on a wire rack set into a jelly roll pan. Pour the warm chocolate glaze over the cake and spread evenly.

Arrange the raspberries atop the cake in concentric circles while the glaze is still warm. Serve the cake at room temperature on a pool of Raspberry Purée.

Raspberry Purée:

Purée the raspberries with the water in a food processor or blender.

Transfer the purée to a saucepan and add the sugar, cooking until it dissolves.

Strain the purée through a sieve and discard the seeds. Stir in the framboise and adjust sweetness as desired.

Floating Island

The French call it Ile Flottante and it's one of those desserts that looks spectacular, never fails to impress, and yet is oh, so, simple to bake. It's ethereally light like a soufflé, but unlike its cousin, this soft meringue doesn't deflate and can be baked hours or even days ahead of serving. The accompanying caramel drizzle and Crème Anglaise (custard) sauce may also be prepared in advance, so that last-minute assembly is all that's required.

Generously butter a 4 qt. baking dish with straight sides that measures at least 3 inches in height. Dust with superfine sugar, shaking out any excess.

Using a heavy-duty or portable electric mixer, begin beating the whites in a large bowl on low speed. Remember, the volume of the whites is going to grow enormously, so use a large capacity bowl. When the whites start to foam, beat in the salt and cream of tartar. Increase the speed to high and beat until the eggs form soft peaks. Then start adding the sugar ¼ cup at a time, beating continuously. When the whites are stiff and shiny, add the vanilla.

Transfer the meringue to the prepared dish and bake at 250° in the lower half of the oven for about 40 minutes. The meringue will rise and color slightly. If a metal skewer or toothpick inserted into the center of the dish comes out clean, the meringue is cooked. Cool completely on a wire rack and then cover with plastic wrap and refrigerate for up to 3 days. It is normal for the meringue to sink as it cools.

To serve, cut the meringue into wedges. Spoon a pool of Crème Anglaise on a dessert plate or in a shallow bowl. Float a piece of meringue atop the sauce and drizzle liberally with Caramel Syrup. Garnish with toasted sliced almonds.

Serves 8
Preparation Time:
  15 Minutes
(note cooling time)
Baking Time:
  40 Minutes
Preheat oven to 250°

- 12 egg whites at room temperature
- ¼ tsp. salt
- ½ tsp. cream of tartar
- 1½ cups superfine sugar
- 2 tsps. pure vanilla extract

- 4 cups Crème Anglaise (see recipe, page 218) Caramel Syrup (see recipe, page 215)
- 1 cup sliced almonds, toasted (garnish)

French Silk Pie

Serves 8
Preparation Time:
20 Minutes
(note refrigeration time)
Baking Time:
15 Minutes
Preheat oven to 350°

1½ cups walnuts
¼ cup brown sugar,
    packed
⅓ cup butter, softened
4½ squares unsweetened
    baking chocolate
6 Tbsps. butter
¾ cup granulated sugar
3 eggs
1 tsp. vanilla
⅛ cup Cointreau or
    orange liqueur
    Pinch of salt

A simple-to-prepare dessert that always elicits rave reviews from any chocolate lover. The pie consists of a very rich, dense chocolate filling flavored with Cointreau, nestled in a buttery walnut crust.

Grind the walnuts in a nut grinder or if using a food processor, grind nuts with the brown sugar to prevent the nuts from becoming oily. The nuts should be finely chopped rather than ground to a paste. Add the butter and sugar, if not added previously, and beat to blend. Press the nut mixture into the bottom and sides of a buttered 9-inch pie plate. Bake at 350° for 10 minutes or until lightly browned. Cool completely.

In a large double boiler, melt the chocolate, butter and brown sugar and stir until smooth.

Add the eggs, one at a time to the chocolate mixture, whisking vigorously. Then stir in the vanilla, Cointreau and the pinch of salt.

Pour the chocolate filling into the cooled walnut crust and refrigerate the pie at least 4 hours. To serve, garnish with whipped cream flavored with Cointreau and chocolate shavings.

Fresh Fig Tart

Fresh figs are sweet and luscious and when they are in season—oh so briefly—I love to use them in everything. They are lovely here combined with custard and the puff pastry adds an appropriately light but luxurious touch to this dessert. The tart is best consumed the day it is baked.

Lightly butter a 9-inch pie plate. On a lightly floured surface roll out the puff pastry into a 10-inch circle and carefully fit the dough into the pie pan. Trim the excess pastry along the outer edge of the pie plate rim and then refrigerate for 30 minutes.

Wash and dry the figs and cut them into thin slices no more than ⅛-inch thick.

Heat the heavy cream with the vanilla bean and seeds until it begins to simmer. Add the brown sugar and stir to dissolve. Turn off the heat and add the spices.

Whisk the 3 eggs and 1 yolk in a bowl and then slowly pour in the hot cream, whisking constantly. Remove the vanilla bean and reserve for another use.

Remove the pastry from the refrigerator and prick the bottom and sides of the pie shell with a fork. Arrange the figs in overlapping concentric circles.

Place the tart on a cookie sheet. Mix the remaining egg with 1 Tbsp. of water to make an egg wash. Brush the edge of the puff pastry crust with this mixture; sprinkle with the sugar.

Carefully pour the warm custard over the figs. Bake at 450° for 30 to 35 minutes or until the custard is set. Cool for 30 minutes before serving. This tart is best when served warm.

Serves 8
Preparation Time:
   30 Minutes
(note cooling time)
Baking Time:
   30 Minutes
Preheat oven to 425°

   1 sheet Pepperidge Farm
      puff pastry dough
   8 fresh figs
1½ cups heavy cream
   1 vanilla bean, split and
      scraped
  ½ cup brown sugar,
      packed
  ¼ tsp. nutmeg
  ¼ tsp. cinnamon
   3 eggs
   1 egg yolk
   1 egg
   1 Tbsp. sugar

Fresh Peach Pie

Serves 8
Preparation Time:
  15 Minutes
(note freezer time)
Baking Time:
  1 Hour
Preheat oven to 425°

  2 **crust pâte sucre (see recipe page 228)**
  1 **egg white**
  ¾ **cup light brown sugar, packed**
  3 **Tbsps. cornstarch**
  1 **Tbsp. flour**
  ½ **tsp. nutmeg**
  ⅛ **tsp. salt**
  10 **to 12 ripe peaches, sliced**
  1 **tsp. lemon juice**
  2 **tsps. almond extract**
  2 **Tbsps. peach brandy**
  ¼ **cup graham cracker crumbs**

This summer-time favorite needs no introduction. If you just happen to have a peach tree laden with fruit or a friend has an over-abundance, make up several pies and freeze them, uncooked, for some dreary November day. When you hanker for a taste of summer's pleasures, cook a frozen pie on a baking sheet in a 350° oven for about 70 minutes.

R oll out the bottom crust and line a 9-inch pie pan with the pastry. Brush the dough with the egg white to seal the crust and then chill for at least ½ hour.

Mix the brown sugar, cornstarch, flour, nutmeg and salt in a small bowl.

In another bowl add the peach slices, lemon juice, almond extract and peach brandy, tossing to combine. Peeling the peaches is optional. Add the sugar mixture to the fruit and stir to distribute. Roll out the top pastry crust to an 11-inch round. Next sprinkle the prepared bottom crust with the graham cracker crumbs and then arrange the peach filling in the pie pan. Place the top pastry round over the fruit and flute or crimp together the edges of the top and bottom crusts to make a decorative rim. Cut several steam vents in the top crust and then freeze the pie for 15 minutes before baking.

Place the pie on a tray and bake at 425° for 15 minutes. Reduce oven temperature to 350° and continue baking for 30 to 40 minutes or until the juices start to ooze and bubble. Cool the pie on a wire rack for 2 hours before serving.

☆

Frozen Passion Fruit Pie

If you've been searching for something new to try for dessert, look no further. The technique is straightforward and the pie can be made days ahead of serving. Passion fruit is an egg-sized, dull-brown fruit with a hard, wrinkled skin. If you don't see them in your grocery, ask the produce manager if he can order them for you. They are somewhat seasonal, but are generally available between March and October.

Serves 8
Preparation Time:
  40 Minutes
(note freezing time)
Baking Time:
  15 Minutes
Preheat oven to 350°

1¼ cups ginger snap or graham cracker crumbs
¼ cup butter, melted
¼ cup sugar
12 passion fruits
5 large eggs
¾ cup sugar
Pinch of salt
Whipped cream and mint leaves (garnish)

Mix the cookie crumbs, melted butter and ¼ cup of sugar in a small bowl to thoroughly blend. Butter a 9-inch pie plate and press the crumbs firmly into place. Bake at 350° for 10 minutes, remove to a wire rack and cool completely.

Cut the passion fruits in half widthwise and scoop the seeds, juice and pulp into a mesh strainer set over a bowl. Press firmly with a back of a spoon to extract every possible drop of liquid. Discard the seeds.

Separate the eggs, placing the yolks in one bowl and the whites in another. Set the bowl with the yolks over a pan of simmering water and whisk the eggs with ½ cup of sugar until the mixture thickens and lightens in color. Add the passion fruit juice and cook until the filling coats a spoon, about 15 minutes. Whisk constantly and do not allow the mixture to boil or it will be ruined. Cool to room temperature.

Beat the egg whites with a pinch of salt until they begin forming soft peaks. Then gradually add the remaining ¼ cup of sugar and beat until the whites are stiff and shiny. Whisk ⅓ of the whites into the cooled filling to lighten, and then carefully fold in the remainder.

Pour the filling into the prepared pie shell. Bake at 350° for 15 minutes. Cool on a wire rack and then place in the freezer. When the pie has hardened, cover with plastic wrap. Note that this pie never freezes rock-hard and is meant to be served room temperature.

To serve, cut with a hot knife. Garnish with whipped cream and mint leaves.

Fruit Cake

Yield: 1 five-pound cake
Preparation Time:
  30 Minutes
(note mellowing time)
Baking Time:
  2 Hours
Preheat oven to 300°

  4 cups sifted flour
  1 tsp. baking powder
  4 tsps. nutmeg
  1 cup butter, softened
  2 cups sugar
  6 eggs
  ½ cup bourbon
  4 cups pecans
  ½ lb. raisins
  1 lb. candied cherries
  ½ lb. candied pineapple
  1 cup bourbon (optional
    for mellowing)

Fruit cake—you either love it or loathe it. I fall firmly into the former category, but I'm fussy. There are many deadly dry versions that appear every Yuletide season. This is my mother-in-law's recipe and it's one of the best. Loaded with nuts and fruit (but no citron!), and bound with a smidgen of batter to hold it all together, it's more fruit than cake. Which is as it should be.

Heavily butter a 10-inch tube pan or two loaf pans and line bottoms with parchment paper. Set aside.

Sift the flour, baking powder and nutmeg. In a separate bowl cream the butter and sugar, beating with a mixer for 5 minutes or until light and fluffy. Add eggs, one at a time. Add the dry mix alternately with the bourbon. Stir in fruits and nuts.

Turn the batter into the prepared pan(s) and bake at 350° for 2 hours or until a skewer inserted into the cake comes out clean. Cover the top of the cake loosely with aluminum foil if it begins to brown substantially before the cake is set.

Remove cake from oven and let cool 15 minutes on a wire rack before turning out of the pan. When cool, liberally sprinkle the cake with additional bourbon and wrap in several thicknesses of cheesecloth. Let the cake mellow for at least a week, preferably longer, dousing with more bourbon every five days if desired.

Ginger Crinkle Cookies

These cookies are simply addictive. I used to make them daily in my restaurant, but finally gave up because staff ate most of the cookies before they could be sold!

Cream the butter and sugar in a medium-sized bowl. Stir in the eggs, molasses and vinegar and beat to combine. Add the flour, baking soda and spices and mix well. Form the cookie dough into 1-inch balls, rolling the dough between your palms to accomplish this.

Sprinkle some sugar on a plate and roll the cookie-dough balls in the sugar.

Grease a cookie sheet and position the cookies 2 inches apart. Bake at 325° for 10 to 12 minutes.

Yield: 3 dozen
Preparation Time:
   15 Minutes
Baking Time:
   12 Minutes
Preheat oven to 325°

- ¾ cup butter, softened
- 2 cups sugar
- 2 eggs
- ¾ cup molasses
- 2 tsps. white vinegar
- 4 cups flour, sifted
- 1½ tsps. baking soda
- 4 tsps. ground ginger
- 1 tsp. cinnamon
- ½ tsp. ground cloves
  Sugar for rolling cookies in

Ginger Ice Cream

Yield: 1 Quart
Preparation Time:
  15 Minutes
(plus chilling and
  freezing time)
Cooking Time:
  45 Minutes

  2 **cups heavy cream**
  2 **cups whole milk**
  ½ **cup grated, peeled**
    ginger root
  8 **egg yolks**
  ¾ **cup sugar**

My favorite!

Combine the cream, milk and ginger root in a saucepan and heat to a simmer. Turn off the heat, cover the pan with a tight-fitting lid and let the mixture steep for 30 minutes. Strain, pressing hard on the solids to extract all of the liquid.

In a clean bowl whisk the egg yolks, gradually adding the sugar. Add the cream mixture to the bowl and stir thoroughly. Return the custard to the saucepan and cook over low to moderate heat, stirring frequently, until the mixture thickens slightly. Take care that you don't overheat the custard and scramble the eggs.

Cool completely and chill for several hours. Follow manufacturer's directions for making ice cream.

Gingerbread

I consider myself something of a connoisseur when it comes to gingerbread. Never able to resist ordering a piece whenever I find it on a restaurant menu, I fortuitously discovered the popular Jeffrey's Grill & Catering in Carmel Valley, California. Chef-owner Jeffrey Thompson has created what I think is the best gingerbread in the world—bar none! He serves it warm with a lemon curd sauce and a scoop of vanilla ice cream. When I'm in a mood to indulge myself (a frequent occurrence), I order this treat for breakfast. It's everything that a gingerbread should be—moist, dense and robust with ginger and molasses. I'm delighted that he so generously agreed to share his secret. Thanks, Jeffrey!

Butter a 9 × 9-inch baking pan and set aside. In a saucepan combine the milk, sherry, spices, molasses and golden syrup. Mix well and warm thoroughly. Pour this mixture into a large bowl and add the eggs, whisking to blend.

In a separate bowl, combine the flour, cream of tartar and the currants. Set aside.

In the bowl of an electric mixer cream the butter, brown sugar and orange rind until fluffy. On low speed add the molasses-egg mixture alternately with the dry ingredients. Do not overbeat.

Mix the baking soda with 2 Tbsps. of hot water and stir until dissolved. Add this to the batter, mixing thoroughly. Transfer batter to the prepared pan and bake in the middle of a 350° oven for 30 minutes. Then reduce the temperature to 300° and bake another 20 to 30 minutes or until the gingerbread is set. Cool on a wire rack.

Serves 8
Preparation Time:
 20 Minutes
Baking Time:
 1 Hour
Preheat oven to 350°

- 5 oz. milk
- 3 Tbsps. sherry
- 2 Tbsps. ground ginger
- 1 Tbsp. cinnamon
- 1 Tbsp. nutmeg
- ½ cup molasses
- 1 cup Lyle's golden syrup (or light Karo syrup)
- 3 eggs
- 2 cups flour
- 1 tsp. cream of tartar
- 5 oz. currants
- 4 oz. butter, softened
- ½ cup dark brown sugar, packed
  Grated rind of 1 orange
- 1 tsp. baking soda
  Hot water

★

Grand Marnier Cake

Serves 8
Preparation Time:
30 Minutes
Baking Time:
40 Minutes
Preheat oven to 350°

Cake:
   10 oz. good quality
      bittersweet chocolate
   ¾ cup butter
   ½ cup Grand Marnier or
      Triple Sec
   ½ cup unsweetened
      cocoa powder
   5 eggs
   1 cup sugar

This dessert is so dense and moist that it is more like fudge than cake. If orange-flavored Grand Marnier is not to your liking, rum, Amaretto, framboise or another sweet liqueur could be substituted. Serve on a pool of Orange Crème Anglaise (see recipe page 227) for a truly chocoholic dessert.

Butter the sides and bottom of a 9×3-inch springform pan; line the bottom with a circle of waxed or parchment paper and butter this also. Dust the insides of the pan with cocoa powder, tapping out the excess.

Chop the chocolate and combine with the butter in a double boiler. Stir and cook until melted. Add the Grand Marnier and cocoa powder, whisking to blend.

Beat the eggs and sugar with an electric mixer for 5 minutes, or until the mixture lightens in color and triples in volume. Carefully fold in the chocolate batter and transfer to the prepared pan.

Bake at 350° for 35 to 40 minutes or until the cake is just set. Cool on a wire rack for 5 minutes. The cake will have risen and then fallen; press down on the edges to even it. Remove the sides of the springform pan and invert the cake onto the rack. Peel off the paper and cool completely.

Italian Chocolate Torte

If you like a delicate but very moist chocolate cake that is quick and simple to prepare, this recipe is for you. The mascarpone cheese is essential to the texture of the torte, but crème fraîche could be substituted if it is drained overnight in a paper coffee filter set over a bowl. The almond flavor is quite predominant, so the torte does not need a sauce to give it impact. If you wish to make a statement, however, serve it on a pool of Crème Anglaise (recipe, page 218) flavored with Amaretto.

Butter an 8-inch springform pan and line the bottom with a circle of parchment paper or waxed paper.

Cut the butter into chunks and combine with the chocolate in a large metal bowl. Set the bowl over a pan of barely simmering water and melt the contents slowly, stirring occasionally.

Meanwhile, whisk the egg yolks with the mascarpone, Amaretto and almond extract in a small bowl. Place the Amaretti cookies and the flour in a large plastic bag and crush to a fine powder with a rolling pin.

When the chocolate is melted, remove the bowl from the stove and add the mascarpone mixture and ½ cup of cookie powder.

Place the egg whites in a grease-free bowl and beat until they begin to foam. Add the cream of tartar and while beating, sprinkle the sugar onto the whites. Beat until the egg whites turn glossy and will hold a peak. Lighten the chocolate batter with ⅓ of the egg whites and then carefully fold in the remaining whites.

Pour the batter into the prepared pan and bake at 350° for 35 to 40 minutes or until the cake is set and pulls away slightly from the sides of the pan.

Transfer the torte to a wire rack, release the clip that tightens the sides of the springform pan and cool completely.

Serve plain or with a dollop of Amaretto-flavored mascarpone or whipped cream, sprinkled with crushed Amaretti cookies. The cake will freeze well if tightly wrapped in plastic and then foil. Defrost overnight in the refrigerator.

Serves 8
Preparation Time:
  30 Minutes
Cooking Time:
  40 Minutes
Preheat oven to 350°

- ½ cup unsalted butter
- 8 oz. bittersweet chocolate chopped
- 4 eggs, separated
- ½ cup plus 1 Tbsp. mascarpone cheese
- 1 Tbsp. Amaretto
- 1 tsp. almond extract
- 50 Amaretti cookies
- 2 Tbsps. flour
  Pinch of cream of tartar
- ¼ cup plus 2 Tbsps. sugar

Luscious Lemon Mousse

Serves 6
Preparation Time:
  30 Minutes
(note refrigeration time)
Cooking Time:
  15 Minutes

- ½ **cup unsalted butter**
- 5 **eggs**
- 1 **cup sugar**
- 1 **cup lemon juice,**
  freshly squeezed
- 2 **cups heavy cream,**
  chilled
- ¼ **cup dark rum**
  Grated rind of 1 lemon

A wonderful dessert that adds a light and refreshing note to the end of a meal. The lemon flavor is tart, but the texture is smooth as silk. I like to serve this with a purée of fresh raspberries or strawberries, as much for the presentation as the contrasting flavor. The mousse will hold for 3 days in the refrigerator if covered tightly.

Melt the butter in a small pan and keep warm. Beat the eggs and sugar with an electric mixer for 5 minutes at high speed until they are pale and fluffy. With the mixer running at slow speed, beat in the butter in a steady stream. Add the lemon juice.

Transfer this mixture to the top of a double boiler and cook until the custard thickens. Remember to stir frequently. Pour the custard into a clean bowl and refrigerate until cold.

When the custard has chilled, beat the heavy cream with the rum until it forms soft peaks. Fold the whipped cream and the lemon zest into the custard base.

Fill a pastry bag with the mousse and pipe the mixture into wine glasses. Refrigerate until serving time.

Malva Pudding

n a large bowl, blend the brown sugar, egg the jam. Sift the dry ingredients together on a piece of waxed paper and set aside.

Add the milk in three additions to the sugar-egg mixture, alternating with the dry ingredients. Next add the butter and vinegar and blend thoroughly. The batter will be thin.

Pour the batter into a 9-inch square baking dish and cover tightly with aluminum foil. Bake at 350° for 45 to 55 minutes or until the cake is a set and is a uniform, rich brown color.

While the cake is baking, combine the cream, butter and sugar in a saucepan. Bring to a boil and then reduce the heat to low and simmer for 15 minutes or until the sauce turns slightly syrupy.

Upon removing the cake from the oven, uncover and pour the sauce over the cake, using it all. Serve warm with whipped cream or vanilla ice cream.

Serves 8
Preparation Time:
  15 Minutes
Baking Time:
  55 Minutes
Preheat oven to 350°

1 cup dark brown sugar
1 large egg
1 Tbsp. apricot jam
1 cup flour
1 tsp. baking soda
  Pinch of salt
1 cup milk
1 Tbsp. butter, melted
1 tsp. white vinegar

1 cup heavy cream
6 oz. butter
1 cup sugar

Mango Shortcake

Serves 8
Preparation Time:
  30 Minutes
Baking Time:
  45 Minutes
Preheat oven to 375°

4½ **cups sliced fresh**
   mango
 ¾ **cup sugar**
 1 **Tbsp. cornstarch**
 ½ **tsp. pure almond**
   extract
   Grated rind of 1 lime
 1 **Tbsp. fresh lime juice**
 1 **cup flour**
 ½ **cup sugar**
 1 **tsp. baking powder**
 ¼ **tsp. salt**
 1 **egg**
 ¾ **cup sour cream**
 ¼ **cup melted butter**

I came across this dessert idea several years ago when I was writing and testing recipes for an African cookbook project entitled, "The Elephant's Kitchen." At that time, I waded through hundreds of recipes, many of them mere lists of unquantified ingredients scribbled on paper napkins and scraps of paper. This was one of the best I adapted. Unlike our American shortcakes, where the fruit is merely piled atop a biscuit or sponge cake, in this recipe the fruit is actually baked into the batter. The result is not heavy, thanks to the addition of sour cream, a tenderizing agent. If you like mangoes, be sure to give this recipe a try. It is also good with juicy ripe peaches and nectarines.

Grease a 9 × 9-inch baking pan and neatly arrange the mango slices on the bottom.

Combine the ¾ cup sugar, cornstarch, almond extract, lime rind and juice and sprinkle this mixture atop the fruit.

Sift the flour, ½ cup sugar, baking powder and salt into a bowl.

In a separate bowl, whisk together the egg, sour cream and melted butter. Pour the liquid ingredients into the dry mix and stir until just combined. If you overbeat, your shortcake will not be tender and light.

Drop the batter by spoonfuls onto the fruit.

Bake at 350° for 35 to 45 minutes or until the cake is golden brown and the mango juices bubble. Cool on a wire rack and serve warm with whipped cream.

Peach Coffee Cake

When I went to work in Africa I had to devise all sorts of down-to-earth recipes to please a largely British clientele. Every day there must be a cake for tea (cookies just won't do), so I make this one occasionally, sometimes using apricots in place of peaches. It also is featured on my brunch menus, because Americans like something sweet for breakfast and can relate to coffee cake or muffins. With tea and brunch in mind, I named this creation peach coffee cake so it would sound appropriate to those meals. The recipe has proven quite popular with all nationalities. On numerous occasions, however, bemused Brits have commented that they cannot taste the coffee flavor.

Serves 8
Preparation Time:
30 Minutes
Baking Time:
1 Hour
Preheat oven to 350°

½ cup butter, softened
1 cup sugar
3 eggs
2 cups flour
1 tsp. baking powder
1 tsp. baking soda
1 tsp. cinnamon
¼ tsp. nutmeg
¼ tsp. salt
1 cup sour cream
1 17-oz. can peach slices, drained
½ cup packed dark brown sugar
2 Tbsps. flour
2 Tbsps. butter

H eavily butter and flour a 9-or 10-inch baking pan. Set aside.

Cream the butter and sugar with an electric mixer until light and fluffy. Beat in the eggs, one at a time.

Sift together the flour, baking powder and soda, cinnamon, nutmeg and salt. Add to the batter alternately with the sour cream; do not overmix. Transfer batter to the prepared pan.

Arrange the peach slices decoratively on top of the batter.

Mix the brown sugar with the 2 Tbsps. of flour, then cut in the remaining butter to make a streusel. Sprinkle over the peaches.

Bake at 350° for about 1 hour or until the cake is set and golden. Remove from the oven and cool completely on a wire rack before unmolding.

☆

Persimmon Pudding Cake

Serves 8
Preparation Time:
  30 Minutes
Baking Time:
  40 Minutes
Preheat oven 325°

  4 **very soft persimmons
     to yield 2 cups of
     purée**
  3 **eggs, beaten**
  ½ **cup melted butter**
  1¼ **cups sugar**
  1½ **cups flour**
  1 **tsp. baking soda**
  1 **tsp. baking powder**
  ½ **tsp. salt**
  2 **tsps. ground ginger**
  ½ **tsp. nutmeg**
  2¼ **cups whole milk**
  1 **tsp. lemon zest**
  1 **tsp. lemon juice**
  ½ **cup raisins**
  ½ **cup chopped pecans**

My good friend Sheila Smith made this wonderful dessert for me one cold winter night. She had a bounty of persimmons and I had a hankering for some comfort food. Sheila didn't really have a recipe, just some vague notion of how her mother used to make this kind of thing in Scotland when she was a wee lass. Anyway, the result was beyond her expectations and we ate every last bit of the pudding in one sitting. Serve it hot out of the oven and top with vanilla ice cream. Yummy!

Butter a 9 × 13-inch baking pan and set aside. Sieve the persimmon purée into a large bowl. Add the eggs and melted butter and whisk to blend.

In a separate bowl, sift the dry ingredients. Add to the persimmon mixture in three additions, alternating with the milk. Stir in the lemon zest, juice, raisins and nuts, mixing just to blend.

Pour the batter into the prepared pan and bake at 350° for 30 to 40 minutes or until set. Serve warm.

Pumpkin-Date Tea Bread

My mother-in-law, Alice, makes this scrumptious tea bread around the holidays when pumpkin is prominently displayed on grocery store shelves. If you like date nut bread, give this recipe a try. The pumpkin purée adds color, moistness and a hint of spice.

Whisk the eggs with the oil in a bowl. Add pumpkin purée, dates and nuts and stir to combine.

Sift the dry ingredients together in a large bowl. Add the fruit and egg mixture and stir briskly to blend. Do not overbeat.

Divide the batter between two greased, full-size loaf pans and bake at 350° for 1½ hours or until the batter has set and a skewer inserted into the center of the bread comes out clean.

Cool 15 minutes on a wire rack, then turn the breads out of the pans to finish cooling. The breads freeze beautifully if tightly wrapped in plastic wrap and aluminum foil.

Yield: 2 Loaves
Preparation Time:
 15 Minutes
Baking Time:
 1½ Hours
Preheat oven to 350°

    4 eggs
    1 cup vegetable oil
    2 cups pumpkin (cooked
      and mashed)
    1 cup chopped dates
    1 cup chopped walnuts
      or pecans
 3½ cups flour
    2 tsps. baking soda
    ½ tsp. baking powder
 2¾ cups sugar
    1 tsp. nutmeg
    ½ tsp. ground cloves
    1 tsp. cinnamon

Roasted Banana Cream

Serves 6
Preparation Time:
  10 Minutes
(note refrigeration time)
Cooking Time:
  15 Minutes
Preheat oven to 425°

  4 **ripe bananas**
  ⅓ **cup sugar (or more to taste)**
  ¼ **cup dark rum**
  ½ **tsp. pure vanilla extract**
1½ **cups heavy cream**
    Whipped cream, macadamia nuts & banana slices for garnish

I make this simple but satisfying dessert at the bush camp when we have a surplus of ripe bananas. The rum flavor is pronounced, so add sparingly if you are not partial to the taste.

Heat the oven to 425° and place the unpeeled bananas directly onto the middle rack. Bake for about 15 minutes or until the bananas are soft. Cool to lukewarm.

In a blender or food processor, combine the sugar, rum, vanilla and peeled bananas. Purée and then add the cream, blending until smooth. If the purée is very stiff you can add a bit more cream. Divide the mixture between 6 custard cups and refrigerate for at least an hour before serving.

To serve, garnish with whipped cream, chopped macadamia nuts and a decorative slice or two of banana.

Sour Cream Pound Cake

There's nothing as rich and satisfying as homemade pound cake. Once you've tasted this version you'll never want store-bought again. I use it for my Tropical Trifle, but it's almost too good for that purpose. Double the recipe and serve one cake unadorned for a proper appreciation of its virtues.

Butter a loaf pan and set aside.

Cream the butter until fluffy. Add the sugar, one-half cup at a time, beating continually. Beat in the eggs, one at a time, and then the vanilla.

Sift the dry ingredients and add to the batter in two stages, alternating with the sour cream.

Transfer the batter to the prepared pan and bake in a slow 300° oven for 60 to 90 minutes or until the cake is set. Cool on a wire rack.

Yield: 1 loaf
Preparation Time:
  20 Minutes
Baking Time:
  60 to 90 Minutes
Preheat oven to 300°

¾ cup butter, softened
1½ cups sugar
 3 eggs
 1 tsp. pure vanilla
1½ cups flour
 ⅛ tsp. salt
 ¼ tsp. baking soda
 ½ cup sour cream

Stem Ginger Pear Cakes

Serves 6
Preparation Time:
   30 Minutes
Baking Time:
   25 Minutes
Preheat oven to 350°

½ cup butter, softened
⅔ cup dark brown sugar,
   packed
½ cup granulated sugar
2 eggs
1 Tbsp. finely minced
   crystallized ginger
   Grated zest of one
   lemon
1 cup flour
1 tsp. baking soda
¼ cup buttermilk
2 ripe pears, peeled and
   sliced thickly
3 Tbsps. stem ginger,
   minced
   Ice cream or whipped
   cream

I'm crazy about ginger. When my friend Sheila gave me a gorgeous jar of stem ginger in syrup for Christmas, I devised this recipe to prevent myself from eating it all straight out of the jar. The cake is light and tender and very easy to make. If you don't have perfectly ripe pears, try using fresh peaches or nectarines—the results will be just as good.

Generously butter six 8-oz. ramekins or custard cups. Set aside.

In a medium-sized bowl using an electric mixer, beat the butter with half the brown sugar and all the granulated sugar for 2 or 3 minutes, scraping down the sides of the bowl occasionally with a rubber spatula. Beat in the eggs and then add the crystallized ginger and the lemon zest.

On low speed add the flour and baking soda, mixing until just barely combined. Fold in the buttermilk with a rubber spatula. Do not overmix.

Divide the cake batter between the prepared ramekins. Don't worry if it appears that you do not have very much batter in the cups—the cake gets quite puffy when baked. Decoratively arrange 3 or 4 pear slices on the top of each ramekin, pushing the fruit down slightly so the batter rises around it a bit. Sprinkle with the stem ginger, then top with the remaining brown sugar.

Place the ramekins on a baking tray and bake at 350° for 20 to 25 minutes or until a toothpick comes out clean when inserted into the cake. Cool on a wire rack for 15 minutes and then run a knife around the cakes to loosen from the ramekins.

Serve warm with whipped cream or ice cream.

Sticky Toffee Pudding

Twenty years ago I discovered this utterly delicious dessert in a small restaurant in the Devon countryside. A little culinary investigation led me to the wonderful Sharrow Bay Hotel in England's Lake District, where this delectable "pudding" was created originally. My personal variation follows and I think you'll love it.

Serves 8
Preparation Time:
  15 Minutes
Baking Time:
  45 Minutes
Preheat oven to 350°

  ¼ cup butter, softened
  1 cup granulated sugar
  2 eggs, room
    temperature
  ½ tsp. vanilla
  1 cup water
  1 tsp. baking soda
  8 oz. dates, pitted
1⅛ cups flour
  ½ tsp. baking powder
1½ cups heavy cream
  ¾ cup butter
  ½ cup dark brown sugar

Place the butter and sugar in the bowl of a food processor and process until well-combined. Add the eggs and vanilla and run the machine for one full minute. Transfer this mixture to a large bowl. Wash the food processor bowl and steel knife in preparation for the next step.

Bring the water and baking soda to a boil in a small pan. Place the dates in the food processor bowl and slowly add the boiling water while the machine is running. Process until the dates are coarsely chopped. Add the dates to the sugar-egg mixture, then fold in the flour and baking powder.

Grease an 8-inch square baking pan and pour in the cake batter. Bake at 350° for 35 to 45 minutes.

Combine the cream, butter and dark brown sugar in a medium-sized saucepan and bring to a simmer over medium-high heat. Cook 8-10 minutes or until the sauce thickens

Cut the pudding-cake into squares. Pour the hot caramel sauce over the cake and broil until bubbly. Serve with whipped cream or double cream, if available.

☆

Sun-Dried Cherry and Peach Crumble

Serves 8
Preparation Time:
  30 Minutes
Baking Time:
  30 Minutes
Preheat oven to 375°

  3 **lbs. peaches, cut into**
    ½-inch-thick slices
  ¾ **cup dried bing cherries**
    (4 oz.)
1½ **tsps. pure almond**
    extract
  4 **tsps. lemon juice**
  ⅓ **cup light brown sugar,**
    packed
  1 **Tbsp. cornstarch**
  ¼ **tsp. nutmeg**

Streusel:
  ¾ **cup flour**
  ⅓ **cup light brown sugar,**
    packed
  ⅓ **cup granulated sugar**
    Pinch of salt
  ½ **cup chopped almonds,**
    optional
  ¼ **lb. cold butter, cut into**
    8 pieces

An old-fashioned dessert as American as apple pie that is quick, easy and especially delicious. I don't bother to peel the peaches unless the skins are very thick and fuzzy, but if you wish to do so, blanch the fruit in boiling water for a minute and then plunge into ice water to facilitate peeling. If you have a bounty of nectarines, they work exceptionally well in this recipe, as do dried blueberries, so feel free to substitute or create new combinations.

Combine the fruits in a large bowl. Toss with the almond extract and lemon juice.

Mix together the brown sugar, cornstarch and nutmeg in a small bowl. Add to the fruit and stir gently to combine.

Divide the fruit mixture between 8 shallow ovenproof dishes or ramekins.

Make the streusel by combining the dry ingredients in a small bowl. Using two knives, cut the butter into the flour mixture until it is pea-sized. Top each dish with about ¼ cup of the streusel mixture.

Bake at 375° for 25 to 30 minutes or until the fruit is bubbly and the topping is golden.

Serve warm with vanilla or ginger ice cream (see recipe page 184).

Tiramisù

Tiramisù is an ambrosial dessert with Italian origins. The principal ingredient of all this goodness is, surprisingly, cheese. Not an ordinary cheese, but mascarpone, a buttery, triple crème dessert cheese with a silky, oily texture. Traditionally, lady fingers soaked in espresso form the base of this dessert. My variation calls for layers of sponge cake, and I have added Amaretto liqueur and cookies for a tastier and more decadent dessert.

Today mascarpone, both imported and domestic, is widely available in many regions. Nonetheless, I have included a simple recipe for making this cheese in the event you encounter difficulty finding it. The homemade version is not as sweet as the commercial product, but it's a reasonable substitute (see recipe page 225).

Serves 10
Preparation Time:
  45 Minutes
(note refrigeration time)
Baking Time:
  15 Minutes
Preheat oven to 350°

- 4 eggs, separated
- 2 cups confectioners' sugar, sifted
  Pinch of salt
- 1 cup flour
- 2/3 cup espresso
- 1 Tbsp. sugar
- 3 Tbsps. Amaretto
- 1 cup heavy cream
- 1½ cups mascarpone cheese (see recipe page 225)
- ¼ cup Amaretto
- ¾ cup confectionery sugar, sifted
- 10 Amaretti cookies, crushed
  Bittersweet chocolate curls

Lightly grease the bottom and sides of two 8-inch cake pans. Cut 2 circles of waxed paper or parchment paper to fit and arrange in the pans. Grease the paper and then lightly flour all interior surfaces.

Place the egg yolks in a bowl and gradually whisk in the confectioners' sugar. Set the bowl over a pan of water that is just barely simmering and whisk until the mixture is thick and almost white in color. Cool slightly.

Beat the egg whites with a pinch of salt in a separate bowl until they form stiff, shiny peaks. Mix about ⅓ of the whites into the yolk base to lighten the mixture, then fold in the remaining whites.

Sift the flour into the batter in 3 additions, folding carefully after each addition. Divide batter between the prepared pans and bake for at 350° 12 to 15 minutes or until the edges of the cake shrink from the sides of the pan.

Cool the cakes and then invert onto a wire rack; remove the paper. Using a long, serrated knife, split the cakes in half horizontally to create four layers.

Heat the espresso with the 1 Tbsp. of sugar and stir until dissolved. Remove from the heat and add the Amaretto liqueur. Brush the cut surfaces of the cake layers with the coffee mixture.

Whip the cream until it is very stiff. In a separate bowl, combine the mascarpone, Amaretto and confectioners' sugar. Lighten this mixture with about ⅓ of the whipped cream and then fold in the remaining cream. Sprinkle the cookie crumbs

★

over the filling and gently fold to mix.

Place one of the cake layers, cut side up, on a large platter. Spread one-quarter of the filling over the cake and then cover with a second layer, placing it cut side down. Spread with more of the filling and then repeat this process with the remaining two cake layers. Cover the top of the cake with the remainder of the filling.

Arrange a dense layer of chocolate curls or shavings over the top of the Tiramisù. Refrigerate for at least 4 hours before serving. The cake will keep for several days if covered with plastic wrap and refrigerated.

To serve, cut into wedges with a serrated knife.

Treacle Steamed Pudding

A traditional English dessert, this pudding (which is really a cake) is steamed rather than baked. The treacle, or molasses as we call it in the United States, does not flavor the pudding but forms a sticky coating on the surface of the cake. If you don't care for molasses, you can use honey or Lyle's Golden Syrup. I like the addition of raisins and cherries because otherwise the cake is very plain, but these items are optional. Sometimes I vary the pudding by adding a cup of apricot purée to the batter. A recipe for the puree can be found on page 212.

Serves 8
Preparation Time:
  30 Minutes
Cooking Time:
  1¾ Hour

- ½ cup butter, softened
- 1 cup light brown sugar, packed
- 2 eggs, room temperature
- 1 tsp. pure vanilla extract
- 1¾ cups flour
- 2½ tsps. baking powder
- ⅛ tsp. salt
- 1 cup milk
- ½ cup raisins
- ½ cup chopped glacé cherries
- ½ cup dark molasses

Heavily butter a 1½ qt. glass bowl or soufflé dish and set aside.

Beat the butter with the brown sugar until smooth, then add the eggs, one at a time, beating thoroughly after each addition. Mix in the vanilla.

Sift the flour with the baking powder/soda and salt. Add the flour in three additions to the batter, alternating with the milk. Stir in the raisins and cherries.

Find a pot large enough to comfortably accommodate your baking dish; it must have a lid. Fill with an inch or two of hot water.

Pour the molasses into the prepared baking dish and tilt to coat the bottom surface. Add the cake batter. Place a piece of parchment or waxed paper on top of the dish and tie with string. Next cover the paper with a layer of heavy-duty aluminum foil and tie this tightly with string. If you have thick rubber bands, these will usually work as well.

Place the cake in the water bath. The level of the water should be about two-thirds of the height of your dish. Cover the pot with a lid and bring the water to a steady simmer, not a vigorous boil. Steam the pudding for 1 hour and 45 minutes, checking occasionally to make sure that the water has not boiled away.

Remove the cake from the pot and let sit 10 minutes. Before serving, invert the pudding onto a serving dish. Cut into slices and serve with whipped cream, ice cream or Crème Anglaise (recipe, page 218).

Tropical Rice Pudding

Serves 4
Preparation Time:
  5 Minutes
Cooking Time:
  30 Minutes

14 oz. unsweetened
  coconut milk
⅓ cup milk
½ cup medium-grain rice
  (not converted)
3 Tbsps. sugar
¼ cup golden raisins
1 tsp. pure vanilla
  extract
4 oz. pineapple chunks,
  drained and diced
  very fine
1 Tbsp. rum (or more to
  taste)

If you're longing for a taste of the tropics on a cold winter night, this variation on an old favorite might be just the thing to remind you of sunny days, warm breezes and whispering palm trees.

Combine the milks, rice and sugar in a saucepan. Bring to a boil and then lower the heat and cover the pan. Simmer slowly for 10 minutes. Stir frequently because the rice has a tendency to stick.

Remove the pan from the stove and add the raisins. Cover pan and let the rice steam, off the burner, for another 10 minutes or until it is tender and creamy. Add the vanilla, pineapple and rum and stir to blend.

Divide the pudding between four 6-oz. cups or ramekins. Serve warm with whipped cream.

Tropical Trifle

Trifle is the quintessential English dessert, although my version frankly does not conform to British standards. There are really few desserts that are as easy as this one to prepare that consistently impress and delight guests when served. If you really want to go all out on presentation, use a proper trifle dish and arrange slices of fruit around the sides of the bowl as well as between the cake layers.

To simplify my recipe, use a packaged pound cake (angel food cake also works well), substitute Cool Whip for the whipped cream and use Bird's custard powder instead of making it from scratch. Strawberries and raspberries work beautifully in any trifle, tropical or otherwise, so mix and match fruits according to what is available. There is no hard and fast rule governing how much custard or cream to use between the layers. Just make sure you add enough to soak into the cake so that as it "matures" it will get moist and soft and even a tad bit mushy.

Bring the milk to a simmer in a saucepan. Whisk the egg yolks in a bowl, adding the sugar gradually. When the milk is hot, slowly add the liquid to the eggs, stirring constantly. Try not to create too much foam at this stage. Pour the contents of the bowl back into the saucepan and return it to the stove.

Cook the custard over low to medium heat, stirring slowly but continually with a wooden spoon. As the custard begins to heat, you must watch carefully so that the eggs don't scramble. When the surface bubbling starts to subside, the custard is almost cooked. Although it can be nerve-racking, the custard needs to thicken until it coats the back of the wooden spoon; when you draw your finger across the spoon, the mark should hold.

When properly thickened, remove the custard from the heat and add the vanilla and passion fruit juice (seeds are acceptable). Transfer to a bowl and chill in the refrigerator for at least an hour, preferably two.

Whip the heavy cream with the sugar until it forms soft peaks.

Cut the pound cake into ¾-inch slices and then cube these. You don't want the pieces to exceed bite-size. Place a layer of cake cubes in the bottom of a trifle bowl or any other

Serves 8
Preparation Time:
  1 Hour
(note refrigeration time)
Cooking Time:
  15 Minutes

  3 cups whole milk
 10 egg yolks
  ¾ cup sugar
  2 Tbsps. pure vanilla
     Juice of 4 passion
     fruits (if unavailable,
     use 2 Tbsps. dark rum)
  1 cup heavy cream
  1 Tbsp. confectionery
     sugar
  1 to 1½ packaged pound
     cakes, such as Sara Lee
     or Entemanns or Sour
     Cream Pound Cake
     (see recipe page 195)
  ⅓ cup dark rum
  3 or 4 mangoes, peeled
     and cubed
  3 bananas, peeled and
     sliced
  4 kiwis, peeled and
     sliced

large, attractive serving bowl you have. Traditionally trifle is served in a straight-sided glass dish, but this is not essential. Sprinkle the cake with some of the rum. Arrange half of the mango pieces on top of the cake. Top with about a third of the custard.

Cover with another layer of cake cubes; sprinkle with rum. Arrange the banana slices in concentric circles. Top with custard and a layer of whipped cream.

Arrange a third layer of cake cubes; sprinkle with remaining rum. Top with the remaining mango cubes. Pour whatever custard is left atop the fruit and cover with a layer of whipped cream. Arrange the kiwi slices on top of the trifle in a decorative manner.

Refrigerate the trifle at least 4 hours before serving it, preferably longer to allow the flavors to marry and the texture to soften.

Volcano Cakes

This is far and away the most popular dessert I ever served in any of my restaurants. The recipe is based on a famous chocolate cake devised by Jean Georges Vongerichten at his New York restaurant, Jo Jo. This version was developed by one of my pastry chefs, Jennifer Larese.

The cakes are a snap to prepare. The key to success is discovering the exact cooking time for your oven. When you cut into the cake, the center should be molten, like lava. It is possible to cook the cakes several hours before serving time. Undercook them slightly; 12 minutes is the ideal length of time for my oven. Remove and set the ramekins on the counter, leaving them at room temperature until you are ready to serve. To reheat, put two ramekins into a microwave oven and cook on high for 1 minute. Repeat with the remaining cakes.

Place a baking sheet in the middle of a 350° oven. Combine the butter and chocolate in the top of a double boiler. Heat until melted, then set aside to cool slightly.

Meanwhile, beat the eggs, yolks and sugar with a mixer for five minutes, until thick and light colored. On low speed, gradually add the flour and then the chocolate mixture.

Butter six 4-oz. porcelain ramekins. Spray oils do not work as well. Dust the insides with unsweetened cocoa powder, tapping out the excess.

Divide the batter between the ramekins. Batter may be refrigerated for several days at this point. Transfer the ramekins to the hot baking sheet and cook for 12 to 14 minutes, or until the tops set, but the centers are still soft.

Remove the cakes to a wire rack and let cool for 3 minutes. Turn out onto serving plates that have been drizzled with caramel sauce (see recipe, page 214). Serve immediately with a scoop of vanilla ice cream.

Serves 6
Preparation Time:
   15 Minutes
Baking Time:
   15 Minutes
Preheat oven to 350°

12 **Tbsps. unsalted butter (1½ sticks)**
 6 **oz. good quality bittersweet chocolate**
 3 **extra-large egg yolks**
½ **cup sugar**
   Scant ½ cup flour
   Unsweetened cocoa powder

Warm Gratin of Fruits

Serves 4
Preparation Time:
  15 Minutes
(note refrigeration time)
Cooking Time:
  1 Hour

1¾ cups heavy cream
1 vanilla bean, split and
  scraped
4 egg yolks
⅓ cup sugar
½ pt. strawberries, sliced
½ pt. raspberries
½ pt. blueberries
4 fresh figs, sliced
1 ripe nectarine, thinly
  sliced
Fresh grated nutmeg
¼ cup sugar

Here is a sensational and trendy dessert, not too sweet, not too fattening, and best of all, surprisingly simple to make. The custard sauce will require the majority of your efforts, although this can be made two days ahead. Arranging the fruit is a snap and you can combine whatever varieties you fancy. If you're pressed for time, assemble the gratins in advance and caramelize just before serving. If caramelizing is just one step too many, simply skip the sugar topping and reheat the gratins under the broiler for 3 to 4 minutes.

Scald the cream with the vanilla bean (pod and seeds). Allow to steep for 15 minutes to infuse the cream with vanilla essence, then remove the vanilla bean and save for future use.

Place the yolks and sugar in a metal mixing bowl and set the bowl over a pan of barely simmering water. Whisk vigorously until the mixture has thickened and the yolks are warm. The consistency of the custard should resemble a thick hollandaise at this point.

Add the scalded cream to the yolk mixture and cook over barely simmering water for 35 to 40 minutes, whisking frequently. Be careful not to let the custard get too hot or the eggs will curdle. When the custard has thickened enough to coat the back of a spoon, strain into a clean bowl.

Divide and artfully arrange the sliced fruit and berries on four ovenproof 7-inch plates. Pour ½ cup of the custard atop the fruit, sprinkle with nutmeg and refrigerate the plates for at least 1 hour. If refrigerating longer, cover with plastic wrap.

When ready to serve, evenly sprinkle 1 Tbsp. of sugar atop each gratin. Place the dishes on a cookie sheet and broil on a rack set closest to the flame. Carefully caramelize the sugar topping. You may also use a propane torch to caramelize the sugar (see description of technique on page 174). The torch method is much faster, but the fruit will not get especially warm.

Whipped Amaretto Pie

A very unusual dessert that is delightful on a hot day. The "secret" ingredient is ricotta cheese but it is indistinguishable in this guise. The almond flavor is dominant and the pie receives its texture from the almonds and chocolate. Definitely not a diet dessert!

Serves 8
Preparation Time:
  30-40 Minutes
(note freezer time)

P ut the graham crumbs in a small bowl and add the sugar, nutmeg and melted butter. Mix well to combine. Press the crumb mixture into the bottom and sides of a foil-lined 9-or 10-inch pie plate and freeze while you prepare the filling.

Mix the ricotta and sugar in a medium-sized bowl until smooth. Add the almond extract and Amaretto and blend well. Stir in the ground almonds and chocolate.

In a separate bowl, whip the heavy cream until it is stiff. Then gently fold the whipped cream into the Amaretto filling.

Spoon the filling into the prepared graham cracker crust, mounding it in the middle. Freeze the pie at least 3 hours before serving. To serve, garnish with shaved chocolate and whipped cream, if desired. If the pie has been frozen overnight or for any length of time, allow it to sit at room temperature for 30 minutes or in the refrigerator for 1 hour before cutting and serving.

1½ cups graham cracker
    crumbs
¼ cup granulated sugar
½ tsp. nutmeg
½ cup butter, melted
2½ cups ricotta cheese
1 cup sugar
1 Tbsp. almond extract
¼ cup Amaretto liqueur
1 cup toasted almonds,
    ground
1 cup chocolate chips,
    ground
1 cup heavy cream

White Chocolate Bread Pudding

Serves 6
Preparation Time:
  20 Minutes
Baking Time:
  30 Minutes
Preheat oven to 325°

- 4 **cups pound cake cubes (about 10 oz. of cake)**
- 6 **oz. white chocolate, chopped**
- 1 **cup half and half**
- 2 **eggs**
- 3 **Tbsps. sugar**
- 2 **tsps. pure vanilla extract**
- 3 **Tbsps. Amaretto liqueur**

This is a grown-up's version of a childhood classic. The recipe is basically a flavored custard that moistens pound cake. If you don't like Amaretto, use Grand Marnier or Chambord or Frangelico to underline the chocolate. I like to serve this dessert warm; it reheats well in the microwave.

Cut pound cake into ½-inch cubes. Place in a bowl and set aside.

Combine the chocolate with the half and half and melt it over low heat.

Using an electric mixer, beat the eggs with the sugar until light and fluffy, about 4 minutes. Add the vanilla and Amaretto. Fold the white chocolate cream into the egg-sugar mixture and pour over the cake cubes. Let sit for 10 minutes, stirring occasionally.

Transfer the pudding to a 1½ qt. baking dish or divide between six individual 8 oz. ramekins. Place the pan or ramekins in a bain-marie or water bath at 325° and bake for 20 to 30 minutes or until the pudding is just set.

White Chocolate Custard Cake

If you love a dense, moist cake, this recipe should please. The addition of banana is wholly optional and may be omitted without jeopardizing the finished product. This cake is excellent plain and simply sensational with a dollop of bittersweet chocolate sauce.

Combine the egg yolks, cream, milk, sugar and vanilla in the top of a double boiler or in a metal mixing bowl set over simmering water. Whisk continually until the custard warms and thickens, about 10 minutes. Do not overheat or the yolks will scramble. If you are using a vanilla bean, remove and scrape the seeds into the custard. Add the white chocolate and stir until it is melted. Let cool completely.

Butter a 9×3-inch or 10×2-inch cake pan and set aside.

Beat the sugar with the butter until it is smooth. Using an electric mixer, add the eggs, one at a time, beating well after each addition. Beat for a total of 3 minutes. Fold in the white chocolate custard.

Sift the dry ingredients together. Add to the batter, alternating with the buttermilk.

Purée the banana by mashing it on a cutting board with a fork. Fold into the batter.

Transfer batter to the prepared pan and bake at 350° in the middle of the oven for 55 to 65 minutes or until the cake is set and the edges have begun to shrink from the side of the pan. Cool for 10 minutes and then turn out, invert and finish cooling on a wire rack.

Serve plain or with slices of fresh banana and chocolate sauce.

Serves 8
Preparation Time:
 45 Minutes
Cooking Time:
 65 Minutes
Preheat oven to 325°

 3 egg yolks
 ⅓ cup heavy cream
 ⅓ cup milk
 ⅓ cup sugar
 ½ vanilla bean, split
  (or ½ tsp. pure vanilla
  extract)
 6 oz. white chocolate,
  chopped fine
 1 cup sugar
 ¾ cup unsalted butter,
  softened
 2 eggs, room
  temperature
 1 cup flour
 1 tsp. baking powder
 ½ tsp. salt
 ⅓ cup buttermilk
 1 large banana
  (optional)

★

White Chocolate Tartufi

Serves 4
Preparation Time:
  20 Minutes
Cooking Time:
  5 Minutes

14 oz. white chocolate,
  chopped
½ cup crème fraîche or
  mascarpone cheese
1 cup heavy cream
¼ cup Frangelico liqueur
6 oz. maraschino
  cherries, drained and
  chopped

Attention lovers of white chocolate: here is a delightful dessert that resembles a mousse, but is richer and less sweet. The cherries and chunks of chocolate contrast nicely with the smooth and creamy texture of the tarufi.

P lace 10 ounces of the white chocolate in the bowl of a food processor.
  Bring the crème fraîche to a boil and add to the chocolate, processing until the chocolate melts. Cool completely.

Beat the heavy cream to soft peaks, add the liqueur and continue beating until the cream is stiff. Fold the whipped cream into the cooled chocolate base.

Chop the remaining white chocolate into small pieces and fold the chocolate and the cherries into the tartufi.

Spoon into goblets and refrigerate, covered, until serving time.

Pantry

Apricot Purée

Brioche

Caramel Sauce

Caramel Syrup

Coconut Milk

Cranberry Chutney

Cranberry Vinaigrette

Crème Anglaise

Crème Fraîche

French Poodle
  Vinaigrette

Guacamole

Hot Fudge Sauce

Lemon Caramel Sauce

Mascarpone Cheese

Nectarine Chutney

Orange Crème Anglaise

Pâte Sucre

Pesto Sauce

Ravioli Pasta Dough

Tangerine Vinaigrette

Tarragon Vinaigrette

Tomato-Basil Vinaigrette

Veal Stock

Apricot Purée

Yield: ¾ cup
Preparation Time:
  5 Minutes
Cooking Time:
  20 Minutes

  1 **cup dried apricots,**
    packed
  ⅓ **cup brandy**
  ⅔ **cup water**
    Grated zest of 1 lemon
  4 **slices fresh ginger root**

Combine all of the ingredients in a small saucepan and cook over low heat until the water evaporates.

Discard the ginger root slices and then purée the fruit in a blender or food processor.

☆

Brioche

This rich, buttery, egg-enriched bread is in a class of its own. Three slow risings contribute to a very fine crumb and delicate texture. I use this brioche for my Brioche Bread Pudding (see recipe page 166) and also like to serve it lightly toasted with lobster salad for an elegant luncheon.

Mix 6 oz. of flour and half the sugar in a large bowl to make the sponge.

In a separate bowl, sprinkle the yeast over the water and stir to dissolve. Whisk in the eggs, beating until smooth. Stir this mixture into the bowl containing the flour and sugar. Place in a warm, draft-free spot and allow to rise until the mixture has tripled and turned bubbly.

Add the remaining flour and sugar and the salt to the sponge. Beat briskly to combine and then turn out onto a floured surface; knead for 10 minutes. If you have a heavy-duty mixer with a dough hook, by all means use it instead.

Cut the butter into 1-inch pieces and gradually knead or beat them into the dough. Transfer the dough to a clean bowl, cover with plastic wrap and let rise overnight in the refrigerator. If you are in a hurry, let the dough rise at room temperature and then proceed to the next step.

Punch down the dough and form it into two loaves.

Place in buttered loaf pans and let the dough rise again until it doubles in size. Because the dough is cold, this third rising will be slow.

Bake for 40 to 50 minutes at 350°. Cool on a wire rack for 15 minutes and then remove the pans to finish cooling. The brioche freezes beautifully if tightly wrapped.

Yield: 2 loaves
Preparation Time:
  30 Minutes
(note refrigeration time)
Baking Time:
  50 Minutes
Preheat oven to 350°

  1 lb., 6 oz. bread flour
  ¼ cup sugar
  1 Tbsp. dry yeast
  ½ cup warm water
  4 eggs, room
    temperature
  2 tsps. salt
  1 lb. unsalted butter,
    softened

Caramel Sauce

Yield: 1½ cups
Cooking Time:
  10 Minutes

1½ cups sugar
  1 tsp. fresh lemon juice
  ¾ cup heavy cream

A quick and simple sauce that will keep for ten days under refrigeration. To use, reheat slowly in a microwave oven or double boiler.

Combine the sugar and lemon juice in a heavy-bottomed skillet. Place over medium-high heat and let the sugar melt without stirring.

Cook the syrup until it takes on a rich brown color and then remove the skillet from the stove. Add the cream all at once. Stir with a clean spoon until the sauce is smooth.

Leave at room temperature if you are serving the same day; otherwise, cover and refrigerate.

Caramel Syrup

I use this simple syrup for Floating Island or other desserts that need a drizzle of caramel for flavor or presentation. It will harden as it cools, but can easily be reheated over low heat at serving time.

Yield: ¾ cup
Preparation Time:
  5 Minutes
Cooking Time:
  15 Minutes

  1 **cup sugar**
  ⅓ **cup water**

P lace the sugar and water in a heavy-bottomed saucepan and bring to a simmer. Cook over low to moderate heat until the sugar particles are completely dissolved and the syrup is clear. Raise the heat to high, cover the pan with a lid and boil the syrup until bubbles form, about 2 or 3 minutes. Uncover the pan and continue to cook, swirling the pan to distribute the syrup. Do not stir at any point or you run the risk of ruining the syrup. The mixture should begin coloring at this stage. When it reaches a light caramel brown, remove from the heat. The syrup will continue to darken, so set the pan in an inch or two of cold water to stop the cooking process.

To serve, pour the caramel into a small pitcher or use a fork to drizzle the syrup over your sauce or dessert.

☆

Coconut Milk

Yield: 2 Cups
Preparation Time:
  5 Minutes
(note cooling time)
Cooking Time:
  20 Minutes
Preheat oven to 400°

  1 **large coconut**
  2 **cups boiling water**

Coconut milk is easy to make if you have a blender or food processor. It's delicious but, alas, qualifies as one of the world's most fattening foods! It is a must for the Satay Sticks (see recipe page 60) however, and I always use it in my curries as well. Most large supermarkets now carry canned, unsweetened coconut milk. Trader Joes markets an excellent and inexpensive light coconut milk that has half the fat and calories.

Find an ice pick or screwdriver, and with a hammer, pierce a hole in one of the eyes of the coconut so that you can discard the coconut water. Place the coconut on a baking tray and bake at 400° for 15 to 20 minutes or until the shell cracks. Remove the nut from the oven and let it cool before further handling.

Wrap the coconut in a towel and smash it into several pieces with a mallet or hammer. Peel off the brown skin with a vegetable peeler and then cut the coconut into small pieces. Place the coconut meat in a blender or food processor and pour in the boiling water. Process until the meat is finely chopped.

Transfer the contents of the food processor to a sieve and strain the liquid into a large bowl. Wrap the coconut meat in a clean linen towel and firmly squeeze any remaining milk into the bowl. Refrigerate the coconut milk if you are not using it right away, as it does not keep well.

☆

Cranberry Chutney

Chutney is so versatile and delicious that I always have some on hand in my refrigerator. It keeps for weeks and it spices up sandwiches, cottage cheese and meats. When I cook for my family I often use chutney in place of higher calorie and more time-consuming sauces.

ombine the vinegar, cranberries, sugar, water and spices in a medium-sized pan and bring to a boil over moderate heat.

Cut the apples, pears and onion into ¼-inch dice and add to the pan with the raisins.

Peel the ginger root and grate. Add this and the orange rind to the chutney.

Cook over low heat until the chutney thickens, about 30 minutes. Cool and then transfer to a container, cover and refrigerate.

Yield: 5 cups
Preparation Time:
  10 Minutes
Cooking Time:
  45 Minutes

  ½ **cup white or cider**
      vinegar
  4 **cups cranberries**
2½ **cups sugar**
  1 **cup water**
 10 **whole cloves**
  2 **cinnamon sticks**
  ½ **tsp. salt**
  2 **tart apples**
  2 **ripe pears**
  1 **small onion**
  ½ **cup raisins**
  1 **piece of ginger root,**
      2 inches in length
      Grated rind of 1 orange

Crème Anglaise

2 cups whole milk
1 vanilla bean, split
6 egg yolks
2/3 cup sugar
1 Tbsp. pure almond
  extract (optional)

Heat the milk and vanilla bean in a heavy-bottomed saucepan and bring to a simmer. Remove the pan from the stove, cover with a lid and let the mixture steep for 10 minutes. Remove the vanilla bean and scrape the seeds into the milk. Wash the bean and save for another use.

In a bowl whisk the eggs and gradually add the sugar. Pour the milk into the bowl in a slow stream, whisking lightly. Return this mixture to the saucepan and cook over low heat, stirring the custard until it thickens. Don't whisk vigorously or the sauce will foam and froth. Take care not to overcook the mixture or the eggs will scramble. The custard should coat the back of a spoon so that when a finger is drawn across the surface, the line holds. Cool slightly and if you're making this Crème Anglaise for the Floating Island dessert, add the almond extract. Refrigerate until cold.

Cranberry Vinaigrette

Cranberries are quintessentially Nantucket. Here is a marvelous vinaigrette that I devised for my Grilled Chicken Salad (see recipe page 75).

Cook the cranberries with the orange juice and sugar until they are soft. Set aside to cool. When cooled, transfer the cranberries to a food processor or blender and purée.

Add the mustard, honey, vinegar and shallots and pulse to blend.

With the machine running, add the oils in a slow, steady stream to emulsify the dressing.

Keep refrigerated until serving time.

Yield: 2 cups
Preparation Time:
15 Minutes
Cooking Time:
15 Minutes

- 6 oz. fresh or frozen cranberries
- ¾ cup orange juice
- ¼ cup sugar
- ¼ cup Dijon mustard
- ¼ cup plus 2 Tbsps. honey
- ½ cup plus 2 Tbsps. Champagne vinegar
- 2 Tbsps. finely minced shallots
- ½ cup vegetable oil
- ½ cup walnut oil

☆

Crème Fraîche

Yield: 2½ cups
Preparation Time:
  5 Minutes
(note refrigeration time)
Cooking Time:
  5 minutes

  1 cup sour cream
  2 cups heavy cream

Crème fraîche is used in much of French cooking to thicken and flavor sauces and soups and in place of whipped cream. It's sometimes carried in the dairy department of large supermarkets, but if it's not available in your area, it's easy to make at home. Do remember, however, that you will need to allow 2 days for the entire thickening process.

Place the sour cream in a medium saucepan and slowly whisk in the heavy cream. Bring the mixture to about body temperature over low heat.

Transfer the cream to a small bowl and cover loosely with plastic wrap. Let sit at room temperature for 8 to 24 hours or until it has thickened. When thick, pour the crème fraîche into a strainer lined with a paper coffee filter. Place the strainer over a bowl and cover loosely with plastic.

Refrigerate overnight, then peel off and discard the filter and any liquid that has accumulated in the bowl.

French Poodle Vinaigrette

There's a small, excellent French restaurant in Carmel that sells the best vinaigrette in the universe. They're not willing to part with the recipe, so I've spent hours trying to duplicate it. This is the closest I've come. Although it's not identical, it is delicious nonetheless.

Place all the ingredients except the oils in a food processor and pulse to combine.

With the motor running, slowly pour the oils in a steady stream to emulsify the dressing.

Yield: 1⅓ cups
Preparation Time:
  15 Minutes

- 2 tsps. very finely minced shallots
- 1 tsp. Dijon mustard
- 1 Tbsp. red vermouth
- 2 Tbsps. lemon juice
- 3 Tbsps. rice wine vinegar
- 2 Tbsps. caper juice
- 2 tsps. anchovy oil
- 2 tsps. fresh ground pepper
- ½ tsp. salt
- ½ cup vegetable oil
- ¼ cup extra-virgin olive oil

☆

Guacamole

Yield: ¾ cup
Preparation Time:
  15 Minutes

  2 **cloves garlic, peeled
    and minced**
  1 **bunch scallions, white
    and green parts, finely
    minced**
  2 **ripe avocados, peeled
    and seeded (save pits)**
  1 **Tbsp. lemon juice**
  2 **Tbsps. oil**
  1 **Tbsp. sour cream**
  6 **drops Tabasco**
  ¼ **tsp. salt**
  1 **small tomato, finely
    diced**

If you own a food processor or blender, mince the garlic and scallions together, then add the avocado and process until smooth. Add the remaining ingredients and pulse to mix.

If you are mixing by hand, mash the avocado in a small bowl and add the remaining ingredients, stirring to mix.

Season the guacamole as necessary.

Bury the reserved avocado pits in the guacamole and pour additional lemon juice over the surface of the mixture to retard discoloration.

Hot Fudge Sauce

Melt the chocolate chips with the butter in a medium-sized saucepan. When smooth, add the evaporated milk and the confectionery sugar and cook for 8 minutes, stirring frequently. Remove from heat and mix in the vanilla.

Yield: 2 Cups
Cooking Time:
  15 Minutes

- ½ cup semi-sweet chocolate chips
- ¼ cup butter
- ½ cup evaporated milk
- 1 cup confectioners' sugar, sifted
- 1 tsp. vanilla

☆

Lemon Caramel Sauce

Serves 4
Preparation Time:
  5 Minutes
Cooking Time:
  10 Minutes

> **Juice and grated zest**
>   **of 1 lemon**
> **2 Tbsps. sugar**
> **2 Tbsps. Cognac**
> **1½ cups duck or veal stock**
> **2 Tbsps. butter**

I devised this sauce for my Confit of Duck (recipe page 125). The flavor is complex, but the sauce is light and boasts a tart sweetness that balances the richness of the duck very nicely.

Combine the lemon juice and zest with the sugar in a small skillet and cook over medium heat until the sugar caramelizes. For maximum flavor allow the sugar syrup to turn a dark amber color.

Add the cognac and cook over high heat until the liquid reduces by half, stirring constantly.

Add the stock and reduce the sauce until the flavor has concentrated.

Whisk in the butter at the last minute, just before serving.

Mascarpone Cheese

Mascarpone is an Italian cream cheese that is all the rage these days. It's very rich, with a hint of sweetness, and is used in desserts, with fresh fruits and in pasta sauces. You can make it yourself with tartaric acid crystals, a by-product of wine making, usually obtainable from your pharmacy.

Bring the cream to the start of a simmer and then remove from the heat. Add the tartaric acid crystals and stir until dissolved.

Line a sieve with a clean cotton or linen towel and set the sieve over a bowl. Pour the cream into the sieve and refrigerate, loosely covered with plastic wrap, for at least 24 hours. Discard the liquid that collects and transfer the mascarpone to a clean container.

Mascarpone will keep under refrigeration for up to a week.

Yield: 3 cups
Preparation Time:
  5 Minutes
(note refrigeration time)
Cooking Time:
  10 Minutes

4 cups heavy cream (not ultra-pasteurized)
1 tsp. tartaric acid

Nectarine Chutney

Yield: 5 to 5½ pints
Preparation Time:
  25 Minutes
Cooking Time:
  1¼ Hours

2 cups brown sugar
1 cup white vinegar
5½ cups diced nectarines
8 oz. crushed pineapple
  with juice
1 cup golden raisins
3 cloves garlic, minced
1 tsp. fresh ginger root,
  peeled and grated
1 tsp. salt
1 tsp. ground cloves
½ cup sliced almonds

Mrs. Roberta Gallagher of Scottsdale, Arizona, zealously maintained the secret of her chutney recipes for many years. An ardent fan of this concoction, I used to beg and connive to get a jar of Aunt Roberta's nectarine chutney from her niece, my friend, Judi. It complements Confit of Duck so beautifully that I just had to have the recipe. Aunt Roberta most graciously complied and now my refrigerator is never without a supply.

Boil the sugar and vinegar for 10 minutes. Add the fruits, garlic, ginger root, salt and cloves to this mixture. Bring to a boil and then reduce to a simmer. Cook until thick, stirring frequently to prevent burning and sticking. This should take about 1 to 1½ hours.

Add the nuts, then pour the hot chutney into hot sterilized jars. Seal tightly. Cool away from a draft.

☆

Orange Crème Anglaise

A twist on the classic French custard sauce, this complements just about any chocolate dessert.

P lace the cream and orange rind in a heavy-bottomed saucepan. Cut the vanilla bean in half, lengthwise, and add it to the pan. Bring to a simmer, then turn off the heat and let the cream steam for 10 minutes. Scrape the seeds out of the bean into the cream. The bean can be washed and dried, then used to flavor granulated or confectioners' sugar.

Whisk the egg yolks and sugar in a bowl. Gradually add the hot cream.

Return the mixture to the saucepan and over low heat, whisk the custard until it thickens enough to coat a wooden spoon. Do not allow the custard to boil or it will scramble the eggs.

Remove from the heat and add the Grand Marnier. Refrigerate until cold.

Yield: 2 cups
Preparation Time:
  5 Minutes
(note refrigeration time)
Cooking Time:
  10 Minutes

2 cups half and half or
  light cream
  Grated rind of one
  orange
1 vanilla bean
4 egg yolks
½ cup sugar
1 Tbsp. Grand Marnier
  or Triple Sec

Pâte Sucre (Sweet Pastry)

Yield: 2 crusts
Preparation Time:
30 Minutes
(note refrigeration time)

2½ cups flour
⅛ tsp. salt
3 Tbsps. sugar
1 cup unsalted butter, chilled and cut into pieces
⅓ cup ice water

This is the recipe that I've always used for pie and tart crusts. It's light and delicate if you handle the dough properly. Delete the sugar if you're making pastry for savory tarts and quiches. I find the food processor technique the quickest and easiest, but you must be cautious not to overmix the dough or it will be tough. My advice to novices of pastry techniques is "practice makes perfect," so don't despair if your initial attempts are less than perfect.

The Food Processor Method (steel knife):
Place the flour, salt and sugar in the work bowl. Pulse 1 second to mix. Add the butter chunks and pulse on and off until the butter has been broken into small pieces. With the machine running, add the ice water and process about 5 seconds. Do not allow the dough to form a solid mass or it will be overworked. Pinch the dough to test its consistency. If the particles do not stick together, more water is needed. Add 1 tablespoon more and process briefly, then test again.

Turn the pastry out onto a clean, dry surface and divide it into 2 equal portions. Gather the dough into a flat, round pancake, kneading only as much as is necessary to form a cohesive mass. Wrap both pastry rounds in plastic wrap and refrigerate at least 2 hours.

The Hand Method:
Place the flour, salt and sugar in a medium-sized bowl. Cut in the butter with a pastry blender or 2 knives until the butter becomes the size of peas. Add the cold water a little at a time, tossing the flour mixture with a fork to distribute the liquid evenly. Turn the pastry out onto a clean, dry surface and divide the dough in half. Squeeze the dough particles together, then gently smear the pastry against the counter surface with the heel of your hand in a straight line away from you. This helps to distribute the butter evenly. Regather the dough and pat it into a flat, round patty. Repeat with the remaining dough. Wrap in plastic wrap and refrigerate at least 2 hours.

Lightly flour a large, clean, dry surface and a rolling pin. Roll the pastry into a circle at least 2 inches larger than the size of the pie plate you are using. To roll a more-or-less circular crust, start by rolling around the edges of the dough. Then roll the dough from the center by pushing the pin away from

★

you, rotating the dough as you continue to roll in this manner. Add flour as needed to prevent sticking. Try to roll the dough to a thickness of 1/8- to 3/16-inch. Any holes or cracks can be patched when the dough is in the pie pan.

Fold the dough in quarters or drape it over the rolling pin to facilitate transfer to the pie pan. Brush off excess flour with a pastry brush and trim the dough edges evenly with a pair of scissors. Refrigerate, uncovered, for at least 30 minutes before baking or filling.

For a single-crust pie, turn the overhanging pastry under to form a slight thickness, then crimp or flute the pastry edges.

For a two-crust pie, roll out the top pastry round, then fill the bottom crust. Arrange the dough over the filling and cut the overhanging pastry with a pair of scissors to form an even round. Moisten the underside edge of the top crust with water and fold the pastry over the bottom crust, gently squeezing the dough layers together. Crimp decoratively.

To avoid a soggy-bottomed crust for a fruit pie or tart, seal the bottom with egg white and refrigerate for 1 hour to set. Then add the fruit filling, top crust and bake.

Pesto Sauce

Yield: 2 cups
Preparation Time:
  15 Minutes

  4 cloves garlic
  2 cups fresh basil leaves,
     packed
  ⅔ cup fresh parsley
  ¼ cup pine nuts or
     walnuts
  ½ cup olive oil
  ¾ cup freshly grated
     Parmesan cheese

If you have a surplus of fresh basil you might consider making a batch of pesto. Although it's readily available in markets these days, good quality pesto is expensive. Make it yourself with the best ingredients you can find. It freezes beautifully and will keep under refrigeration, covered with a layer of olive oil, for many months.

I n a blender or food processor purée the garlic, basil, parsley and pine nuts. When smooth, add the olive oil and process again briefly. Stir in the Parmesan and season to taste. If the pesto is very stiff or dry, add more olive oil.

Ravioli Pasta Dough

P lace the flours and salt in the bowl of a food processor and pulse to blend. Add the eggs and 2 Tbsps. of the olive oil. Process for 40 seconds, then test the dough, pinching to see if it sticks together. If it seems dry, add the remaining Tbsp. of oil.

Turn out onto a semolina-dusted surface and knead vigorously for 5 minutes. Shape into a loaf and cover with plastic wrap; let rest at room temperature for 30 minutes. The dough can be refrigerated at this point for up to 2 days. Return to room temperature before rolling it into sheets.

Cut the dough into 6 or 8 slices. I find it difficult to work with long sheets, so I divide it into eighths. Completely cover the pieces you're not working with so they don't dry out.

Pass one piece of dough through the flat rollers of the machine with the thickness-regulating knob set on the widest position, usually #1. Fold the resulting sheet in half and pass it through the rollers again. Repeat this process two more times, lightly dusting the sheet with semolina if it's sticking. Reduce the thickness of the pasta by adjusting the knob, one notch at a time, until you reach the desired thinness. I stop at #5; anything higher than this rips the dough on my machine.

Place the pasta strip on sheets of waxed paper that have been dusted with semolina. Continue rolling out the rest of the pieces.

Using the filling of your choice, pipe or spoon small mounds onto one of the pasta strips. Leave about 1½ inches between mounds. Cover with a second sheet, taking care to drape the dough over the filling. Because of the mounds, the top sheet needs to be a bit longer (and wider), if possible. Gently press your fingers around the filling to create small pockets. Cut into individual squares or circles with a ravioli cutting tool.

Transfer the ravioli to a tray lined with semolina-dusted waxed paper. Do not stack. If you wish to freeze the pasta, find a shelf in your freezer where you can lie the ravioli flat, in a single layer, until they harden. Once solidly frozen, they can be bagged in plastic without danger of sticking together.

**Yield: 1½ lbs. of dough;
50 to 60 ravioli
Preparation Time:
One Hour**

1½ cups all purpose flour
1½ cups semolina flour
2 tsps. salt
4 extra-large eggs
2 to 3 Tbsps. olive oil

Tangerine Vinaigrette

Yield: 2 cups
Preparation Time:
  15 Minutes
Cooking Time:
  5 Minutes

- ½ **cup duck or chicken stock**
- ½ **cup frozen tangerine juice concentrate (undiluted)**
- 1 **Tbsp. Dijon mustard**
- 2 **Tbsps. fresh lime juice**
- 2 **Tbsps. sherry vinegar**
- 1 **cup vegetable oil**
  Pinch of salt

A simple yet versatile salad dressing that will keep for two weeks under refrigeration.

Heat the duck stock and juice in a small pan until boiling. Cook over high heat for 2 minutes. Pour the liquids into a blender or food processor and add the mustard, lime juice and vinegar. With the machine running, add the oil in a slow, steady steam to emulsify the sauce.

Add a pinch or two of salt to heighten the flavor of the vinaigrette. Keep refrigerated.

Tarragon Vinaigrette

Place the onion, vinegar, lemon juice, mustard, salt, pepper and sugar in the bowl of a food processor or blender and blend briefly. Add the egg and the tarragon and process again to combine. With the machine running, add the oil in a slow, steady stream until the dressing emulsifies. The vinaigrette may be kept, covered, in the refrigerator for up to one week. Refrigeration tends to thicken the dressing slightly and to intensify the onion flavor.

Yield: 1½ Cups
Preparation Time:
  10 Minutes

  1 **small onion or**
     2 shallots, minced
  ¼ **cup tarragon vinegar**
  2 **tsps. lemon juice**
  2 **tsps. Dijon mustard**
  ½ **tsp. salt**
  ½ **tsp. white pepper**
  1 **tsp. sugar**
  1 **egg**
  1 **Tbsp. tarragon, dried**
1¼ **cups vegetable oil**

☆

Tomato-Basil Vinaigrette

Yield: 3 cups
Preparation Time:
30 Minutes

- 2 **Tbsps. balsamic
  vinegar**
- 1 **shallot, minced**
- 2 **cloves garlic, minced**
- ½ **cup extra-virgin olive
  oil**
- 5 **ripe tomatoes, peeled,
  seeded and diced**
- 25 **fresh basil leaves,
  shredded**
  **Salt and fresh ground
  pepper to taste**

A lovely, fresh condiment that complements grilled fish nicely and adds zest to simply prepared vegetables. I especially like it as a colorful and piquant counterpoint to the smooth, understated flavor of Rotolo di Prosciutto and Formaggi (see recipe page 57).

Combine the vinegar, shallot and garlic in a bowl and whisk in the olive oil. Add the tomatoes and basil and stir to combine.

Season to taste with salt and pepper. If necessary, add 1 tsp. of sugar to balance the acidity.

☆

Veal Stock

If you haven't yet tried your hand at making stock, it's time to take the plunge. It's easy and there is just no substitute for a high quality, homemade veal stock. If freezer space is at a premium in your house, just reduce the stock to a manageable quantity. The greater the reduction, the stronger the concentration of flavor. Once you have mastered this process, you'll never want to be without homemade stock again.

Yield: Quantity Varies
Preparation Time:
  10 Minutes
(note refrigeration time)
Cooking Time:
  8 Hours
Preheat oven to 400°

O il a large roasting pan or tray and fill with the bones. If you do not have a large enough pan, use two. Bake for 1 hour at 400°.

Add the carrots, celery, onions and garlic and bake an additional 30 minutes.

Remove the roasting pan from the oven and put the contents into your largest stock pot (divide the meat and bones into 2 pots if necessary and split remaining ingredients accordingly). Add hot water to the roasting pan and scrape up all of the browned meat juices that are stuck to the pan. Add this liquid to the stock pot. Add enough cold water to almost cover the bones, then pour in the white wine. Bring the stock to a simmer and skim off any foam that collects on the surface. Add the remaining ingredients and cook over low heat for about 6 hours, or until the liquid reduces by about one-third.

Strain the stock into a clean pot and discard the solids. Allow the liquid to cool for several hours and then refrigerate until cold. This will allow for any fat to rise to the surface and solidify; discard.

Reheat the stock over medium-high heat and reduce until the liquid reaches the desired flavor intensity or quantity.

- 8 lbs. veal bones
- 2 lbs. beef bones
- 1 lb. carrots
- 3 stalks celery
- 2 large yellow onions
- 4 cloves garlic, unpeeled
- 1 lb. mushrooms, cut in half
- 2 cans of whole, peeled Italian plum tomatoes, 35 oz. each
- ½ cup tomato paste
- 4 cups dry white wine
- 1 Tbsp. whole black peppercorns
- 6 sprigs fresh tarragon or thyme
- 2 bay leaves

★

Conversion Index

LIQUID MEASURES

1 dash	3 to 6 drops
1 teaspoon (tsp.)	⅓ tablespoon
1 tablespoon (Tbsp.)	3 teaspoons
1 tablespoon	½ fluid ounce
1 fluid ounce	2 tablespoons
1 cup	½ pint
1 cup	16 tablespoons
1 cup	8 fluid ounces
1 pint	2 cups
1 pint	16 fluid ounces

DRY MEASURES

1 pinch	less than ⅛ teaspoon
1 teaspoon	⅓ tablespoon
1 tablespoon	3 teaspoons
¼ cup	4 tablespoons
⅓ cup	5 tablespoons plus 1 teaspoon
½ cup	8 tablespoons
⅔ cup	10 tablespoons plus 2 teaspoons
¾ cup	12 tablespoons
1 cup	16 tablespoons

VEGETABLES AND FRUITS

Apple (1 medium)	1 cup chopped
Avocado (1 medium)	1 cup mashed
Broccoli (1 stalk)	2 cups florets
Cabbage (1 large)	10 cups, chopped
Carrot (1 medium)	½ cup, diced
Celery (3 stalks)	1 cup, diced
Eggplant (1 medium)	4 cups, cubed
Lemon (1 medium)	2 tablespoons juice
Onion (1 medium)	1 cup diced
Orange (1 medium)	½ cup juice
Parsley (1 bunch)	3 cups, chopped
Spinach (fresh), 12 cups, loosely packed	1 cup cooked
Tomato (1 medium)	¾ cup, diced
Zucchini (1 medium)	2 cups, diced

APPROXIMATE EQUIVALENTS

1 stick butter = ½ cup = 8 Tbsps. = 4 oz.

1 cup all-purpose flour = 5 oz.

1 cup cornmeal (polenta) = 4½ oz.

1 cup sugar = 8 oz.

1 cup powdered sugar = 4½ oz.

1 cup brown sugar = 6 oz.

1 large egg = 2 oz. = ¼ cup = 4 Tbsps.

1 egg yolk = 1 Tbsp. + 1 tsp.

1 egg white = 2 Tbsps. + 2 tsps.

Metric Conversions

OUNCES TO GRAMS

To convert ounces to grams, multiply number of ounces by 28.35

1 oz. ....30 g.	6 oz. ....180 g.	11 oz........300 g.	16 oz. ......450 g.
2 oz. ....60 g.	7 oz. ....200 g.	12 oz. ......340 g.	20 oz. ......570 g.
3 oz. ....85 g.	8 oz. ....225 g.	13 oz........370 g.	24 oz. ......680 g.
4 oz..........115 g.	9 oz. ....250 g.	14 oz. ......400 g.	28 oz. ......790 g.
5 oz. ....140 g.	10 oz. ......285 g.	15 oz. ......425 g.	32 oz. ......900 g.

QUARTS TO LITERS

To convert quarts to liters, multiply number of quarts by 0.95

1 qt. ....1 L	2½ qt........2½ L	5 qt. ....4¾ L	8 qt...........7½ L
1½ qt. ......1½ L	3 qt. ....2¾ L	6 qt...........5½ L	9 qt...........8½ L
2 qt. ....2 L	4 qt. ....3¾ L	7 qt...........6½ L	10 qt.........9½ L

FAHRENHEIT TO CELSIUS

To convert Fahrenheit to Celsius, subtract 32 from the Fahrenheit figure, multiply by 5, then divide by 9

OTHER METRIC CONVERSIONS

To convert **ounces to milliliters,** multiply number of ounces by 30

To convert **cups to liters,** multiply number of cups by 0.24

To convert **inches to centimeters,** multiply number of inches by 2.54

Glossary of Ingredients

ACHIOTE: a spice blend made from ground annatto seeds, garlic, cumin, vinegar and other spices.

ACORN SQUASH: a oval-shaped winter squash with a ribbed, dark-green skin and orange flesh.

ANAHEIM CHILE: elongated and cone-shaped chiles that are red or green with a mild flavor.

ANCHO CHILE: a shiny-skinned red or green cone-shaped chile with medium heat.

ARBORIO RICE: a large-grained plump rice which equires more cooking time than other rice varieties. Arborio is traditionally used for risotto because its increased starchs lend this classic dish its creamy texture.

ARMENIAN CUCUMBER: a long, pale, green-ridged cucumber with an edible skin, also known as the English cucumber.

ARUGULA: also known as rocket or roquette, noted for its strong peppery taste. Arugula makes a lively addition to salads, soups and sautéed vegetable dishes. It's a rich source of iron as well as vitamins A and C.

ASIAN NOODLES: though some Asian-style noodles are wheat-based, many others are made from ingredients such as potato flour, rice flour, buckwheat flour and yam or soybean starch.

BALSAMIC VINEGAR: made from the juice of Trebbiano grapes and traditionally aged in barrels, this tart, sweet, rich vinegar is a versatile ingredient.

BARTLETT PEAR: this large, sweet, bell-shaped fruit has a smooth, yellow-green skin that is sometimes blushed with red.

BASMATI RICE: translated as "queen of fragrance," basmati is a long-grained rice with a nut-like flavor and fine texture.

BÉCHAMEL SAUCE: a basic French white sauce made by stirring milk into a butter-flour roux. Béchamel, the base of many other sauces, was named after its inventor, Louis XIV's steward Louis de Béchamel.

BELGIAN ENDIVE: a white, yellow-edged bitter lettuce that is crunchy.

BLOOD ORANGE: a sweet-tart, thin-skinned orange with a bright red flesh.

BOK CHOY: resembles Swiss chard with its long, thick-stemmed, light green stalks. The flavor is much like cabbage.

BOUQUET GARNI: a group of herbs, such as parsley, thyme and bay leaf, that are placed in a cheesecloth bag and tied together for the use of flavor in soups, stews and broths.

BULGAR WHEAT: wheat kernels that have been steamed, dried and crushed, offering a chewy texture.

CAPERS: available in the gourmet food sections of supermarkets, capers are a small, green, pickled bud of a Mediterranean flowering plant; usually packed in brine.

CARDAMOM: a sweetly pungent, aromatic cooking spice that is a member of the ginger family.

CHANTERELLE MUSHROOM: a trumpet-shaped mushroom that resembles an umbrella turned inside out. One of the more delicious wild mushrooms.

CHÉVRE: cheese made from goat's milk is lower in fat and offers a delicate, light and slightly earthy flavor.

CHICKPEAS: also called garbanzo beans, they have a firm texture and mild, nut-like flavor. Available canned, dried or fresh.

CHICORY or CURLY ENDIVE: a crisp, curly, green-leafed lettuce. Best when young. Tend to bitter with age.

CHILE OIL: a red oil available in Asian stores. Chile oil is also easily made at home by heating 1 cup of vegetable or peanut oil with 2 dozen small dried red chiles or 1 Tbsp. cayenne.

CHIPOTLE PEPPERS: ripened and smoky-flavored jalapeño peppers have a fiery heat and delicious flavor.

CHOW-CHOW: a mustard-flavored mixed vegetable and pickle relish.

CLARIFIED BUTTER: also called drawn butter. This is an unsalted butter that has been slowly melted, thereby evaporating most of the water and separating the milk solids, which sink to the bottom of the pan. After any foam is skimmed off the top, the clear butter is poured off the milk residue and used in cooking.

COCONUT MILK: available in Asian markets, this milk is noted for its richly flavored, slightly sweet taste. Coconut milk can be made by placing 2 cups of finely grated chopped fresh coconut in 3 cups scalded milk. Stir and let stand until the milk cools to room temperature. Strain before using.

COULIS: a general term referring to a thick purée or sauce.

COURT BOUILLON: a broth made by cooking various vegetables and herbs in water.

CRÈME FRAÎCHE: a bit richer than sour cream, yet more tart than whipped heavy cream. It can be purchased in most supermarkets or made by whisking together 1/2 cup heavy or whipping cream, not ultra-pasteurized, with 1/2 cup sour cream. Pour the mixture into a jar, cover and let stand in a warm, dark area for 24 hours. This will yield 1 cup which can be kept in the refrigerator for about 10 days.

CRESS: resembles radish leaves, with a hot peppery flavor.

EGGPLANT: commonly thought of as a vegetable, eggplant is actually a fruit. The very narrow, straight Japanese or Oriental eggplant has a tender, slightly sweet flesh. The Italian or baby eggplant looks like a miniature version of the common large variety, but has a more delicate skin and flesh. The egg-shaped white eggplant makes the name of this fruit understandable.

FAVA BEANS: tan flat beans that resemble very large lima beans. Fava beans can be purchased dried, canned or fresh.

FLOWERS, EDIBLE: can be stored tightly wrapped in the refrigerator, up to a week. Some of the more popular edible flowers are the peppery-flavored nasturtiums, and chive blossoms, which taste like a mild, sweet onion. Pansies and violas offer a flavor of grapes. Some of the larger flowers such as squash blossoms can be stuffed and deep-fried.

FRISÉE: sweetest of the chicory family, with a mildly bitter taste. The leaves are a pale green, slender but curly.

FROMAGE BLANC CHEESE: fresh, day-old curds with some of the whey whipped back into the cheese. The texture is similar to ricotta cheese and is available plain or flavored.

GADO-GADO: this Indonesian favorite consists of a mixture of raw and slightly cooked vegetables served with a spicy peanut sauce.

GANACHE: a rich chocolate icing made of semisweet chocolate and whipping cream that are heated and stirred together until the chocolate has melted.

GNOCCHI: the Italian word for "dumplings," gnocchi are shaped into little balls, cooked in boiling water and served with butter and Parmesan or a savory sauce. The dough can also be chilled, sliced and either baked or fried.

GORGONZOLA CHEESE: a blue-veined Italian creamy cheese.

GRAHAM FLOUR: whole-wheat flour that is slightly coarser than the regular grind.

GRITS: coarsely ground grain such as corn, oats or rice. Grits can be cooked with water or milk by boiling or baking.

HABANERO CHILE: tiny, fat, neon orange-colored chiles that are hotter than the jalapeño chile.

HAZELNUT OIL: a lightly textured oil with a rich essence of hazelnut.

HUMMUS: this thick Middle Eastern sauce is made from mashed chickpeas seasoned with lemon juice, garlic and olive oil or sesame oil.

JALAPEÑO CHILE: these plump, thumb-size green chiles are known for wonderful flavor.

JICAMA: grows underground like a tuber, yet is part of the legume family. Beneath the thick brown skin, the flesh is creamy-white and sweet. Tastes like a cross between an apple and a potato.

KALAMATA OLIVES: intensely flavored, almond-shaped, dark purple Greek olives packed in brine.

KOSHER SALT: an additive-free, coarse-grained salt that is milder than sea salt.

LEMON GRASS: available in Asian food stores, this citrus-flavored herb has long, thin, gray-green leaves and a scallion-like base. Available fresh or dried.

LENTILS: the French or European lentil is grayish-brown with a creamy flavor. The reddish-orange Egyptian or red lentil is smaller and rounder. Lentils should be stored airtight at room temperature and will keep about 6 months. Lentils offer calcium and vitamins A and B, and are a good source of iron and phosphorus.

MÂCHE: also known as lamb's lettuce, has a delicate, sweet-nutty taste. The lettuce is a deep green.

MANGO: grows in a wide variety of shapes: oblong, kidney and round. Its thin, tough skin is green and, as the fruit ripens, becomes yellow with red mottling. Under-ripe fruit can be placed in a paper bag at room temperature.

MARJORAM: there are many species of this ancient herb, which is a member of the mint family. The most widely available is sweet marjoram or wild marjoram. Early Greeks wove marjoram into funeral wreaths and planted it on graves to symbolize their loved one's happiness, both in life and beyond.

MARSALA: a wine with a rich, smoky flavor that can range from sweet to dry.

MESCLUN: a traditional French mixture of tiny lettuces, including curly endive, red lettuce, Romaine, oak-leaf, butter lettuce and rocket.

MIRIN: a sweet cooking sake.

MISO: a fermented salty soybean paste made by crushing boiled soybeans with barley.

MOREL MUSHROOM: a wild mushroom that is cone-shaped with a spongy beige cap. Has a nutty taste.

NAPA CABBAGE: also known as Chinese cabbage, it looks like a cross between celery and lettuce, very much like romaine lettuce. The flavor is more delicate with a slight peppery taste.

NASTURTIUM FLOWERS: edible sweet and peppery flowers in a rainbow of colors. Nasturtiums are beautiful in salads and easy to grow.

NORI: paper-thin sheets of dried seaweed ranging in color from dark green to dark purple to black. Nori is rich in protein, vitamins, calcium, iron and other minerals.

OPAL BASIL: a beautiful purple basil with a pungent flavor.

OREGANO: this herb belongs to the mint family and is related to both marjoram and thyme, offering a strong, pungent flavor. Greek for "joy of the mountain," oregano was almost unheard of in the U.S. until soldiers came back from Italian World War II assignments raving about it.

OYSTER MUSHROOM: a beige fan-shaped wild mushroom with a mild flavor and soft texture.

PARMESAN CHEESE: a hard dry cheese made from skimmed or partially-skimmed cow's milk.

PECORINO CHEESE: a cheese made from sheep's milk

POLENTA: cornmeal—ground corn kernels, white or yellow, often enriched with butter and grated cheese. A staple of northern Italian cooking.

PORCINI MUSHROOM: The parasol-shaped mushroom cap has a thick stem, with a meaty, smoky flavor.

QUINOA: served like rice or as a base for salads. Pale yellow in color and slightly larger than a mustard seed with a sweet flavor and soft texture.

RADICCHIO: this peppery-tasting lettuce with brilliant, ruby-colored leaves is available year-round, with a peak season from mid-winter to early spring. Choose heads that have crisp, full-colored leaves with no sign of browning. Store in a plastic bag in the refrigerator for up to a week.

RICE WINE VINEGAR: a light, clean-tasting vinegar that works perfectly as is, in salads, as well as in a variety of Asian-inspired dishes.

RISOTTO: an Italian rice specialty made by stirring hot stock in Arborio rice that has been sautéed in butter.

ROMAINE: known for a sweet nutty flavor, this lettuce has long, crisp, green or red leaves.

ROUX: a mixture of melted butter or oil and flour used to thicken sauces, soups and stews. Sprinkle flour into the melted, bubbling-hot butter, whisking constantly over low heat, cooking at least 2 minutes.

SAFFRON: a bright yellow, strongly aromatic spice that imparts a unique flavor. Store saffron in a cool dark place for up to 6 months.

SAVOY CABBAGE: also known as curly cabbage, has lacy leaves with a white or reddish trim.

SERRANO CHILE: a fat, squat, red or green hot chile. They are milder when roasted with the ribs and seeds removed.

SHIITAKE MUSHROOM: a Japanese mushroom sold fresh or dried, which imparts a distinctively rich flavor to any dish. The versatile shiitake is suitable for almost any cooking method including sautéing, broiling and baking.

SNOW PEAS: a translucent, bright green pod that is thin, crisp and entirely edible. The tiny seeds inside are tender and sweet. Snow peas are also called Chinese snow peas and sugar peas.

SORBET: a palate refresher between courses or as a dessert, the sorbet never contains milk and often has softer consistency than sherbet.

SOY MILK: higher in protein than cow's milk, this milky, iron-rich liquid is a non-dairy product made by pressing ground, cooked soybeans. Cholesterol-free and low in calcium, fat and sodium, it makes an excellent milk substitute.

SPAGHETTI SQUASH: a yellow watermelon-shaped squash whose flesh, when cooked, separates into spaghetti-like strands.

STRUDEL: a type of pastry made up of many layers of very thin dough spread with a filling, then rolled and baked until crisp.

SUN-DRIED TOMATOES: air-dried tomatoes sold in various forms such as marinated tomato halves, which are packed in olive oil, or a tapenade, which is puréed dried tomatoes in olive oil with garlic.

TAHINI: Middle Eastern in origin, tahini is made from crushed sesame seeds. Used mainly for its creamy, rich and nutty flavor as well as for binding food together.

TEMPEH: made from cultured, fermented soybeans; comes in flat, light, grainy-looking cakes.

TOFU: a versatile fresh soybean curd, tofu is an excellent and inexpensive form of protein. It is characteristically bland in taste, but can be enhanced with seasonings.

TOMATILLOS: green husk tomatoes; small with a tart, citrus-like flavor .

TRUFFLE: a fungus that grows underground near the roots of trees prized by gourmets for centuries. Truffles should be used as soon as possible after purchase, but can be stored up to 6 days in the refrigerator or for several months in the freezer. Canned truffles, truffle paste and frozen truffles can be found in specialty stores.

VIDALIA ONION: the namesake of Vidalia, Georgia where they thrive. This yellow onion, sweet and juicy, is available in the summer or by mail- order year-round.

WATERCRESS: this spicy-flavored green is dark in color with glossy leaves.

Mail Order Sources

If you are unable to locate some of the specialty food products used in *Cooking Secrets From Around the World,* you can order them from the mail order sources listed below. These items are delivered by UPS, fully insured and at reasonable shipping costs.

❦ DRIED BEANS AND PEAS

Baer's Best
154 Green Street
Reading, MA 01867
(617) 944-8719
Bulk or 1-pound packages of over 30 different varieties of beans, common to exotic. No peas.

The Bean Bag
818 Jefferson Street
Oakland, CA 94607
510-839-8988
Dried beans, including many heirloom and organic beans, and bean mixes; hot sauces; sun-dried tomatoes; gourmet rices, specialty grains.

Corti Brothers
5801 Folsom Blvd.
Sacramento, CA 95819
(916) 736-3800
Special gourmet items such as: imported extra-virgin olive oils, wines, exotic beans, egg pasta.

Dean & Deluca
560 Broadway
New York, NY 10012
(800) 221-7714
(212) 431-1691
Dried beans, salted capers, polenta, arborio rice, dried mushrooms, dried tomatoes, parmesan and reggiano cheeses, kitchen and baking equipment.

Phipps Ranch
P.O. Box 349
Pescadero, CA 94060
415-879-0787
Dried beans such as cannellini, cranberry, fava, flageolet, borlotti, scarlet runner, Tongues of Fire, and more. Also dried peas, herb vinegars, grains, herbs and spices.

❦ DRIED MUSHROOMS

Dean & Deluca
560 Broadway
New York, NY 10012
(800) 221-7714
(212) 431-1691
Dried beans, salted capers, polenta, arborio rice, dried mushrooms, dried tomatoes, parmesan and reggiano cheeses, kitchen and baking equipment.

G.B. Ratto & Co.
821 Washington St.
Oakland, CA 94607
(800) 325-3483
(510) 836-2250 fax
Imported pasta, dried beans, amaretti cookies, semolina flour, dried mushrooms, dried tomatoes, parmesan and reggiano cheeses.

Gold Mine Natural Food Co.
1947 30th St.
San Diego, CA 92102-1105
(800) 475-3663
Organic foods, dried foods, whole grain rice, Asian dried mushrooms, condiments, sweeteners, spices.

❦ FLOURS AND GRAINS

Arrowhead Mills
Box 2059
Hereford, TX 79045
806-364-0730
A large variety of whole grain products, including specialty grains, grain mixes, flours, cereals.

Barbara's Bakery, Inc.
3900 Cypress Drive
Petaluma, CA 94954
707-765-2263
Whole grain and cereal products.

Butte Creek Mill
P.O. Box 561
Eagle Point, Oregon 97524
503-826-3531
A large assortment of cereals, whole grains, rolled grains, stone-ground flours and meals.

Continental Mills
P.O. Box 88176
Seattle, WA 98138
206-872-8400
Specialty whole grains, including bulgur.

Dean & Deluca
560 Broadway
New York, NY 10012
(800) 221-7714
(212) 431-1691
Dried beans, salted capers, polenta, arborio rice, dried mushrooms, dried tomatoes, parmesan and reggiano cheeses, kitchen and baking equipment.

G.B. Ratto & Co.
821 Washington Street
Oakland, CA 94607
(510) 832-6503
(800) 325-3483
Flours, rice, bulgar wheat, couscous, oils, and sun-dried tomatoes.

Gold Mine Natural Food Co.
1947 30th St.
San Diego, CA 92102-1105
(800) 475-3663
Organic foods, dried foods, whole grain rice, Asian dried mushrooms, condiments, sweeteners, spices.

King Arthur Flour Baker's Catalogue
P.O. Box 876
Norwich, VT 05055
(800) 827-6836
Semolina flour, all types of flours, wheat berries, kitchen and baking equipment.

Lundberg Family Farms
P.O. Box 369
Richvale, CA 95974-0369
916-882-4551
Premium short-grain and long-grain brown rice. California basmati brown rice, organic brown rice, specialty brown rices and rice blends, rice cakes and rice cereals.

Specialty Rice Marketing Inc.
P.O. Box 880
Brinkley, AR 72021
501-734-1234
Whole grains and cereals, including brown rice cereal.

U.S. Mills
4301 N. 30th Street
Omaha, NE 6811
402-451-4567
Whole grains and cereals, including brown rice cereals.

The Vermont Country Store
P.O. Box 3000
Manchester Center, VT 05255-3000
(802) 362-2400 credit card orders
(802) 362-4647 customer service
Orders are taken 24 hours a day.
Many different varieties: whole wheat, sweet-cracked, stone-ground rye, buckwheat, cornmeal and many more. They also sell a variety of items which are made in Vermont.

FRUIT & VEGETABLES

Diamond Organics
Freedom, CA 95019
(800) 922-2396
Free catalog available. Fresh, organically grown fruits & vegetables, specialty greens, roots, sprouts, exotic fruits, citrus, wheat grass.

Giant Artichoke
11241 Merritt St.
Castroville, CA 95012
(408) 633-2778
Fresh baby artichokes.

Lee Anderson's Covalda Date Company
51-392 Harrison Street (Old Highway 86)
P.O. Box 908
Coachella, CA 92236-0908
(619) 398-3441
Organic dates, raw date sugar and other date products. Also dried fruits, nuts and seeds.

Northwest Select
14724 184th St. NE
Arlington, WA 98223
(800) 852-7132
(206) 435-8577
Fresh baby artichokes.

Timber Crest Farms
4791 Dry Creek Road
Healdsburg, CA 95448
(707) 433-8251
Domestic dried tomatoes and other unsulfured dried fruits and nuts.

❦

SEEDS FOR GROWING HERBS AND VEGETABLES

Herb Gathering, Inc.
5742 Kenwood Ave.
Kansas City, MO 64110
(816) 523-2653
Seeds for growing herbs, fresh-cut herbs.

Shepherd's Garden Seeds
6116 Highway 9
Felton, CA 95018
(408) 335-6910
Excellent selection of vegetable and herb seeds with growing instructions.

The Cook's Garden
P.O. Box 535
Londonderry, VT 05148
(802) 824-3400
Organically grown, reasonably priced vegetable, herb and flower seeds. Illustrated catalog has growing tips and recipes.

Vermont Bean Seed Company
Garden Lane
Fair Haven VT 05743
(802) 273-3400
Selling over 60 different varieties of beans, peas, corn, tomato and flower seeds.

W. Atlee Burpee & Co.
Warminster, PA 18974
(800) 888-1447
Well-known, reliable, full-color seed catalog.

Well-Sweep Herb Farm
317 Mount Bethal Rd.
Port Murray, NJ 07865
(908) 852-5390
Seeds for growing herbs, fresh herb plants.

❦

SPECIALTY FOODS AND FOOD GIFTS

China Moon Catalogue
639 Post St.
San Francisco, CA 94109
(415) 771-MOON (6666)
(415) 775-1409 fax
Chinese oils, peppers, teas, salts, beans, candied ginger, kitchen supplies, cookbooks.

Corti Brothers
5801 Folsom Blvd.
Sacramento, CA 95819
(916) 736-3800
Special gourmet items such as: imported extra-virgin olive oils, wines, exotic beans, egg pasta.

Festive Foods
9420 Arroyo Lane
Colorado Springs, CO 80908
(719) 495-2339
Spices and herbs, teas, oils, vinegars, chocolate and baking ingredients.

G.B. Ratto & Co.
821 Washington St.
Oakland, CA 94607
(800) 325-3483
(510) 836-2250 fax
Imported pasta, dried beans, amaretti cookies, semolina flour, dried mushrooms, dried tomatoes, parmesan and reggiano cheeses.

Gazin's Inc.
P.O. Box 19221
New Orleans, LA 70179
(504) 482-0302
Specializing in Cajun, Creole and New Orleans foods.

Gold Mine Natural Food Co.
1947 30th St.
San Diego, CA 92102-1105
(800) 475-3663
Organic foods, dried foods, whole grain rice, Asian dried mushrooms, condiments, sweeteners, spices.

Knott's Berry Farm
8039 Beach Boulevard
Buena Park, CA 90620
(800) 877-6887
(714) 827-1776
Eleven types of jams and preserves, nine of which are non-sugar.

Kozlowski Farms
5566 Gravenstein Highway
Forestville, CA 95436
(707) 887-1587
(800) 473-2767
*Jams, jellies, barbecue and steak
sauces, conserves, honeys, salsas,
chutneys and mustards. Some products are non-sugared, others are in
the organic line. You can customize
your order from 65 different products.*

Williams-Sonoma
Mail Order Dept.
P.O. Box 7456
San Francisco, CA 94120-7456
(800) 541-2233 credit card
  orders
(800) 541-1262 customer
  service
Vinegars, oils, foods and kitchenware.

SPICES AND HERBS

**Apple Pie Farm, Inc.
(The Herb Patch)**
Union Hill Rd. #5
Malvern, PA 19355
(215)933-4215
A wide variety of fresh-cut herbs.

Festive Foods
9420 Arroyo Lane
Colorado Springs, CO 80908
(719) 495-2339
*Spices and herbs, teas, oils, vinegars,
chocolate and baking ingredients.*

Fox Hill Farm
444 West Michigan Avenue
P.O.Box 9
Parma, MI 49269
(517) 531-3179
*Fresh-cut herb plants, topiaries,
ornamental and medicinal herbs.*

Meadowbrook Herb Gardens
Route 138
Wyoming, RI 02898
(401) 539-7603
*Organically grown herb seasonings,
high quality spice and teas.*

Nichols Garden Nursery
1190 N. Pacific Hwy
Albany, OR 97321
(503) 928-9280
Fresh herb plants.

**Old Southwest Trading
Company**
P.O.Box 7545
Albuquerque, NM 87194
(800) 748-2861
(505) 831-5144
*Specializes in chiles, everything from
dried chiles to canned chiles and
other chile-related products.*

Penzey Spice House Limited
P.O. Box 1633
Milwaukee, WI 53201
(414) 768-8799
*Fresh ground spices (saffron, cinnamon and peppers), bulk spices, seeds,
and seasoning mixes.*

Rafal Spice Company
2521 Russell Street
Detroit, MI 48207
(800) 228-4276
(313) 259-6373
*Seasoning mixtures, herbs, spices,
oil, coffee beans and teas.*

Spice Merchant
P.O. Box 524
Jackson Hole, WY 83001
(307) 733-7811
Specializes in Asian spices.

Recipe Index

APPETIZERS AND FIRST COURSES

BREAKFAST AND BRUNCH

DESSERT

FISH AND SEAFOOD

MEAT

PANTRY

PASTA

POULTRY

SOUPS AND SALADS

VEGETABLES AND ACCOMPANIMENTS

About the Author

Pam McKinstry began her professional cooking career in 1979, when she started the Morning Glory Cafe on Nantucket Island, Massachusetts. She eventually opened two other establishments on the island—the Dockside Restaurant and the Sconset Cafe. She and her husband, Mark, also owned and operated the Sconset General Store. During her 16-year tenure on Nantucket, Pam authored four cookbooks highlighting the cuisine of her restaurants.

Inveterate travelers, Pam and Mark have journeyed around the world extensively since 1983, indulging a passion for adventure that shows no signs of abating. In love with Africa since her first visit in 1986, Pam has written three travel guides about the continent as well as a book of narrative essays chronicling some of her adventures. She currently lives for most of the year in Zambia, where she works at Chinzombo Safari Lodge in the South Luangwa National Park. During the winter rainy season she returns to her home in Carmel, California, where she recuperates from the rigors of bush living. Pam is currently at work on an African cookbook.

Bon Vivant Press a division of the Millennium Publishing Group

PO Box 1994 Monterey, CA 93942
408-373-0592 • 800-524-6826 • FAX 408-373-3567
Visit our web site at - http://www.millpub.com

Send _____ copies of *Cooking with the Masters of Food & Wine* at $34.95 each.

Send _____ copies of *Cooking Secrets from Around the World* at $15.95 each.

Send _____ copies of *Cooking Secrets from America's South* at $15.95 each.

Send _____ copies of *Louisiana Cooking Secrets* at $15.95 each.

Send _____ copies of *Pacific Northwest Cooking Secrets* at $15.95 each.

Send _____ copies of *Cooking Secrets for Healthy Living* at $15.95 each.

Send _____ copies of *The Great California Cookbook* at $15.95 each.

Send _____ copies of *The Gardener's Cookbook* at $15.95 each.

Send _____ copies of *The Great Vegetarian Cookbook* at $15.95 each.

Send _____ copies of *California Wine Country Cooking Secrets* at $14.95 each.

Send _____copies of *San Francisco's Cooking Secrets* at $13.95 each.

Send _____copies of *Monterey's Cooking Secrets* at $13.95 each.

Send _____ copies of *New England's Cooking Secrets* at $14.95 each.

Send _____ copies of *Cape Cod's Cooking Secrets* at $14.95 each.

Send _____ copies of *Jewish Cooking Secrets From Here and Far* at $14.95 each.

Add $3.00 postage and handling for the first book ordered and $1.50 for each additional book. Please add $1.08 sales tax per book, for those books shipped to California addresses.

Please charge my ☐ Visa
☐ MasterCard **#**_____

Expiration date_____Signature _____

Enclosed is my check for _____

Name _____

Address_____

City_____State_____Zip_____

☐ This is a gift. Send directly to:

Name _____

Address_____

City_____State_____Zip_____

☐ Autographed by the author
Autographed to_____

NOTES

NOTES